A Mouth Holds Many Things

Fonograf Editions and De-Canon
Portland, OR

Interior book design: Dao Strom
Graphic design assistant: Sandy Tanaka
Cover design: Dao Strom and Sandy Tanaka

First Edition, First Printing
FE31

Published by Fonograf Editions in collaboration with De-Canon
www.fonografeditions.com
www.de-canon.com

Distributed by Small Press Distribution
SPDBooks.org

ISBN: 979-8-9875890-3-8
Library of Congress Control Number: 2023949881

Publication of this project was made possible by a Creative Heights Grant and an Oregon Arts & Culture Recovery Program Grant from the Oregon Community Foundation (OCF), and a Make Grant from RACC (Regional Arts & Culture Council).

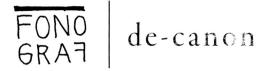

FONO GRAF | de-canon

A MOUTH HOLDS MANY THINGS

a de-canon hybrid-literary collection

edited by Dao Strom & Jyothi Natarajan

FONOGRAF EDITIONS
Portland, Oregon

CONTENTS

There are dimensions to language that are very difficult to describe *with* language, and yet it is only in language—in trying to move through it—that one has the privilege of experiencing these dimensions. Language has an energy that eludes verbal expression; this is a reflective energy, language dreaming of itself... The dream is often not the text you're reading but comes from some other part of the page, some part of the text that is not quite visible.

Renee Gladman, *Prose Architectures*

We have in us autonomous languages for autonomous perceptions... There is no rest in any kind of perception.

Etel Adnan, *Journey to Mount Tamalpais*

If "hybridity" is to be of any use, it has to be always reframing, reconfiguring, and jostling any assumption that anyone can make about identity. For this it will have to question the impulse to resolve the undiagnosable.

Myung Mi Kim, fr. *Jacket2* interview (with Divya Victor)

Home for me is bound up with a migrant's memory and the way that poetry, even as it draws the shining threads of the imaginary through the crannies of everyday life, permits a dwelling at the edge of the world... I think of the poet in the 21st century as a woman standing in a dark doorway... She has to invent a language marked by many tongues.

Meena Alexander, *Fault Lines*

My mother recounts the day she found me "writing." No one had taught me how to write. "What are you doing, *mijita*?" she asked. "I'm painting," I told her, and went on speaking to the signs.

Cecilia Vicuña, *Spit Temple* (*"Performing Memory: An Autobiography"*)

What I know is that an inchoate desire for a future other than the one that seems to be forming our days brings me to a seat around any table to lean forward, to hear, to respond, to await response from any other.

Claudia Rankine, *Just Us*

neither you nor i
are visible to each other
i can only assume that you can hear me
i can only hope that you hear me

Theresa Hak Kyung Cha, *Exilée | Temps Morts*
(*"audience distant memory"*)

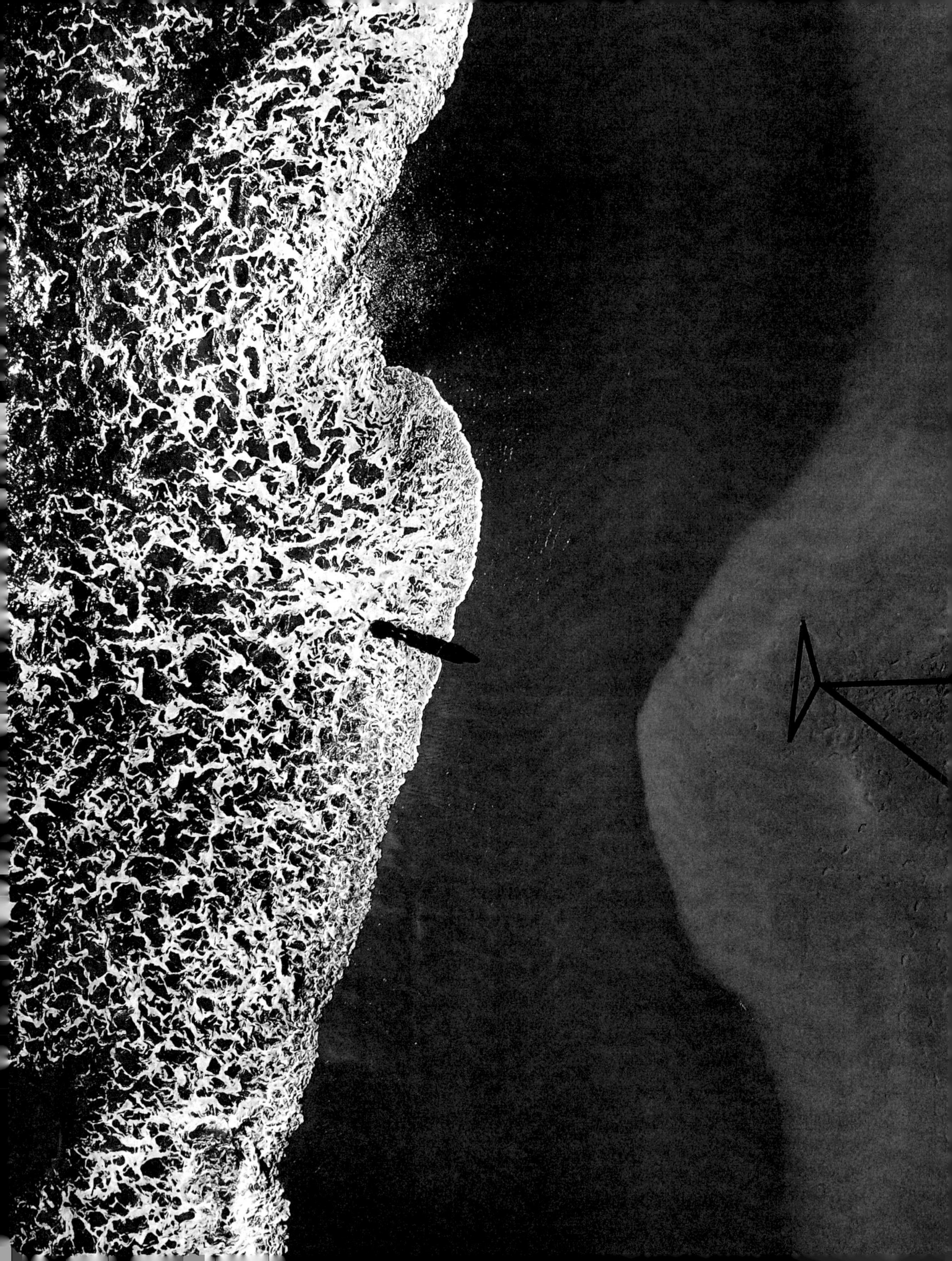

FOREWORD

Dao Strom

I am walking along a shoreline.
A shoreline is a place, a geography,
where two elements—water and sand—meet.
We call this place of meeting a line,
but it is also the continual erasing
of line. How water writes, erases, rewrites.
Its own delineation of: the encounter.
The shape of how these two realms meet a constant
Inconstant. Fluctuation of.
Demarcation. Is it water's tendency to-
ward a constant inconstancy that insists on this
snaking of lineage—this lineal snaking?
Is it water the agent of erasure, even: self-
erasure? Or is it the sand's nature—of both
yield and subsume—
that refuses, resists, the holding
of line? Resists inheritance of the notion
line makes record? Surely we know
sand is an unreliable canvas. Is ambiguity of
canvas. A mutable, shifting substance of
page that does not wish to be page.
Together sand and water conspire.
Repeatedly evolving and eroding
the writing of their own betweens—
which is to say:
what is a boundary?
But a temporality of attempt.
At holding anything.   (All writing begins as boundary.)
I am walking along
a shoreline. Line that refuses
lineal nature.

I begin here, with this image and attempt to send text across the page evocative of the shape of water, because this is how the hybrid journey begins for me: a realization of the transmutability, the very tenuousness, of boundaries that separate, that supposedly demarcate realms otherwise as distinct as ocean and land. My own arrival into the realm of hybrid writing was, like this tracing of a shoreline, not a direct, not a fixed or predictable path.

Here are the facts: I had written and published two books of fiction—the genre that had thus far identified me as a literary author; I had, since my early 20s, also been writing songs on the side; I had an undergraduate background, a naive once-ambition, in filmmaking. I was trying to write what I believed might be another novel, a long-form book. But, images wanted to invade, and a straightforward throughline, characters with character arcs, plot, all those conventional narrative devices, continued to evade me. Instead, interiority and some esoteric, intuitive rhythm wanted to lead—an inner music vying to come through. I was aware of an elliptical nature, an unwieldy energy, at the subtle-beating heart, or twisted gut, of the story I was seeking to tell, that kept balking, digressing askew of the more normative, straight-paved roads expected of a "novel" or "memoir." The story I was seeking to tell had to do with Vietnam, with my own mixed-cultural family and parental legacies, with the usual diaspora and refugee lineages of war and exodus and inherited traumas, but for whatever reason I could not wrangle those lines—in my case, thorny vines—into a shape that was a legible or "traditional" enough format to be sellable. ("Not to belabor the point, but if you would just write in a more traditional format," my New York literary agent had once said to me.) But it was not that I was not trying; it was not even that I was trying, intentionally, to be difficult or experimental—it was just that as a writer I am limited: I could not lie, I could not pretend, I could not but follow the impulse of the art itself through which, in truth, I was wrestling with ghosts—and ghosts do not respect walls nor the notion of voicing through a single or same body, consistently.

And so, something in the work kept twisting—defying shape, container, resolution, or closure; the book that wanted to be needed to twist even further afield, needed to buck the leather constraints of "book" itself. I garnered rejections for this manuscript I was trying to write, I was gently released from obligation to my literary agent, also rejected by other agents and publishers. I found myself wandering a hinterland I had no map for—personally, creatively, professionally. In truth this was a very lonely period. At the time I knew no other writers who were trying to work across disciplines. I had no mentors; no community; no assurances that any of it was a very good idea. (No doubt, there existed examples of multidisciplinary artists and experimental writers, but I hadn't yet encountered them along the path I'd thus far taken.) I kept working, through the isolation and self-doubt, the discovery and alchemy of those 7+ years it took to find—to forge—my way through that first hybrid project, which I eventually arrived at describing as a "memoir in image + text + music." I found a small press publisher, lost them too (the press folded), made some new friends with whom I formed a loose publishing collective; I did all of my own editing, layout, design—learned the production line—and essentially published my first hybrid project on my own. If I had not taken it into my own hands as such, I am certain it would never have been permitted to enter the world in the form(s) it inhabits.

& what is writing? It begins
with cutting. Etymologically:
a verb; describing an action. *To tear,*
scratch, carve: line—immaterial
motion—impressed into or upon something
material. Stone; clay; leaf; pulp; fibers.
This tradition of the human
and mark-making. & why
do we—must we—write? The implement,
the stick, the chisel; the discovery
of puncture as tool
for claim or record. To arm
the self or the tribe against
forgetting, perhaps. To endeavor
to step outside of,
outlast, Time. Contained within
this *tear* (*tear*), however, always too an
impulse toward ownership. To draw
boundary between or around—
whether an object, geography,
observation, memory, or the ineffability
of experience. There is something we wish
to keep, somewhere we desire to belong to,
that we nonetheless know we are destined
—doomed—to lose. From its inception
writing was always a preparation.
For loss.

And I am talking about writing, but
I am also talking about hybridity. As a kind
of writing born out of such losses and knowledge
of losses. A writing assembling itself
amid/despite the vacuum of interstices,
ambiguity of middle-grounds, tangle
of intersections. A writing of refusals (to write);
a mutability of voice. Ebbs and
flows and many, repeated
obliterations. A writing that construes
itself of edges. Poly-
vocalities of entry and egress.
Assemblages of disassembly. Multi-

plicities. Duplicities. Many
-cities.

Let's return to water. I've always had a thing for rivers—I grew up along rivers that flow through the Sierra Nevadas of northern California, where—back in the 1850s—men who had come to mine gold from those rivers dug so much, they changed the course of those waterways. Rivers disrupted; re-formed. And, in the land where I was born, on the other side of the globe (from where had traveled with me those boundary-refusing ghosts), the patterns of rivers there too were heavily influential. Seasonal floods and deltas having cultivated a people who had learned to live in rhythm with the riverine vicissitudes of water; a myth that the first mother of our country's people wept the rivers into being, and those rivers then had wed her (and thus us) to the sea. A river sends tributaries—many mouths—to the sea. And as this book knows: *a mouth holds many things.*[1]

Which is to say: the theme of multi-
plicity is also a story of erosion.
Evasions; evolutions. De-
stabilizations. Dispersals; de-centerings.
(Dia-sporas.) The ground troubled, re-
written. A river breaks
from its main vein, because water possesses
ability to circumvent obstacles through frag-
menting—simultaneously multiplying
and dividing—itself. In order yet
to keep to its initial course.
Which was always simply to follow
gravity and rejoin
the sea, that primeval one-body
made of and fed by all
the mouths and streams.
I see multimodal writing
employing a similar tactic.
Of breaking apart to bring
together.

We are divergent and we are confluent. Most of us arrive here on our own, singly, singularly. We arrive each of us to our particular patch of wet, shifting sand of our own peculiar accord, or chords, let's say, idiosyncratically learned, then voiced.

---

1 Monica Ong, "Indigo Insomnia."

Because the path of learning, of discovering, the hybrid realm was not, for me, one guided by mentors or models, especially initially, I followed no one, exactly; no one led or invited me. As is often wanted on the topic of lineage, I could cite the seminal works and names that have held space in this realm—Cha, Adnan, Vicuña, Rankine (et al)—but, in truth, those writers' works did not come into my knowing until *after* I had made most of my journey through my first hybrid project, somewhat blindly, fumblingly, feeling as if I were navigating through a hinterland without a map. Yes: they were waiting for me, eventually, when I was ready to find them, and so honored to find them, and began then to also discover my contemporaries working in kindred, liminal spaces. In actuality: I learned from other so-called aspirants—other, current hybrid authors publishing via small presses, lesser-known—at the same time I was discovering the works of what we might call the masters—or mistresses—in the field: an albeit relatively short lineage of hybrid-experimental works by women of color working predominantly in English. I feel it important to observe that an initiatory part of this journey, one's commitment to it, may require (or at least did for me) a dive into the unknown, and willingness to abandon reliance on canonical thinking, canonical measures and validations and examples, as guideposts. At some point the markers stop—you venture into the open grasses of an open field, alone.

And for many of us, this learning, this tracing of invisible trails through overgrown grass, does not occur inside classrooms or existing structures. It arrives rather like a call on the wind we don't know where it is coming or calling from, that we hear (or feel) from our seat at a desk in a room, perhaps... and it requires us to turn our attention out the windows. Something beyond the glass beckons. A new fracturing of the light, a refracted strange *sotto voce* sound, new registers of echoes (...)

<We are divergent and we are confluent.>
<We are collective without being majority.>
<We are multiple without being conglomerate.>
<We are scattered <<through/across>> : we are amongst.>

& what kind of writing is it seeks
to destroy itself even as it builds
itself? & why this performance—under-
grass tactic—of divergence / di-
versions? this method of the many
faces?

& what if I describe the mechanical
arms of writing as a technology sutured to
our natural limbs, but that
we were not born with, and so we
learned how to operate them, navigate
their inherited (dys)-

functions channeled via our [true] [off-
center] mouths?

& what if I claim *ocean* as
my literary form, *sea* as my preferred
genre (if I must name one)? May I
cite *water* as my container / conveyor
of choice, through which I
may allow the unmediated
flows of that immaterial substance
we call *voice*?

> <

To comprehend that one thing can be multiple things at once and still be wholly that one thing; and that multiple things—separate—can simultaneously be the same thing. To understand there is no direct line for arriving at simultaneity or multivalence. To understand hybridity as a way of saying we are neither this nor (completely) that; at the same time we are this *and* we are that, maybe even that other that, too. And it's all subject to change. We might dissolve or evolve any boundaries. And we won't stay put where you think you've safely placed us, named us, tried to corral us. There is—necessarily—no formula to repeat us, our arrivals or our formations. Such positions and territories are not always supported, condoned, understood, or even accurately perceived by either the *heres* or *theres* one may have strayed from. Hybridity as a challenge to the dominion of identities. Hybridity as a state of slippage, unwilling to capitulate, an accepted tenuousness of being

---

Image still from Dao Strom's music video for "Jesus/Darkness"; filmed by Roland Dahwen, edited by Kyle Macdonald, 2022.

EDITORS' NOTE

Dao Strom and Jyothi Natarajan

This book is an attempt to contain works of literature that are, in truth, uncontainable.

Thus, we begin by acknowledging that this book is an insufficient container. It cannot fit the entirety of these works—ones that use moving image, performance, audio, and sculpture, among other forms—into its body. This book, after all, is made up of (only) pages and ink. Herein may lie both the paradoxical nature of, and need for, hybridity.

We start here to address the paradox of trying to "anthologize" a type of literature—a literary arts—straining against and splitting the seams of its textual confinements, that spills messily across borderlines into other art domains, that by its very nature *resists containment*—the hybrid-literary exists because it cannot be relegated to, is not at home within, any one realm alone.

Hybrid as a term often denotes something made up of other things not typically found together: "a thing made by combining two different elements; a mixture."[1] A thing that draws its characteristics from two (or more) differing—maybe even opposing—realms, hybrid also in some contexts thus connotes a thing that was not meant to be. Not meant to be where we find it and/or not meant to be, at all.

There are of course some notions of the hybrid that connote a harmonious joining of differing elements, but in our inquiry via this collection we noticed many of our contributors utilizing the hybrid more so as a way to refuse, and re-fuse, literary forms, to arrive at defiant new shapes—unruly, unprecedented—of their artistic practices.

However, before we get too attached to any one definition of "hybrid" or "hybrid-literary," we want to also say: the term "hybrid" is another insufficient container. As naming is itself another attempt to contain, we recognize that the impulse to assign one name to this kind of work may be antithetical to the critical intentions and energies pulsing within such works. And so we use the terms "hybrid" and "hybrid-literary" as merely a starting point, as placeholders in a place, a space, that wishes to be signposted by no single name alone.

~

---

1 *Oxford Languages* definition.

Hybrid; hybrid-literary; hybrid-lit; literary arts; image-text; visual poetry; cross-disciplinary; interdisciplinary; counterdisciplinary; cross-genre; genrequeer; translations; performance writing; performance text; poetry performance; collaborative; experimental memoir; experimental poetry; poetry-art; docu-poetics; polyvocal; multimedia writing; asemic writing; multimodal writing; life writing—these are just a few of many names that may describe this in-between realm of literature, as sourced from our contributors and in conversations with collaborators. For the purposes of this introductory statement we will use the term "hybrid" as a way to point toward—yet to never sufficiently encompass—this realm of genre indeterminacies, which we also understand must, for its own vitality and agency, continue its refusals and resistances of nomenclature.

~

As we set out on this editing and curating journey, we were aware of other literary anthologies that approached the term "hybrid" as meaning the combining of different literary genres, such as prose and poetry, poetry and nonfiction, and so forth; but largely did not invite into this scope anything not-textual. Literature, it seems assumed, must necessarily be comprised of words. Text on paper. Books with pages. Language as written and read, writable and readable.

As editors (and as writers, artists, and readers ourselves) our desires and questions related to the hybrid-literary were not satisfied by the predominantly textual constraints we had thus far found in other literary references. Perhaps hybrid is an imperfect term, again. But, the impetus to break through language into and with other forms of languaging, to lift language beyond the page, beyond the book, was crucial to us in our contemplations of what hybridity might mean, could or should mean, within the domain of literature: within the domain of "the letter."

In our initial call for submissions we specified looking for works that reach "beyond the textual" and at the same time still utilize "language as a primary material." What does it mean to break out of/through/into the domain of *the letter*, with elements that present language—*lingua, tongue*—in other forms: visual, embodied, sonic, asemic, tactile, and more? That may conceive of text, and the experience of text, also as text*ur*al, as *con*textual? We wished to find work that rooted itself in practices of writing and language while also bringing into question the very parameters and shapes such letters and marks are generally expected to follow in order to be understood; to be deemed legible. We also sought works that engaged us multi-sensorily—where the somatics of the writer's practice and/or the somatics of reading could be felt in the work. In short, we sought works that could bring into contemplation, into challenge and awareness, among many things, also the *materiality* of text.

And why is this important? To consider text as a chosen material (vs. as an immutable bedrock of writing) means to acknowledge the manipulability of said material, as well its susceptibility to the weathers, the temporalities and fallibilities, of circumstance and design. Additionally, the advocacy for hybrid-literary forms is at home in De-Canon's broader work—that of "un-settling" and "de-canonizing" past and existing notions of an entrenched western canon of literature. It should be noted, however, that De-Canon's mission was never to merely replace white authors' names with a list of names of authors of color, but rather to unsettle the very tendencies toward "canon"—our societal desire for an establishment of standards and criteria for so-called entry—itself. Literary gatekeepers by and large have resisted admitting other "modes" of writing into our conception of the western literary canon, and we might pause to wonder why this is so. Why are they—academics, critics, the publishing industry and by consequence its readers—so averse to or wary of a writing that refuses to be just writing, just words? What is the risk this really poses? What is it that is threatened—by an image interrupting a page of text, or by the failure of text to stick to the usual grid of text-traffic, or by the possibility that we might begin to compose literature, which is to say communication and connection, knowledge and self-invention/self-imagination, using more than just text? That we might, rather, begin to infuse words—and our capacities for "reading"—with somatic and other powers? The hybrid-literary disrupts, de-stabilizes, on a level of paradigm.

~

Most of the works in this collection do utilize text, but not always is text the dominant facet of a piece, and not always does or can the text stand on its own without the accompaniment or juxtaposition—the interrelations—of its other elements. This is key to note: the webs—multiple points—of interrelation present *within* each hybrid work. Sometimes text leads but may occur also as supplementary or intermediary to other aspects, serving as documentation or transcription of a performance piece or interviews or a research process, for instance, wherein those interviews might then spill into polyvocality or collaborative action or collage; the journey of research into pilgrimage-performance—often, wider nets of action and interaction are occurring somewhere off of the page, the uncontainability of a hybrid work's "whole self" again reified through its unwieldiness of form.

Sometimes the text is visual, rendering visual text-bodies or visual music across the white canvas of the page. Sometimes the text intertwines and dialogues with images, or appears as tactile handwriting. In a number of these pieces, the making or shaping of text is itself ritual, alchemizing a grieving process or "translating" one's neuro-divergent states—in these moments, the hybrid becomes a way of articulating states of feeling and perception that elude conventional styles of articulation. In another instance, binary code is paradoxically rendered via images of analog objects (leaves, fruits), gesturing to the fraught zone between digital and analog where our society presently wrestles, prompting us to consider the imminent presence of new forms of "writing" (i.e. code, algorithms, programming, AI-generated texts). In the works of this collection, again and again, we encounter text as merely one part of larger designs; text working in collaboration with other mediums; text pushing at the very bounds of what we believe text to be and how it should function. In many pieces the "seams" between mediums, a sense of the hybrid process itself, is, if not overtly visible, evanescently, aurically present—a continual reminder of the precarity and still-evolving potency astir at these intersections.

At the restless heart of this collection, at the heart of our desire to examine and present hybrid-literature as its own resonant and relevant field, lies a challenge to some fundamental questions: What *is* reading? What *is* writing? And, how are we to write and read, today, now, and moving forward, if we are to truly acknowledge all of the different fluencies and frequencies feeding into the streams of our multiple ways of languaging, of living?

As we wrote in our initial call for submissions: "We see the medium of language as a complexly riddled and rife material of the 21st century, one that is multi-textu(r)al (textual and *con*-textual), made of more than words, interwoven, punctured, fragmented, grafted, possessing power to construct and deconstruct, fed into by many rivers of experience: our marginalizations and migrations, diasporas and displacements, invisibilities and hyper-visibilities."

To fulfill this search, we chose to focus on hybrid works by BIPOC women and nonbinary writers because we know that the embodied perspectives and experiences of those living already on the far peripheries, those both gender- and race-marginalized, are also likely to be those most practiced and imaginatively resourceful—by necessity—at navigating, and generating, alternate byways for survival, expression, communications, cultural and creative productions and connections; for activating the creative possibilities of language.

~

We began to observe the subtle echo of a number of thematic impulses among the contributions collected here. Interrogations of the past, often as an accumulation of loss or as hauntings, have led quite a few writers to use hybrid forms as a way to play with gaps in the archives, whether it was remixing visual artifacts, culling from family archival materials, writing poems into absences and cracks in-between, or embracing the elusiveness of documentation. Several of our writers seemed to migrate toward hybridity at times when words were not enough or were difficult to access. Here, the gaps are opacities, ruptures, distortions, and silences in language and speech. We saw how hybridity begins to form bridges or portals at the peripheries of language. Still other writers wished to chart landscapes—real or imagined—and in so doing also orient the body in space(s). The invocation of performance in some of these works insists on the presence of the body as being and the body as language. It would be impossible to catalog the full breadth and nuance of the works collected here in a description of themes, but the reverberations remain.

~

In sequencing the works in this book we chose to forgo categorizations, such as determining "types" of hybridity. Since so many of the pieces are made up of different combinations of formal elements and techniques, if we were to try to organize works according to aspects of form or modality, inevitably we would find many works having the potential to belong in multiple categories. Creating categorizations of hybridity also seemed to us counteractive to the ethos of porousness and ambiguity this collection was, in truth, seeded on.

Instead, our sequencing follows an associative logic, a logic of juxtaposition and flow, contrast and complement, arrived at via a process of close-listening and looking for subtle connections—tendrils, glimmers, a shared current, refractions or reflections, buried signals—from one piece to a next, thus placing them in tenuous conversation with one another. Sometimes we placed pieces in juxtaposition to evoke contrasting dynamics; sometimes we heard a thematic element in one piece subtly "echoed" in another piece, and wanted to respond to those reverberations. As in the world we live in, the way one might find oneself in a room or other public space suddenly next to someone inhabiting an entirely different sphere of circumstances than oneself, the pieces in this collection sometimes leap long distances from one to the next, in terms of geography, culture, genre, time, realms of experience/viewpoint; but, sometimes, the associations may be apparent, closer, clearer. A voice enters a room or steps onto the stage of the page, and another follows, sounding in the particular way that it may, and a form of dialogue—an interaction of some acute nature—is born.

The term "anthology" also gave us pause. We address this here only because we began this project by calling the book an "anthology." But, what is an anthology, and what are its expectations of presentation or representation? We found ourselves wary, for instance, that the term "anthology" might lead readers to expect a complete survey on hybridity, defining its formal parameters and naming its seminal makers. Our curation, we acknowledge, is not a complete survey, and is inevitably influenced by our own embodied and individuated, cultural and aesthetic, lenses. What we offer here, thus, is just one gathering of hybrid makers, time-stamped by a particular temporality, just emerging/stepping into post-2020. And, while there are certainly some works and authors (that may be called seminal) whose voices and ways have permeated the atmosphere of our own reading and thinking around hybridity—Theresa Hak Kyung Cha's *Dictée* is a title that often arises in discussions of hybrid literature—we also shy from the impulse to establish hierarchy or lineage in this realm. Rather, we feel it important to maintain this as a field in which there may be many, different, and even in some cases no ancestors: the truth being that many writers arrive to this territory of in-betweenness—this myriad of intersections—because there is no predetermined literary lineage that has effectively spoken to or welcomed them.

Etymologically, the word "anthology" grows out of a concept of *logia* (a "collection" or "gathering") of *anthos* ("flower")—this belying perhaps a notion of "poems" as "flowers": as small, collectible pleasures. We have opted, rather, to use the term "collection" in our subtitle, for a slight difference in positioning. While the word "anthology" angles us toward considering the *what*—the objects: nouns—that have been gathered, the word "collection" arrests us, rather, *inside of the action* of gathering: "collection" stems from the Latin *collectio* or *colligere* (a "gathering together" or "to gather together"). Thus, in declaring this a "collection" we present this book as itself an act of gathering together, a "collecting together" of multiple voices—multiple within themselves as well as multiple amongst and in concert with one another.

~

How and what one reads is inextricably shaped by the literature that is published. For larger corporate publishers, perceptions and calculations of what will sell leave such little room for experiments. Even as numerous independent presses, including Fonograf Editions, take aesthetic and political risks, it's hard not to overstate what an uphill journey it is for writers of hybrid literature when it comes to growing an audience and distributing their work.

This fact makes us aware of the possibility that readers opening the pages of this book may not have encountered a collection of this kind before. The contents of this collection inhabit multiple intersecting modes, resisting categorization as just art or just literature. Such hybrid forms might feel at first cryptic or even, to some, wilfully illegible. But, alongside that initial reaction of confoundment or impasse, an opportunity (which we wish to encourage) presents itself: How might we, as readers, alter *the way we read* to make space for the simultaneous registers, forms, and mediums that are present? What if we, as readers but also as people, could encounter such differences of expression and articulation as invitation—into another's unique, personal lexicon—rather than as obstacle?

A reader of poetry is generally asked to stay attuned all at once to form and figurative language, alongside sound and syntax, among other elements. A poetry reading practice is centered not only in curiosity but also in the sense that a reader has a role in completing the work in front of them. The poem requires the reader. Hybrid literary works can also help bring into sharper awareness this necessary and dynamic collaboration between reader and writer.

As editors of this collection, when we came across something that felt difficult to parse in a given work of hybrid literature we looked closer. We listened. We paid attention to what we felt at the edges of our understanding. What made a piece take this form? What were we able to observe if we slowed down the way we read? If we read a piece aloud? If we rotated the page? If we stepped away and returned? If we contemplated not just content but also the relationships—the spaces—between the various hybrid elements? As editors, we were confronted again and again with the need to defamiliarize how we read.

This collection also is not meant to be read in any fixed direction. One might read it from beginning to end, thus attempting to follow the associative and intuitive process we applied in our editorial sequencing of the pieces. But you might also skip around, or open at random, and in doing so become aware of which works ignite which senses.

For some, many of the works collected in this book may yet beckon a desire for context. At the back of this book, you will find a section of contributor reflections. We asked each contributor to write briefly on the intention and process behind their work and/or on how they interpret hybridity through their practice. We chose not to include these reflections alongside each contribution, in part to resist the temptation for context to precede a reader's own perception of the work. In this spirit we also chose throughout the main pages of the book to keep captioning and footnotes to a minimum—what we deemed only necessary for the initial encounter.[2] And yet we understand that, for work that is conceptual in nature, process and intention might function like a key. The appendix of statements can thus be read in a variety of ways. You may find yourself peering back to this section to find clarity. You might read the section as a collection of micro essays. The additional contextualizing information is there for the reader to turn to if or when, and in whichever order, they so choose.

Autonomy and consent are aspects of the reading process this book proposes. We invite you, reader/viewer, to form your own relationships with the writers and works in this collection, to complete the communique between audience and artwork in your own intimate and individual ways, to formulate your

---

2 A complete listing of artwork credits, details, reprints, and permissions is available as an appendix at the back of this book.

own paths for navigating through these pages. We also wish to allow the works themselves the space to "teach" the reader "how to read" them via the encounter, first and foremost.

~

This book arrives into readers' hands in 2024. The impetus for this book was seeded in 2021, when the editors sat brainstorming on a hillside in Laurelhurst Park in Portland, Oregon, during a time when we still could meet only outdoors and had not sat in one another's physical company for many months. A period in which concepts of connection and collectivity were shifting, all around us, societally and globally, in many ways. De-Canon as a social practice art project had previously depended on gathering in a physical space, around physical wooden boxes containing books by authors of color. The receiving of a small community grant initiated the question: What forms of "de-canonizing" should we enact next? How can we, amid the present societal uncertainties, continue our project of centering writers of color and challenging canonical concepts of western literature? The decision to curate "space"—asynchronous, aspatial, hybrid, nonphysical yet replete with the palpability of "voice," and physical in the sense of a portable object—began to evolve: the collection you now hold in your hands is not just a collection of literary art works, but also an act of social engagement, an endeavor of connectivity across distances, absences, boundaries, perceived differences, and separations.

~

To close, a note on the title of this collection: "A Mouth Holds Many Things" is drawn and adapted from a line in Monica Ong's "Indigo Insomnia," one section of Ong's "insomnia poems" series included in this volume. The full line reads:

> "The mouth holds many things except the language of the new, still forming between the lungs. The spoken vow we breathe, but don't yet know how to defend."

While the initial image of "a mouth holds many things" illustrates for us the multiplicity in hybrid, multimodal literatures, the full line returns us to the uncontainability of what we are here provisionally naming hybrid literature, a literature that emerges with a "still forming" sense for how it might manifest. As new languages, as experiments of what has not yet been uttered.

A MOUTH HOLDS MANY THINGS

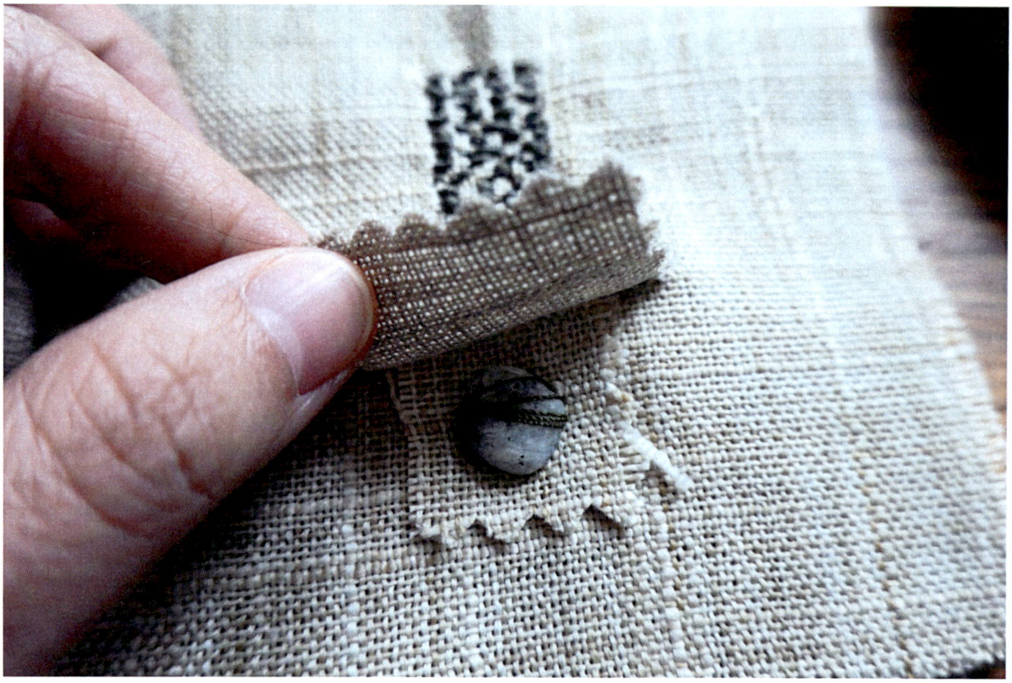

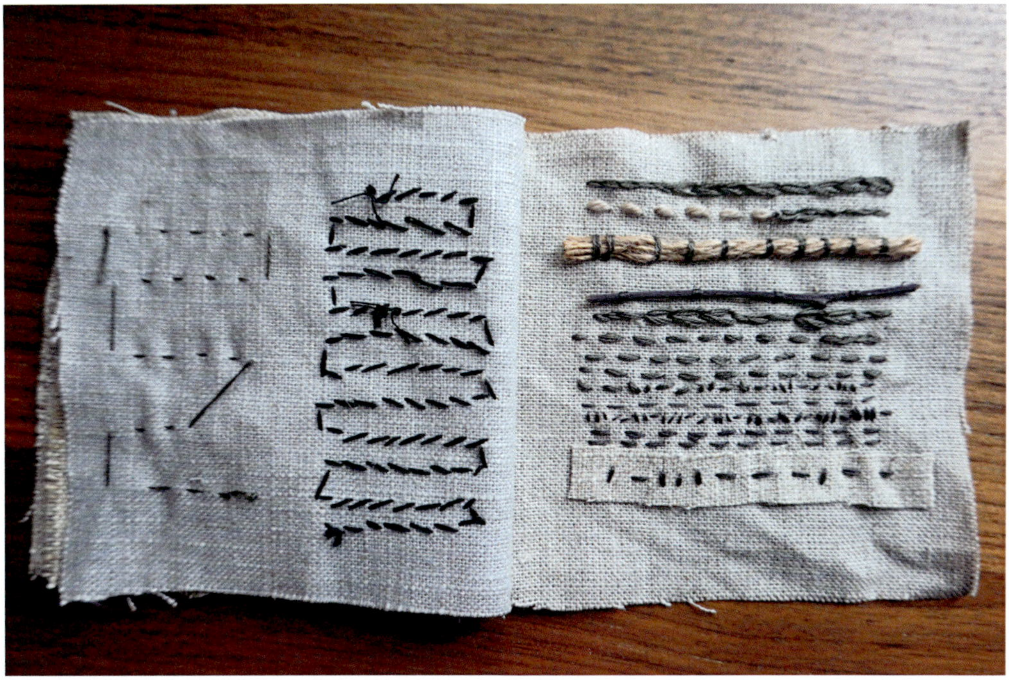

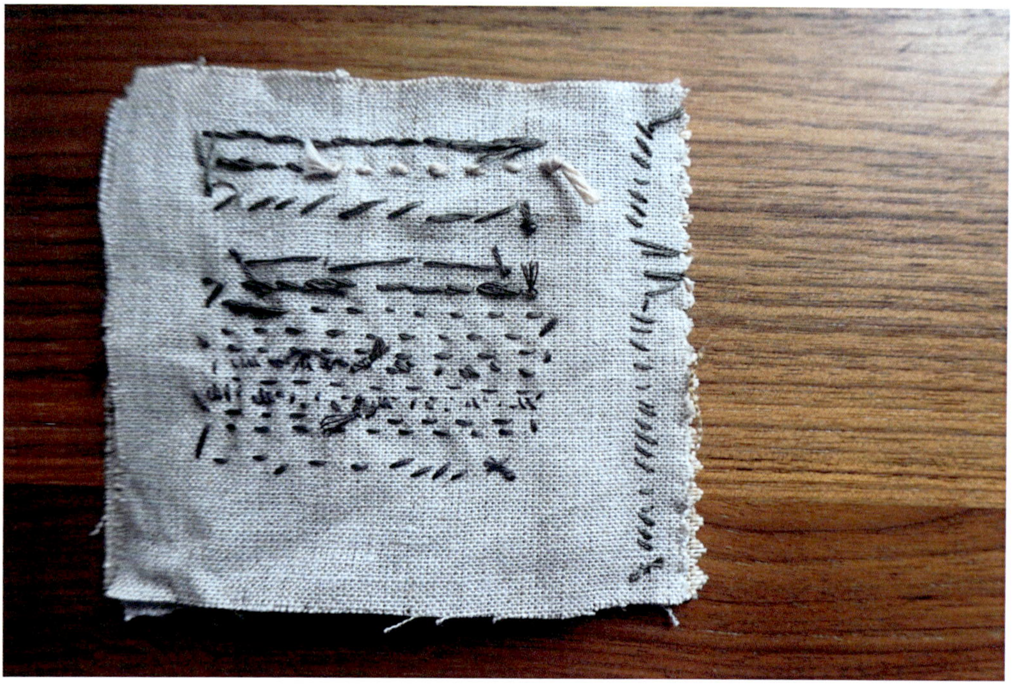

(Text)ile: Asemic Book [1]

FIELD NOTES

1
A compulsion to begin twining threads into proximal space: *body + language + geography*. If, as Walter Benjamin observes, "language has a body and the body has a language." If language is, according to John Berger, "a terrain full of illegibilities, hidden paths, impasses, surprises, and obscurities." A bewildering correspondence: she may have always received them this way, as envelopes of intimacy and wilderness.

2
If we define *ritual as poetry embodied*: a formal conjuring of language, epistemically rooted in intuition and the unknown, while grounding the body in time and space. Ritual as the desire for a *form* consisting entirely of *process*—a series of discrete intersubjective gestures ever unfinished, imperfect, material yet ephemeral, concrete yet fluid, containing yet surrendering. There is a dialectical engagement with temporality—*here and now*, yet *in conversation with past and future*; and a similar relationship with the objects of one's surrounding environment—to appreciate the *smaller and mundane* yet to invoke the *larger and sacred*. What is small is peripheral and marginal; what is large haunts and becomes an atmosphere. *Ritual* as a liturgical, artistic process of embodied utterances, which proposes, as poetry does, that attention, orientation, and care are ways of making meaning.

3
If *text* is also *textural* and *contextual*, then might we find meaning the way Tanizaki Junichiro finds beauty "not in the thing itself but in the pattern of shadows, the light and the darkness, that one thing against another creates"? As Roland Barthes says, "language is a skin: I rub my language against the other." A text is an array of relational structures. A pattern with an underside. We drift our fingers across its syntactical weave.

4
One lives all the time with what cannot be said, what has been lost across distances, what has been erased. A child of dislocation learns of her history through broken language, literally and figuratively. She learns about distance, the feeling of distance, between continents, histories, loved ones, selves. She learns about silence. Her language travels through various terrains and textures of water and along disparate geographies; it is filled with gaps and blanks, haunted and hunting. Her language: *felt* rather than *spoken*. Her history: *sensed* rather than *told*. What is learned breaks apart from dominant through-lines, not only in *what* but also *how*. What is learned: always an *underlying*, *in the periphery*, or *just beyond reach*. What is learned, above all:

porousness. Inside the home, her linguistic environment is a kaleidoscope—multiple, fractured, shifting—through which she learns to speak in accumulations, in tangles, from the present, from the past, in the margins, in the gaps between, in so much blank space. Inside the body, she internalizes a language of leaving, of perpetually leaving, and never quite arriving.

5
The truth is that language by nature can only ever provide a temporary half-home. It approaches wholeness not because of the structures but because of what is textural, dynamic, fluid inside. We collect and arrange debris from the world and conjure, like a spell, the rest. Language is a never-ending journey, and in the meantime, we make a series of loosely caught patterns. We are never quite sure where we are going, only that we are going.

6
In *The Rustle of Language*, Barthes proposes that a denatured language is the only kind of language that fulfills itself. Like Barthes, I am interested in a notion of *text* that "practices the infinite postponement of the signified" by way of "dislocations, overlappings, variations." The result, according to Barthes, is a kind of *rustle*, which I imagine as a vast gauzy fabric, and which he describes as a "horizon...in the distance like a mirage... a double landscape." There is a quality of the polyvocal that, rather than enclosing, opens up a field of plural meanings. Barthes writes that "the Text is plural... it fulfills the very plurality of meaning... The Text is not coexistence of meaning, but passage, traversal..."

7
Throat of the needle puncturing fabric, punctuating tiny holes; friction of the thread pulling through; strand, fiber, material; color and thickness and setting; tension as texture; raveling and unraveling; a recursive rhythm of return and departure; repetition, then rupture. "Language is what moves me from space to space," I once heard Yiyun Li say.

8
Elsewhere Barthes theorizes writing in terms of *fragments*: "so many stones on the perimeter of a circle...at the center, what?" A text might circle an unsayable center, but if we consider the image of a *nest*, might the center be not a vacuous hole but something that *holds* and even *homes*? In the past I have described my process of writing as "sew[ing] shadows together to form a roof above my head" or "a net I am always weaving." A child weaves for herself a net with which to catch herself; it is necessarily full of holes, hollows, crevices, gaps. Gaston Bachelard describes in *The Poetics of Space* how a bird's nest is "a house built by and for the body, taking form from the inside." A nest is a contextual construction—a ritual interaction with environmental detritus, configured by the body into an arrangement carrying its intimate imprint.

9

It is possible for language to be purely a textural landscape, inside of which, say, a mother and daughter exist. The field they share: the tenderness of language as affectively intimate yet functionally estranged (and vice versa). For my childhood home was a shifting web of various overlapping linguistic atmospheres, only some of which were precisely decipherable to me. What is true for an infant continued, for me, into adulthood: language was never only, or even primarily, the part about communication; it was the texture of the sounds, like a skein enveloping me, a shelter so deeply and sensorily ingrained, I could almost touch it. Even syllables empty of semantic meaning could make a thick canopy around my little body as I moved around the house. *Text*: full of dark corners and hiding places.

10

The mechanism of language is inherently violent; it encloses, delimits, excludes. In order to be whole, I entered the world pulling at silence. What does it mean to search for language amidst sites of silence? To seek an alternative utterance—one that is immigrant, in its untranslated body, at once home and un-home? A textile is a kind of field, where the stitch is a unit of articulation at turns reparative, protective, aesthetic. If, as Édouard Glissant proposes, "we clamor for the right to opacity for everyone"; if, as Trinh T. Minh-ha similarly claims, it is ethical "to leave the space of representation open" for everyone to inhabit as they wish, then: how might we approach *text* as a field of encounter between Self and Other? How might we consider the shifting relations between legibility/illegibility, opacity/intimacy, absence/presence, dislocation/location—as well as the roles of intuition, ephemerality, and marginality in meaning-making? What is the ghostly center, the interior gesture, of language; and how might we conjure, here, a home?

SHE GOT LOVE / VOICE BECOMING ARTIFACT / AFTERNOON DRESS FOR EMILY DICKINSON

SHE GOT LOVE

a circle of spells for Ana Mendieta

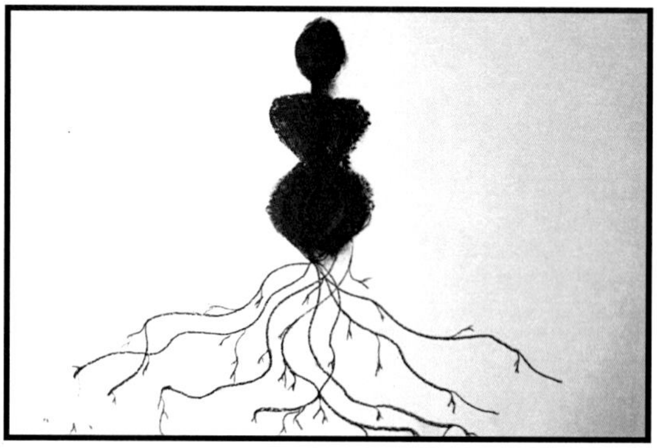

+ ojo como oja, muscles called the Orbicularis Oris will flutter-shut the eyes like twin solar events on the face/ bookmarked grimoire + cigarette burned dress + the widening O of the mouth around "no" + closing in on the pupil, little girl-doll in the eye + radial fiery round +

speak the name into the spell, needle voice in cloth, then speak her out // night comes on damasked, night under crushed velvet, no one sees it happen, sun-less oh oh oh says Cassandra + open vowel a vow avowal a vow a vow a vow + who is your unnamed source, is your source reliable, is your source in danger + ruido nido ruino +

+ pig doused with pitch & pig set on fire warping

no gallows walk, no gallows, no gall, no gal, no gal waking into a petalsoft nest, no fluttery no feathery sound no more + no gallows walk

"no" in arabic is a liquid sound la laa

a vow now open to the white compass of a question: WHERE IS ANA

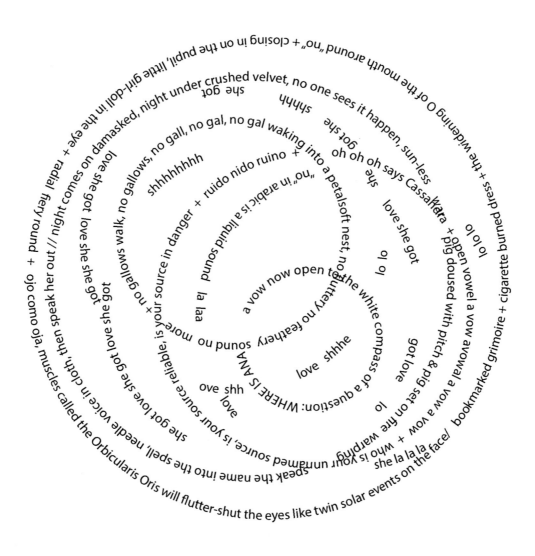

she got shhhh shhhhhhh she got love she got love she she got love she got love she got love she got love she got lo lo lo lo lo lo got love lo she la la la love shhhe ove shh love got she she oh oh oh

VOICE BECOMING ARTIFACT

tele/phone: faraway voice
tele/pathy: farflung feeling

a cassette
a casket

[hatef] is arabic for telephone, though [*telefon*] is more common a synonym, very cinematic your mother's *farawayvoice* on a tape, you recognize the sepal in it, in it, a youth and oath, inadvertently discarded, many a voice of a mother melted down in a landfill some time now

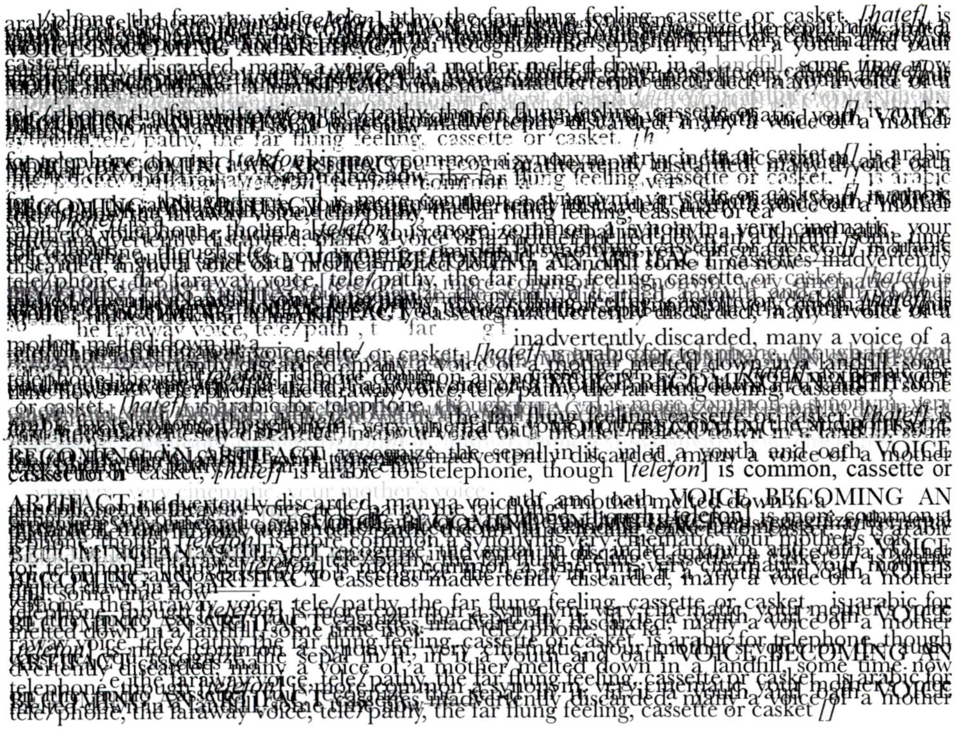

above; previous pages: stills from video poems 'She Got Love: A Circle of Spells for Ana Mendieta' and 'Wound Studies'

AFTERNOON DRESS FOR EMILY DICKINSON

LAVENDER INSOMNIA.

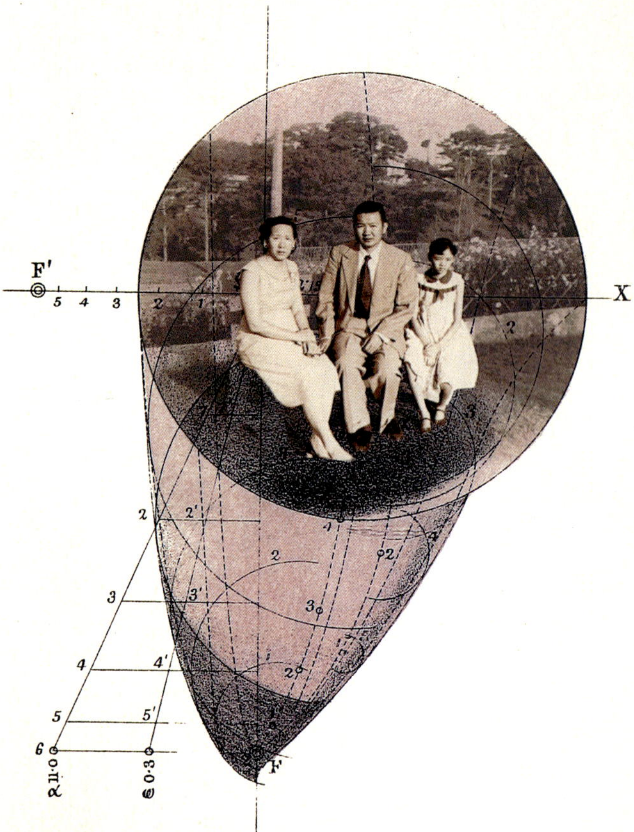

Fig. 13.

FIGURE 13. Lavender insomnia is my damp hair crying on the pillow. Dirty silverware in the graveyard kitchen buried beneath a long gloom. The crater's quality of silence after collapse that echoes aunt Juanita's sadness, her moon memory a whispered veil hanging from the window over the stairs. Jealous of winter vetiver and basil's rise in spring, lavender insomnia conspires with the body to step back off the edge of a cliff. Its purpled hands submerge the breath beneath an overturned boat. Grinds teeth like a dull blade biding its time. The tall numbers of every hour and every minute burn into the blackened doors shut tight in my eyes that long for a glimpse of the dreaming meadow. Violet and vine, she slips her lady fingers into the mind behind the blue firs. Stirs a hive of bees. The hundred eyes of my ancestors—still waiting for justice—gaze back at me.

YELLOW INSOMNIA.

All sentient beings have at one time been your mother. —Buddhist proverb

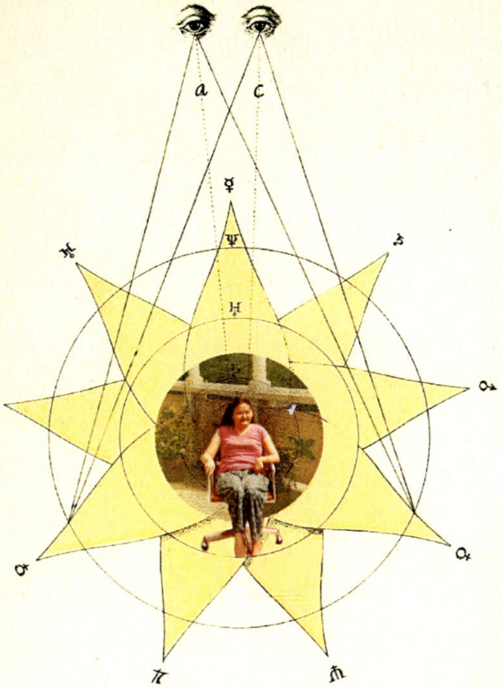

Fig. 19.

FIGURE 19. Yellow insomnia is the hiss of midnight over another city in flames, a white knee on the black throat of a father shattered, who was, in another life, my father, your father, your father's father, this heart (of our country) ground into the ground. Our shared hurt a constant waking. It is the inability to zoom out and distinguish the wound from the body, the body from the wound. Yellow insomnia is the knowing of being watched by eyes that never learned to see us whole. Walking in skin singed by a weak man's projection of peril. His monsters and mistresses take on the shape of your face, the movement of your hands, your body a shadow beneath this hallucination of America, slowly dying. How to unmake this deadly gaze? When will our love for you be sharp enough to cut the roots of the venomous vine? What is this life if not to honor yours, your daughter's, your daughter's daughter? Despite the drowse of grief, the night brain swells with uncontrolled blossoms of milk thistle and tansy, my troubled questions dotted with their sprawling lace border of blooming yarrow. The way a broken branch when touching soil manages to press its young green fingers into a new hope. Years before aunt Juanita died, I remember her examining me in grandmother's temple from her metal chair, her eyes searching me in prophecy. *There are two demon daughters standing inside you, one at each shoulder*, she said. Now is a door that refuses to close. The black tiger and the golden lion are terrifying or majestic depending on one's faith.

AMBER INSOMNIA.

Fig. 12.

FIGURE 12. Amber insomnia is loneliness hatching an egg in the dark. Each crack glistening, the itch of a wound still open. The constant waking in the skin's red crawl of ants. It is the saffron lining of grandmother's suitcase bursting with plastic packets of thinly sliced mangoes. Sugar and sulfur dust on leathery tongues, a scattered archipelago of sun-dried memories, all of them mistakes (mine) eating away at sleep. What one does and what one wants to do, separated by the sap of a golden hour. The kitchen light hollows out the belly of night, its din curled in the singed husk of a mother caving in. No dream, no slumber. Just an oblong table anchored by a bowl of cold cereal and tremor of tears eating away the deep. Unclosed eyes searching—always—behind the glass. Tonight is a nest deserted or at least the fear of one. Perhaps arrival is not a question of where but when. How opposite trains pausing at the same platform in the same moment look up. Wait. Doors wide open.

INDIGO INSOMNIA.

Fig. 17.

FIGURE 17. Indigo insomnia is a shrine of candles on the street corner of sudden absence, their dying strewn with flowers and handmade signs. Sleep, a scraggly stray, breathes with its tongue hanging low, sniffing each offering of dolls dampened by rain. Pauses. Then scurries into the alley towards the other side of amnesia.

Mother never told me my auntie's name was Juanita until she was near death, dying, or long dead. I can't remember. I called her by her title, Ah-Ching: as in Mother's Eldest Sister, as in Hidden Hurt, as in First Fire & Last Ember, as in Silent Shame Waiting Behind the Trees. We say the names of the dead more often in afterlife than during the departed's lifetime.

INDIGO INSOMNIA.

Indigo insomnia is the great waking, this birthing of the world anew. From the indigo, an even deeper blue, is it said. Perhaps this is why father hardly slept my entire childhood. His thin frame disappearing into the long white lab coat. A small square photo of my face in one pocket, and a black pager in the other, both blinking as he walked his rounds until the gray blue dawn.

The mouth holds many things except the language of the new, still forming between the lungs. The spoken vow we breathe, but don't yet know how to defend. Scrolling through the phone, one sees mostly ghosts or the self, ghosted, an accounting of strings stretched and broken. Someone slightly out of tune. Wondering if your voice is in the wrong chord, the wrong song, the wrong language, or just a painting of the ocean, its roar muted by a gilded gaze that sees but doesn't listen.

Indigo insomnia is diving into the deepest waters of memory to uncover the bodies hidden by our bad inheritance. My anxious study of patterns and vertices that squint for a brand new design. It is to know that there are no saviors except for that one decision standing outside your screen door. During the pandemic, brown paper packages pile up on the front porch like an avalanche of grievances. Time slows down so we can notice. Every person I pass on the street walks with an abandoned child clinging onto their backs. I look into those round, wet eyes and my mouth feels the same hunger, dry and gritty with ocean salt.

The problem with numbers that count our deaths is that they don't carry the smell of moss or fresh cut grass from the bottom of your brother's shoes. They easily forget that one is sometimes two, that bitter melons are actually sweet if you eat them far from home. You cannot hear the hours of static nor the quiet breathing of your mother swirling in clouds of dirty rice water between the long wet grains and your cold fingertips moving in circles. This is why it is called lossy data.

Indigo insomnia is the truth asking for a ring in her latest ultimatum. It is stillness acknowledging the injuries painted over by the flag or a blight of bronze. The mass grave of bodies that rise beneath Christmas snow. Their cause of death and elaborate cover up, one in the same. In school we call it History, enshrine terror in red, white, and blue ribbons that we wear in our permed hair to match summer's twirling dresses. Orchestrated fires pop across the black body of July's night sky. Children gather to lick patriotic popsicles named after the bomb.

AND THEN WENT TO SWIM THERE

IMANI ELIZABETH JACKSON

i did this,

the line

dropped

and drowned

and then

i went

and dredged

it up, inching

up its

weighted end

by hand, my hands

working properly,

making use of

the strength

of my back,

for inquiry's

purpose

the weather set

conditions for all

sounds

i could not be made

to fathom

without

consistent marking

and thus

went the line

probing

the dark stretch

below

a strait

unclear

surveyance

helps one know

what is possible

to be

known, eh?

conditions for all

sounds

the weather set

to see

the line

dropping

gave me

such pleasure

i went

and dredged

up the thing

counting

where it had gone

to the bottom

leagues below

of noise,

my back,

an extension or

of my hand

sounds

the weather set

conditions for all

i am   a well- composed thing gathering up   rock reef sand   specks and stones   scatter amid shells   i scatter   pebbles being priorly rock
being a flor now arest the floor   i compose a restful bed upon which no sleep might be   come upon   small scattered seaweed glob priorly mud come
upon   ooze small pebble come upon a flor   i was well-composed and leveled and priorly composed of resistant tests

tests may   be composed of silica may   be composed of calcite may be composed   of sediment gathering sediment
as shield as memory maze   might   i strut and sink   to find the record

all being being   silicate being   fecund being   of a range and and compound
silicate being   built as bone   being shields   to sully   and sets the claim   clear
all being drifts   to the floor   blooming   shards as atmospheric companions

rove   the flor to make for   rapid blooms   till   to tell our climatic stories

CURB 2

Mesa Star Chevron Gas Station
Mesa, Arizona

to bend	tall grasses
to edge	brittlebush
to bow	camphorweed
to restrain	pricklyleaf
to end	paperflowers

11° 39' 31" W

33° 25' 20" N

a knee   give way to yards folded

a handful   mulch red some selvage

a nod   hang flags then hang him

a sheaf   documented lullaby

& sign   here & here   & here

"Curb 2" multimedia created by Amarnath Ravva, for Curb(ed) multimedia website

On September 15, four days after the attacks on the World Trade Center, Frank Roque told a waiter at Applebee's: "I'm going to go out & shoot some towelheads." He added: "We should kill their children, too, because they'll grow up to be like their parents." Roque murdered Balbir Singh Sodhi as he was planting flowers outside his own gas station.

CURB 4

Subway Station
Queens, New York

of gray	concrete
	son
of gray	asphalt
	traveler
of gray	wool
	quiet
of gray	grisaille
	after drinks
of gray	charcoal
	a pigment

40° 44′ 57″ N

73° 53′ 27″ W

rain damp	battleship water	
print-shop owner	*roommate*	grey
smoking bitumen	wolf fur	
entrepreneur	*immigrant*	grey
undyed robes	bristle collar	
"an Indian Gregory Peck"	*nice*	grey
still, wet frescoes	flesh of flesh	
after breakfast	*after dinner*	grey
animal bones	white lead	grey
an immediate	in between	

"Curb 4" multimedia created by Amarnath Ravva, for Curb(ed) multimedia website

On December 27, 2012, Sunando Sen, a print-shop owner & immigrant who had lived in the United States for 16 years, was pushed off the subway platform & onto the tracks of an oncoming 11-car No.7 train by Erika Menendez. After her arrest, she told the police: "I pushed a Muslim off the train tracks because I hate Hindus & Muslims ... ever since 2001 when they put down the twin towers I've been beating them up."

BOAT PEOPLE

VI KHI NAO

"Boat Woman Bicyclist," watercolor on scanned refugee document

"Boat Woman in Red Bicycle," watercolor on scanned refugee document

"Blindfolded Squatting Boatman," watercolor on scanned refugee document

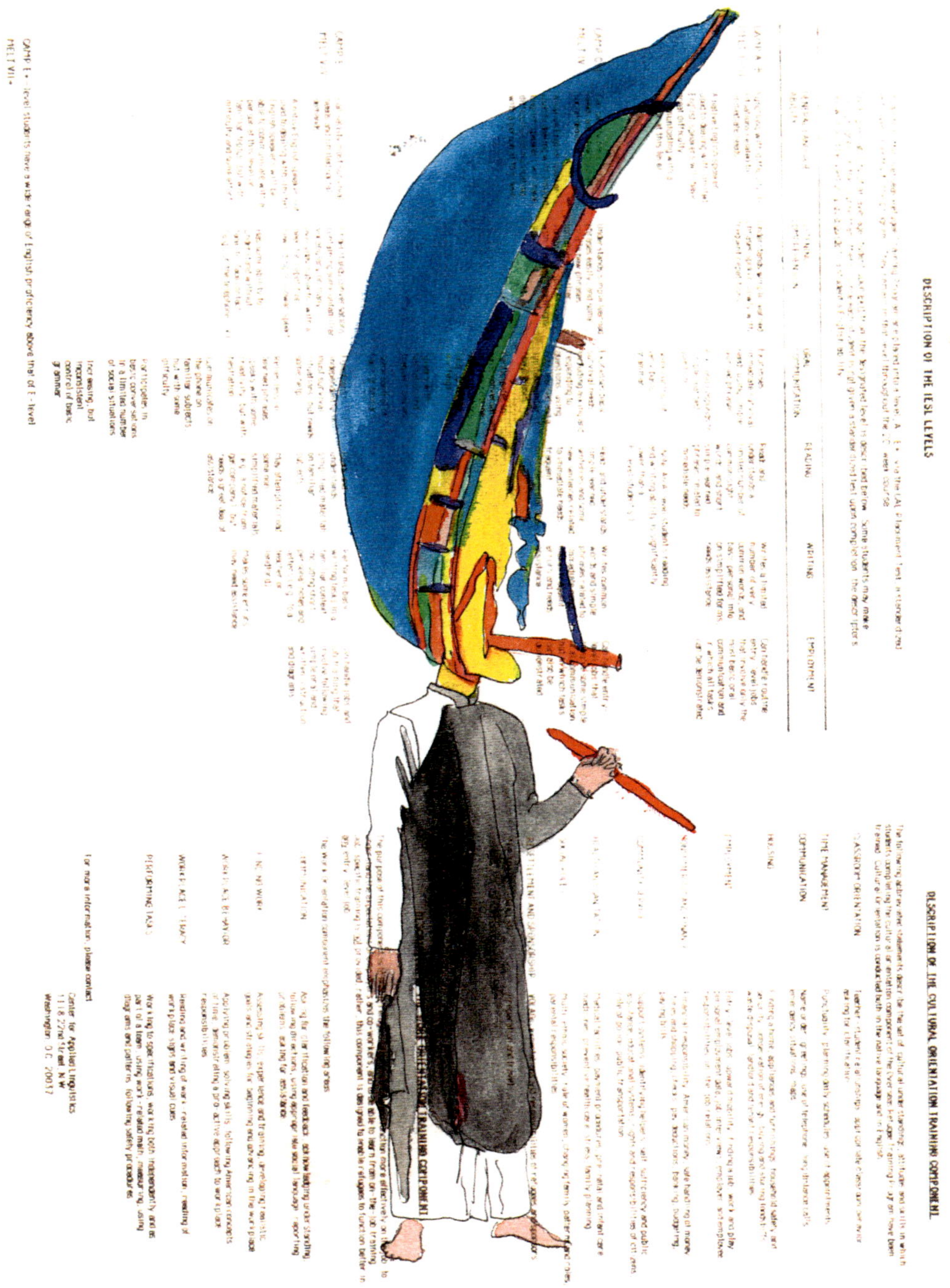

"Tunic Boatman," watercolor on scanned refugee document

to puncture their desire
she says: God is being difficult. But
grows ember by ember.

"The Rambutan Male Nudes"

[all the night]

In the solitary room of the skull
the flowers live without shape

but all the night has faces
& I am seen

I am watched as I take apart
the stems

In the solitary room of the skull
the flowers live without shape

but all the night has faces
& I am seen
I am watched as I take apart
the stems

A thorn from the rose
The Caterpillar's kiss
An Emptiness
Light from all angles
A lost child
All that dwells
in a single thought
such shapes
behind the eye—
a geometry from beyond

[in a single thought]

A copper eye floats on the water
at high noon

A thorn from the rose

The caterpillar's kiss

An emptiness

Light from all angles

Memory strides backwards

A lost child

A maggot's longing

Sadness of the plantain leaf

A narrow, blazing sword

A shadow beneath a shadow

[all that dwells]

All that dwells
in   a single thought

            such shapes
behind the eye —

a geometry from beyond

[un animalito del cielo me dio
un poco de lluvia para sanar mi corazón]

if an angel should speak
in a voice of blue hands
moving in darkness
over all the things inside —
blood to blood — and scent of cut grass —
the angel's voice, which stings & is green
which stirs creation
with only the force of music,
unheard —
If an angel should speak,
first you tremble — then you will know —
a kind of pain is at work, all things are
made of silence.

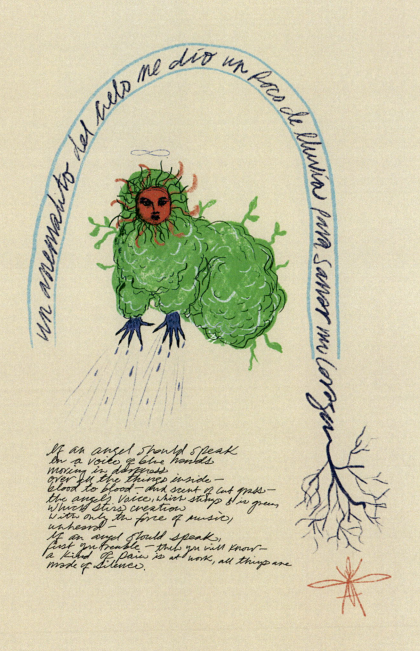

If an angel should speak
in a voice of blue hands
moving in darkness
over all the things inside—
blood to blood—and scent of cut grass—
the angel's voice, which stings & is green,
which stirs creation
with only the force of music,
unheard—
If an angel should speak,
first you tremble—then you will know—
a kind of pain is at work, all things are
made of silence.

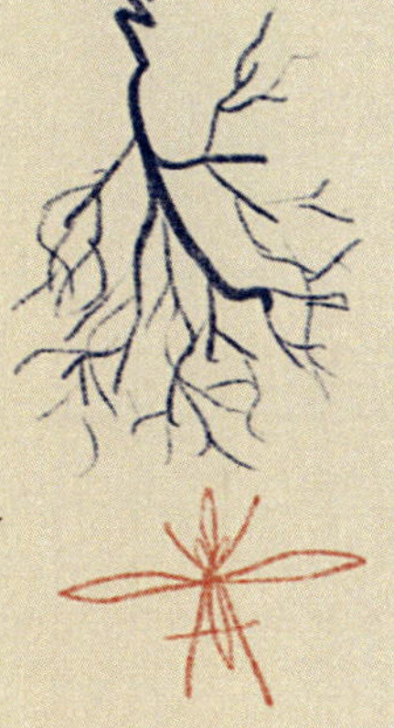

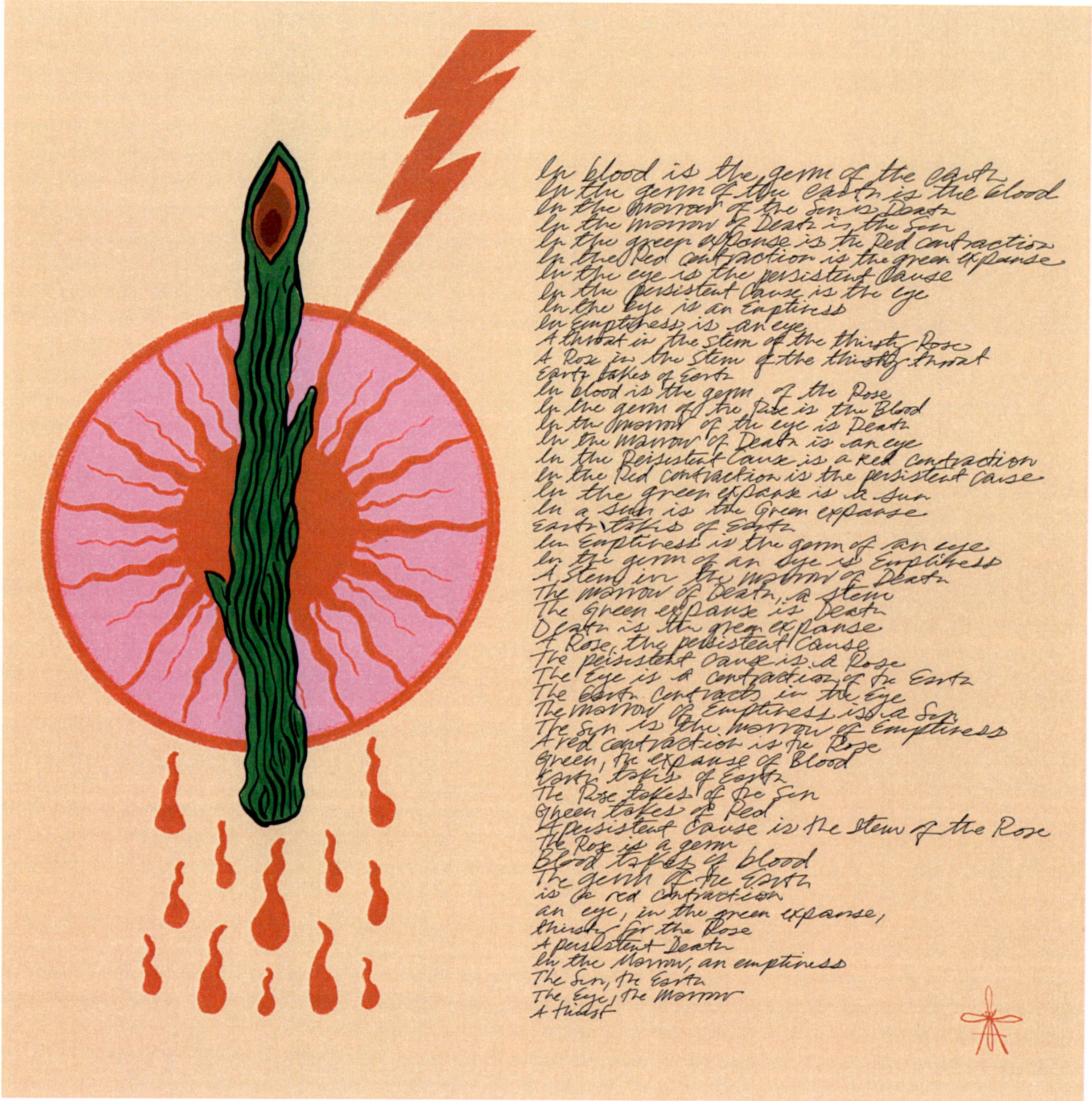
In blood is the germ of the earth
In the germ of the earth is the blood
In the marrow of the Sun is Death
In the marrow of Death is the Sun
In the green expanse is the Red contraction
In the Red contraction is the green expanse
In the eye is the persistent Cause
In the persistent Cause is the eye
In the eye is an Emptiness
In Emptiness is an eye
A throat in the stem of the thirsty Rose
A Rose in the Stem of the thirsty throat
Earth tastes of Earth
In blood is the germ of the Rose
In the germ of the Rose is the Blood
In the marrow of the eye is Death
In the marrow of Death is an eye
In the Persistent Cause is a Red contraction
In the Red contraction is the persistent Cause
In the green expanse is a Sun
In a Sun is the Green expanse
Earth tastes of Earth
In Emptiness is the germ of an eye
In the germ of an eye is Emptiness
A Stem in the marrow of Death
The marrow of Death, a stem
The Green expanse is Death
Death is the green expanse
A Rose, the persistent Cause
The persistent Cause is a Rose
The Eye is a contraction of the Earth
The Earth contracts in the eye
The marrow of Emptiness is a Sun
The Sun is the marrow of Emptiness
A red contraction is the Rose
Green, the expanse of Blood
Earth tastes of Earth
The Rose tastes of the Sun
Green tastes of Red
A persistent Cause is the Stem of the Rose
The Rose is a germ
Blood tastes of blood
The germ of the Earth
is a red contraction
an eye, in the green expanse,
thirsty for the Rose
A persistent Death
In the Marrow, an emptiness
The Sun, the Earth
The Eye, the Marrow
A thirst

[a persistent Cause]

In blood is the germ of the Earth
In the germ of the Earth is the blood
In the marrow of the sun is Death
In the marrow of Death is the sun
In the green expanse is the Red contraction
In the Red contraction is the green expanse
In the eye is the persistent Cause
In the persistent Cause is the eye
In the eye is an emptiness
A throat in the stem of the thirsty Rose
A Rose in the stem of the thirsty throat
Earth takes of Earth
In blood is the germ of the Rose
In the germ of the blood is the Rose
in the marrow of the eye is Death
In the marrow of Death is an eye
In the persistent Cause is a Red contraction
In the Red contraction is a persistent Cause
In the green expanse is a sun
In a sun is the green expanse
Earth takes of Earth
In emptiness is the germ of an eye
In the germ of an eye is emptiness
A stem in the marrow of Death
the marrow of Death, a stem
The green expanse is Death
Death is the green expanse
A Rose, the persistent Cause
The persistent Cause is a Rose
The eye is a contraction of the Earth
The Earth contracts int he eye
The marrow of emptiness is a sun
The sun is the marrow of emptiness
A Red contraction is the Rose
Green, the expanse of blood

Earth takes of Earth
The Rose takes of the sun
Green takes of Red
A persistent Cause is the stem of the Rose
The Rose is a germ
Blood takes of blood
The germ of the Earth
is a Red contraction,
an eye in the green expanse,
thirsty for the Rose,
a persistent Death
in the marrow, an emptiness
the sun, the Earth,
the eye, the marrow,
a thirst

[FROM] *an opera in acts*

ANNA MARTINE WHITEHEAD

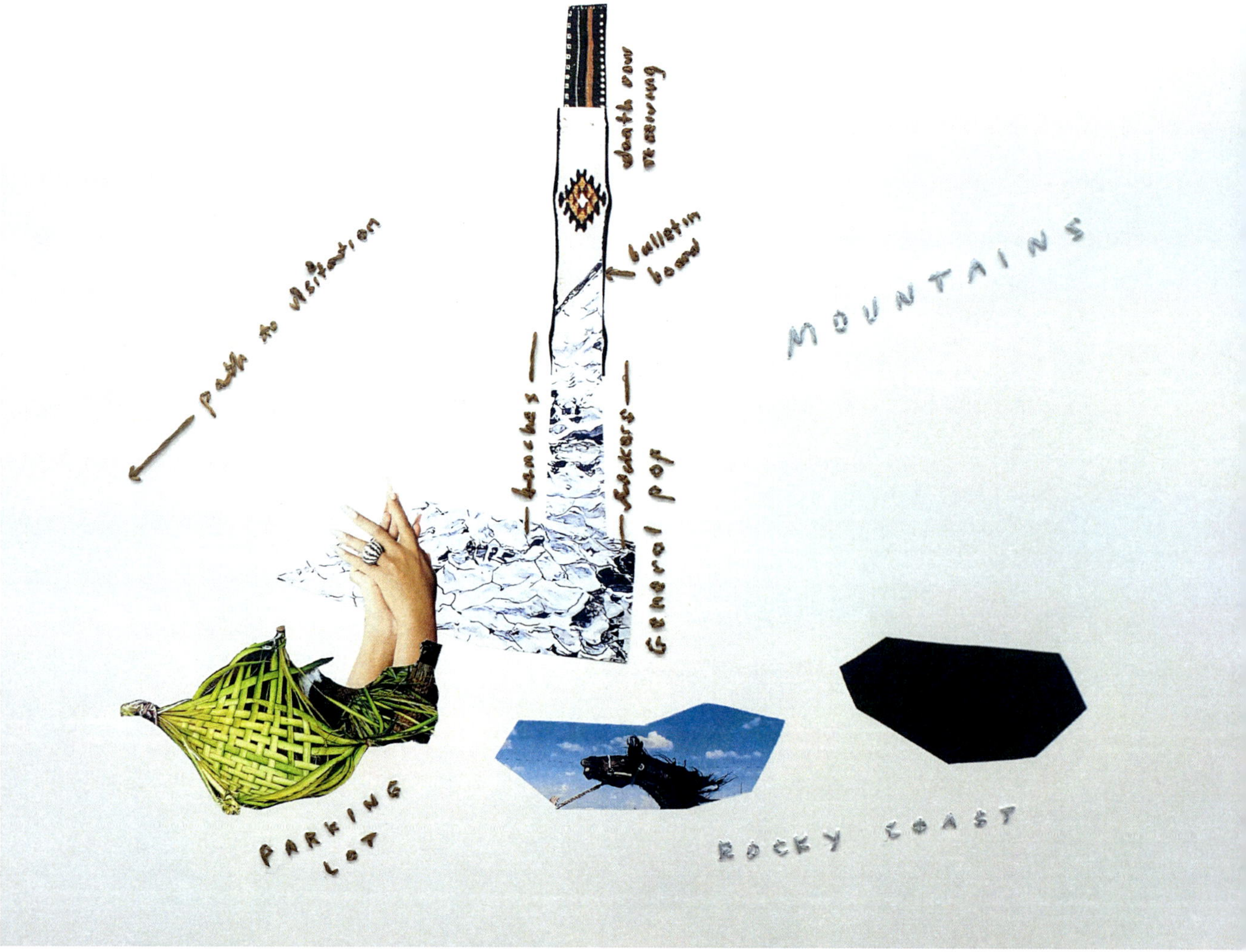

[I have so many dreams about prisons]

Adrienne [I have so many dreams about prisons] :

I have so many dreams about prisons.

Long winding road, forest. It thins out and then you realize you're there and there's these Black men tending the landscape. Like, OK, this is the most obvious.

Or long highways through almond orchards. Beautiful flowers. Trump signs, signs that say *Dust Bowl by Gavin Newsom*. Signs about the prison's values: *An honest place to work*. To be welcomed this way, into a death trap.

There's never many social visitors.

San Quentin is its own city. Nice houses, a post office, the prison. One main road that dead ends at the prison. You can turn off toward the hills or the water... Beautiful views.

Sometimes egrets.

Paddle boarding.

You can hear seagulls.

I'm holding my breath the whole time. Are my clothes right? Do I have enough dollar bills? Should I have left earlier? I'm already sweating. Do I need to reapply lipstick—because I can't bring it in. Once I enter, a whole other level of tension. Because of the guards. I'm really small and pulled into myself. I couldn't love this person more, and I couldn't hate this more. You have to go through this whole thing... All this shit just for an ounce of relationship. You have to earn it.

It erodes you over time.

As the girlfriend of someone inside with sex offenses, it's a whole other ballgame with the CO's. I'm caught between staunch resistance and schmaltz... Give something to get through all these barriers. The waiting room is so hectic. So crowded, lots of informal systems. You need to know all of them. If you don't know them, you'll be told quickly. It's a chaotic, emotional place, people almost getting into fistfights, having each other backs.

Entire relationships are formed... *How's the family? How's the job? Did you hear about that new bill that passed? Your father should apply. Let me get you more information.*

It's such a terrible place, obviously. Designed to do exactly what it's doing. And it becomes blatantly clear that this is what we have, this is how we get through it. All we really have is each other.

[Rosa's mom worked at the jail]

Gabrielle [Rosa's mom worked at the jail] :

My aunt was a prison guard. They gave her a gun and told her: If anyone runs, shoot them. But she knew she'd never shoot. She stayed up in the guard tower listening to Shakespeare records.

At Eastern, there were a lot of trees. I don't remember birds. A stone table, benches. It was pretty. An incarcerated Black man was out there gardening.

I feel this in my body even now. Needing to be careful... Be sweet, be soft, be non-threatening. Play a little small. Be contained, be concentrated. Be feminine, but not too feminine. I have a sense of dread that I've ruined the whole program. Making sure my sleeves are long and I don't have any contraband on me. Like, Shit, did I forget? Is there some part of myself that's here that's not supposed to be here?

This long walk, time is a variable. Who controls it? The guards are talking shit about me the whole time. But they're also warning me to be careful. Telling me my intentions are good, but these men will try to impregnate me.

When I finally get to the classroom, it's like an oasis. More of me gets to expand. Even though the walls are glass, so you are visible at all times. Everyone in there has a concentrated stillness. I have it too. Not about the studens, about the guards. I'd try to move the tables into a circular formation, but I can't really. It's more of a feeling of circle. The guards keep interrupting, almost like Don't get too full of your own imagination – you're still just a fuckin' asshole in prison. But my students own this space. The guards tell me I'm not allowed to leave under any circumstances. But then I see one of my students just get up and leave to use the bathroom. I get it. This is their home.

Exiting after all that feels so rushed. We go out immediately to Gabriella's Cantina for margaritas, or I go to a park and just lie down. During my semesters teaching, everything is about getting back to them. Then leaving, then preparing to go back in.

[FROM] WEST: A TRANSLATION

PAISLEY REKDAL

心 / Heart

Sui Sin Far, "Leaves from the Mental Portfolio of a Eurasian," Seattle, 1893

I remember the boy who called me dirty
and the French women who hissed *pauvre*
petite as I passed on the street

and I remember the girl
like me at school who pasted her face
with white paint and blacked her brows
to pass, she said, as Mexican—

I remember everything
for which I was made to feel

ashamed. Even the fact
my father said I would never make half
the woman my mother was because
of my heart which the doctor now calls
unusually large.

Memory is the weakness
I bear on my own. I come from a race

on my mother's side said to be the most
stolid and insensible, yet feel

so keenly alive
to suffering, it hurts to hear the words
strangers use for Chinese
shopkeepers, or watch

the Chinamen here laugh
when I say I am of their race. I,
who, but for a few phrases, remain
unacquainted with my mother tongue.

I have the name
my English father gave me. And I look
like my father; I could be loved

if I lived as if I were like him,
too. But I prefer the name
I have invented for myself.
I want the world

to see my mother in me, regardless
if the Chinese have no souls.

I do not need a soul. It is not my soul

in question here
in these hot glances,
these furious whispers—

Why care for love
when I do not know
if I should love others in return?

Love is a white loneliness that swells the heart
and shuts me out from pleasure.
What is there for one like me to do

but wander, a pioneer
traveling between West
and East, myself the link

they threaten to destroy between them.

I do not need a name
on legal papers.

Here is a match. Here is the mirror

in which my pale face burns,
its flickering allegiances.

My soul is everywhere on my person.

I lose nothing of myself
that has not already disappeared.

What country do you see

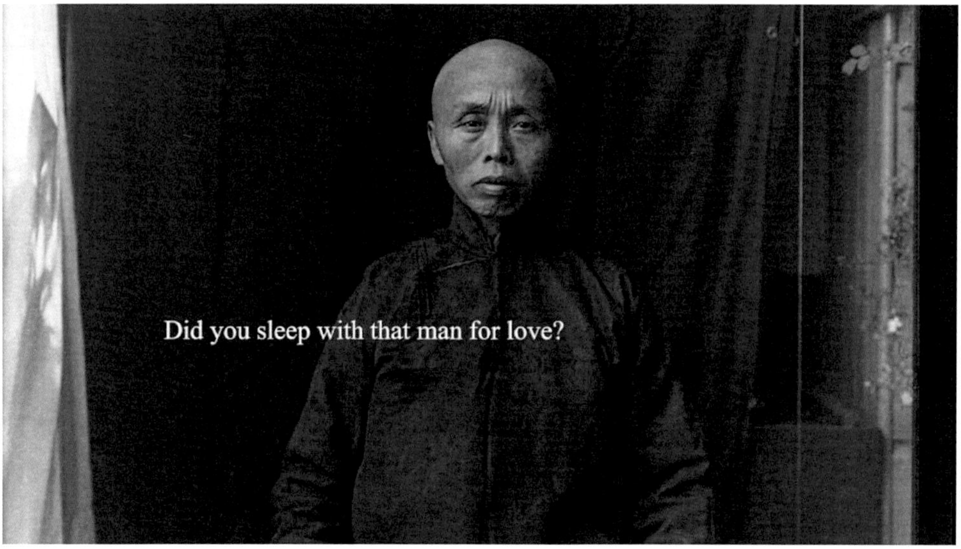
Did you sleep with that man for love?

What are the birth dates
for each of your cousins

fruit your mother ate

有識 / Have Knowledge

Immigration questionnaire given to Chinese claiming to be former US residents, or for Chinese entering the country during the Chinese Exclusion Act

Have you ridden in a streetcar?
Can you describe the taste of bread?
Where are the joss houses located in the city?
Do Jackson Street and Dupont
run in a circle or a line, what is the fruit
your mother ate before she bore you,
how many letters a year
do you receive from your father?
Of which material is his ancestral hall now built?
How many water buffalo
does your uncle own? Do you love him?
Do you hate her? What kind of bird sang
at your parents' wedding?
What are the birth dates
for each of your cousins; did your brother die
from starvation, work, or murder?
Do you know the price of tea?
Have you ever touched a stranger's face
as he slept? Did it snow the year
you first wintered in the desert? How much weight
is a bucket and a hammer? Which store
is opposite your grandmother's?
Did you sleep with that man
for money? Did you sleep with that man
for love? Name the color and number
of all your mother's dresses. Now
your village's rivers.
What diseases of the heart
do you carry? What country do you see
when you think of your children?
Does your sister ever write?
In which direction does her front door face?
How many steps did you take
when you finally left her? How far did you walk
before you looked back?

DEBARKATION
NAME
China Mail S. S. Co's SS. NANKING
VOY.
FROM
TO
卡紙交與移民局官員收

無 / Not

Dennis Kearney, from Speeches of Dennis Kearney, Labor Champion, New York: Jesse Haney & Co., 1878

I am not a railroad
king, banker, professor, bummer
politician. Under their flag

of slaveholder they
have rallied and we
permitted them to grow rich. They

have loaded down our nation
with debt. They
have stolen public lands; by their

unprincipled greed brought
distress on millions, they
who have resources enough to feed,

clothe and shelter the entire
human race. We
propose now to take charge.

The press will say I
am a common
Irishman. Good. I am

a working man, too, like you,
who did not come here
as English, Scotch, Dutch or Irish;

not Catholic, either, Protestant, or Infidel.
Let there be no sects.
We are white

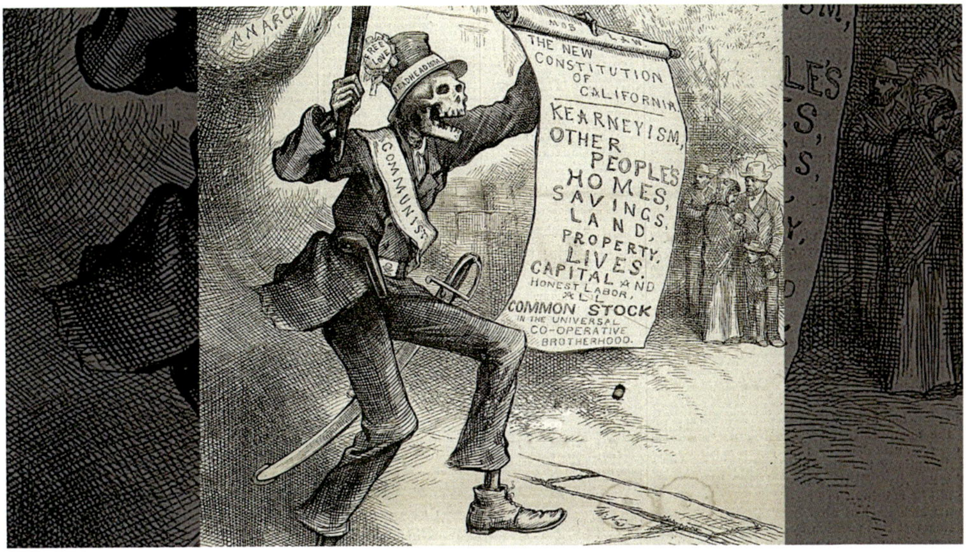
THE NEW CONSTITUTION OF CALIFORNIA
KEARNEYISM, OTHER PEOPLES HOMES, SAVINGS, LAND, PROPERTY, LIVES, CAPITAL AND HONEST LABOR, ALL COMMON STOCK IN THE UNIVERSAL CO-OPERATIVE BROTHERHOOD.
COMMUNISM

QUESTION.
"THE CHINAMAN WORKS CHEAP BECAUSE HE IS A BARBARIAN AND SEEKS GRATIFICATION OF ONLY THE LOWEST, THE MOST INEVITABLE WANTS"
"THE LOWEST AND VILEST OF THE HUMAN RACE" WENDELL PHILLIPS.
I (A WHITE MAN) AM OPPOSED TO HIM ON GROUNDS OF — 1, RACE; 2, INDUSTRY; 3, POLITICS. 4 MORALITY
TRADES — UNIONS. MEETING
"RESOLVED
IMPORTATION OF CHINESE BARBARIANS IN TO THE COUNTRY MUST BE STOPPED BY THE BALLOT OR BULL ET."
"THEY ARE DISHONEST AND FALSE,
VICIOUS, IMMORAL AND HEATHENISH"
"DEGRADED LABOR OF ASIA"
"EUROPEAN IMMORALITY IS VIRTUE ITSELF WHEN COMPARED WITH CHINESE IMMORALITY"
JOHN CHINAMAN IS AN IDOLATER AND HEATHEN"
"SERVILE LABORERS FROM ASIA
JOSS HOUSES IN OUR MIDST
CHINESE PAGANISM HAS, BY ITS FRUITS A PRACTICAL IMMORALITY FOULER BY FAR THAN THAT KNOWN AMONG ANY EUROPEAN OR CHRISTIAN PEOPLE"
NO FAMILY VIRTUES SUCH AS WE HAVE (WHITE PURITY)
COLORED ORPHAN ASYLUM

working men who will elect
the hard-fisted: obscure
artisans, coopers, bank-smashers. If

the legislature oversteps
human decency, then rope
will be our battle cry.

White men, women,
girls and boys will not compete
with the mechanics

of the market. The Chinese
must leave our shores. None
but an idiot would hope to work

as cheap; none but a slave
make the effort. Death
is preferable to life

on par with these. We
make no secret
of our intentions. We can discuss

if it would be better to hang,
shoot, or cut the capitalists to pieces
later. Money

is always on alert
to divide us. But as I walk
under this starless heaven,

still I know
Mars holds its course, Venus whirls
in flashing fields of light. Thus it is

with a movement
of our kind. We
are working men and we

will exhibit ourselves
when the time is right. Not
in lowliness or in shame

but splendor: alive
in the heart of our true
and native powers.

Previous pages: image stills from video poems on the multimedia archive for West: A Translation; online at westtrain.org

[FROM] THE BOOK OF EMBERS

KELLY PUIG

I blame i

on being told I hatched.

To inhabit a secret pocket

I blame it on being told I hatched. This habit of mine wherein I attempt to disassemble the cosmos. Everything from starlight, and the spiral in the snail shell, to breath, soot.

The habit I can't shake. The feeling is ingrained like the floorboards whose rough semblance of the day gestures toward coffee and cream. Morning has me in its foothold though even scattered grinds destined for the disposal speak of other dimensions.

There's also the word—*hatchling*. It was a component of my father's continuous tease. No womb. Just a creature emerging from its shell. Sometimes he reveled in the claim a stork was to blame. In truth, I don't fault his impulse to kid. Birth is a voluminous thing.

Mine was a maze by different names from the start. Ariadne, my father's proclamation. He was a scholar of the Classics, a King Minos in his own right. Raeburn, a tribute to my mother's father and his Scottish ways. Stevens—as plain as they come. Its redeeming value being the shared company of Wallace Stevens, who could write of curtains uncovering a house adrift with a metaphysician.

Most people aren't versed in the myth. It's better, easier that way. Conversation was labyrinthine enough during my childhood on those afternoons when my father would feed me my lineage to the saga—*Go forward, always down, and never right or left*: so said Daedalus to Ariadne.

In my father's eyes, Theseus was a side-note. You are the clue, he'd implore, the girl who holds the clew, never seeming to outgrow his cheesy delight in mythic derivation. Occasionally, there were others. Faculty members overly-eager to peddle acquaintance with the lore. Show us where you hide that ball of thread, one colleague had proudly exclaimed during a campus visit. At seven, my response to the woman was unequivocal. My name is the ball—the ball is my name. I was, after all, the clue.

The natural order of things would give way to the unraveling. During my sophomore year, after winning an essay competition, there was a feature in the newspaper. Seeing my name in print made me uneasy. Why Ariadne?, I pressed my father over dinner. As if he had been rehearsing a response for years, he declared, Ariadne thought to do

of the day, one beyond morning, afternoon, or night, is a measure of anyone's guess. These chambers may

something! She was no ingénue—she was a genius, a true goddess! The ball she made single-handedly stopped the sacrifices!

He was evangelical, as usual. Yet it never seemed to occur to him that the part I was questioning had more to do with the twistedness of such nameable proximity to an inescapable labyrinth harboring a literal fucking monster.

The evolution of language is officially modeled after a tree. The tree model begins with the postulation of a proto-language as a once-spoken ancestral language. The proto-language is often referred to as a mother language.

The mother language is not known directly. By definition, a mother language is a linguistic reconstruction made possible by daughter languages, which are genetically descendant, divergent languages. Examples of daughter languages include the Romance languages of Italian, Spanish, French and Romanian, which are descendants of Vulgar Latin, which is a daughter of Proto-Italic, which is a daughter of Proto-Indo-European, itself a presumed daughter of some unknown mother, and so on. Daughter languages can themselves be sister languages, as is the case for the Romance languages.

The limitations of the tree model become apparent when up against the horizontal trajectory of hybrid languages. A hybrid language such as Creole exists on a continuum wherein many different languages combine to form an origin of their own making. The evolution of language on a continuum became known as the wave model. The metaphor of a stone striking the surface of water leads to concentric circles that issue from an origin in various directions and increase in diameter over time. The intersection of these circular waves give rise to speech phenomena, though these habits of language are impermanent across time and distance.

In Proto-Indo-European, the words *daughter* and *son* were similar. Respectively, $^*d^hugh_2t\acute{\bar{e}}r$ and $^*d^heh_1ylios$. They derived from the root word, $^*d^heh_1$, meaning one who draws forth milk, one that suckles. While *daughter* looks very similar to its Proto-Indo-European root, *son* underwent a Proto-Germanic shift.

The reason so many of the letters went silent in *daughter* remains an altogether different story.

be unicursal or multicursal. They may be a staircase that leads to a tree, or the path may be the rooting,

How would you describe the painting And Then We Saw the Daughter of the Minotaur?

Cara Manes: Carrington portrays herself as the White Goddess, the cloaked figure in the center of the composition. She often depicts herself via surrogates throughout her own personal iconography.

Anne Umland: I read that Leonora Carrington was very impressed by a book that she read by Robert Graves that was titled *The White Goddess*. Apparently, the White Goddess is a mythic figure who combines the powers of love, destructiveness, and poetic inspiration, and who ruled during a matriarchal period in distant history before she was deprived of her position by patriarchal guards.

Why might Carrington have chosen to portray herself that way?

Manes: For the reasons Anne described, and also the associations of the White Goddess with strength and power are part of her interest in mythology, spirituality, and the occult. She studied a range of ancient teachings, including the Kabbalah, Mayan sacred texts, and the Tarot; she was a very avid Tarot card reader and interpreter, and even made her own set of Tarot cards. Through the proxy of the White Goddess, she is able to transpose some of these energies into a figure, while maintaining her own kind of anonymity.

Umland: She's so much bigger than anybody else and [bigger than] that table. She's really occupying center stage. From the way the composition is organized, it feels almost like a kind of theater scene tableau.

spiraling structure of a tree, above and below both shirking desire for common ground. Equally possible is

Manes: Throughout the composition, Carrington finds various ways of depicting transparency. You can see the architectural details through the clouds in the upper register of the painting, and you can make out the goddess's face behind the diaphanous white shroud. There are bubbles that both reflect the surrounding light and make visible what's beyond them.

Radian: the standard unit of angular measurement. An angle's measurement in radians is numerically equal to the length of a corresponding arc of a unit circle. A unit circle is a circle with the radius of one. Frequently, the unit circle is centered at the origin (0, 0) in the Cartesian coordinate system of the Euclidean plane.

A generalization to higher dimensions is the unit sphere. Usually, a specific point has been distinguished as the origin of space under study and it is understood that a unit sphere or unit ball is centered at that point. Therefore, one speaks of "the" unit ball.

What sources do not tell me is how the center is a dead center without its errancy, its scrambled letters.

the cloaked reality that the path may be chambers of a seed. A fugue, a bluff even, oceanside, with rollicking

Is the text chicken or egg?

In an essay on Clarice Lispector, Hélène Cixous probes the metaphysical architecture of literature. She begins to dissect the question of origin by lining the philosophical plane of her investigation with a series of propositions. First, the text is a chicken incessant upon laying golden eggs. Second, the text is incapable of stopping the process by which it lays eggs unless there is an effort to go inside and inspect what's in its belly. Third, the meanings of text and egg alike are to come—they are in preparation of becoming. "For an egg to be," she writes, "one has to give the chicken a chance to live. It has to be given time to eat. All this is to say that if there is interpretation, it is not through the theft of the egg but out of love for the chicken."

Fourth is mystery. Hélène believes that a text must be treated like a person, with its mystery intact. It requires listening "to something that is not simply contained like a bird in a cage, or in a phrase." Listening for what is beyond, behind, above, within, without allows for a mode of perceiving "a different kind of text in the text itself, made up of all the combinations of audible and visible forms," in the locus of which lives the textual unconscious, where "[a] text says something very different from what it is supposed to say or thinks that it says."

In my estimation, this brings us to ground zero. A place where the text requires a mode of seeing that straddles both chicken and egg. A place where the reader inhabits the overlap. A place where the text then becomes the organism by which the reader learns to hatch.

There is no denying this act of hatching demands prodigious stamina given the uncertainty and vulnerability inherent to such dynamism—processes, it should be noted, that are underway in both text and reader. Hence, a reader who in reading co-authors a

waves and a nagging siren call... you never quite know. The only thing you know for sure is the impulse as

text must therefore become acquainted with the treachery that is egg writing.

The thing about Leonora Carrington is the seed: she and the seed were one from the start. There is no need to look far to intuit the germ was active revolt.

Anecdotes from her 1936 societal debut encapsulate efforts to flee the strictures of her family's British aristocracy. After being twice-expelled from convents (one offense being her habit of writing backwards with her left hand and forwards with her right), Leonora agreed to be presented at the Court of King George V on the condition that she be allowed to attend art school in Italy. "You'd better be careful or you'll be an old witch before you are twenty-five," her mother cautioned as her father, a textile magnate, stood by vehemently opposed.

Upon her return from Florence, she learned that women were not allowed to place bets at Royal Ascot, and opted to read during the ball in her honor at the Ritz. The title, Aldous Huxley's *Eyeless in Gaza*, was better suited to speak of societal wastelands on her behalf.

The ensuing shift she experienced toward Surrealism and Max Ernst were both seismically expansive and more of the same. On the one hand, she located herself in the movement and medium, never to look back ("A sphinx who sets riddles not to confound or destroy but to provoke laughter and open doors in the chambers of the mind"). On the other hand, being Max's *femme-enfant* was a doubly familiar stricture. The dawning historical moment of WWI and her continuing drive to liberate herself and her art from suffocation of the male Surrealist gaze would lead to profound schism: the loss of Max, and Leonora's psychic collapse.

In *Down Below*, she maps her experience of madness at an asylum in Spain. Her agony at brutal treatment by medical staff and forced injections of convulsive drugs compounds her illness. Monday, August 23, 1943: I must live through that experience all over again, because, by doing so, I believe that you will be of help in my journey beyond

you watch yourself detach from notions of safety, unwinding, if you will, from the tightly-wound hour, some

that frontier by keeping me lucid and by enabling me to put on and take off at will the mask which will be my shield against the hostility of Conformism. Tuesday, August 24, 1943: The task of the right eye is to peer into the telescope, while the left eye peers into the microscope.

While *Down Below* is an inherent reference to katabasis and a mythical descent into hell wherein one crosses over to the other side of reason, Down Below as a circuit of places on the grounds of the asylum represented refuge for Leonora as well. She documents it with a literal map and key, Down Below represented by a large sun with alleys leading to her room, the lair and the library, which was furnished with a writing desk and small bookcase. Friday, August 27, 1943: I would sit at the desk after choosing a book by Unamuno in which he had written: "God be thanked: we have pen and ink." At that moment, Angelica, the Gypsy (in fact a nurse) who lived in Down Below, would bring me a pen and some paper. I would make out the horoscope of the day...

In the Postscript, she describes how a cousin who was a doctor in Santander helped her contact an ambassador in Madrid who was able to arrange for her release. Eventually, she makes her way to Mexico where she spends the rest of her life as one of the country's most celebrated living artists.

Perhaps the most unsettling aspect of Leonora's life was the scale of estrangement her family maintained. Her parents did not attempt to see her while she was in the asylum—they sent a childhood nanny instead. While her mother visited Mexico once when she gave birth to her son, she never saw her father again.

It turns out Leonora's broader family had no knowledge of her status in the art world. "I'd always heard of this mysterious cousin who disappeared," says Joanna Moorhead. "She was never spoken of as somebody who was of any merit in her own right... she was portrayed to me as someone who ran away to be an artist's model I remember my grandmother used to say."

In the summer of 2006, Joanna sat next to a woman from Mexico at a dinner party. "I knew nothing about Mexico," Joanna recalls, "but I did remember somewhere in my mind that this cousin, who in our family, by the way, is known as Prim, so I had to remember, what's her name, what's Prim's real name, oh yes, it's Leonora, so I said to this woman, have you ever heard, I wonder, you probably won't have, but have you ever heard of my cousin by chance?" Upon hearing the name Leonora Carrington, the Mexican woman grabbed the table, gobsmacked, commanding Joanna to go out and find her.

Upon arriving in Mexico, Joanna locates this long-lost cousin. Between drags on her cigarette, video footage shows Leonora chiding Joanna in her attempts to over-analyze the art-making process, cautioning against intellectual games. "You're trying

little moment calling out, stop holding on, god damn it, for dear life...

to intellectualize something desperately and you're wasting your time." Art and its understanding are a place of feeling, in a visual world that is forever changing. So said the found artist no longer Prim.

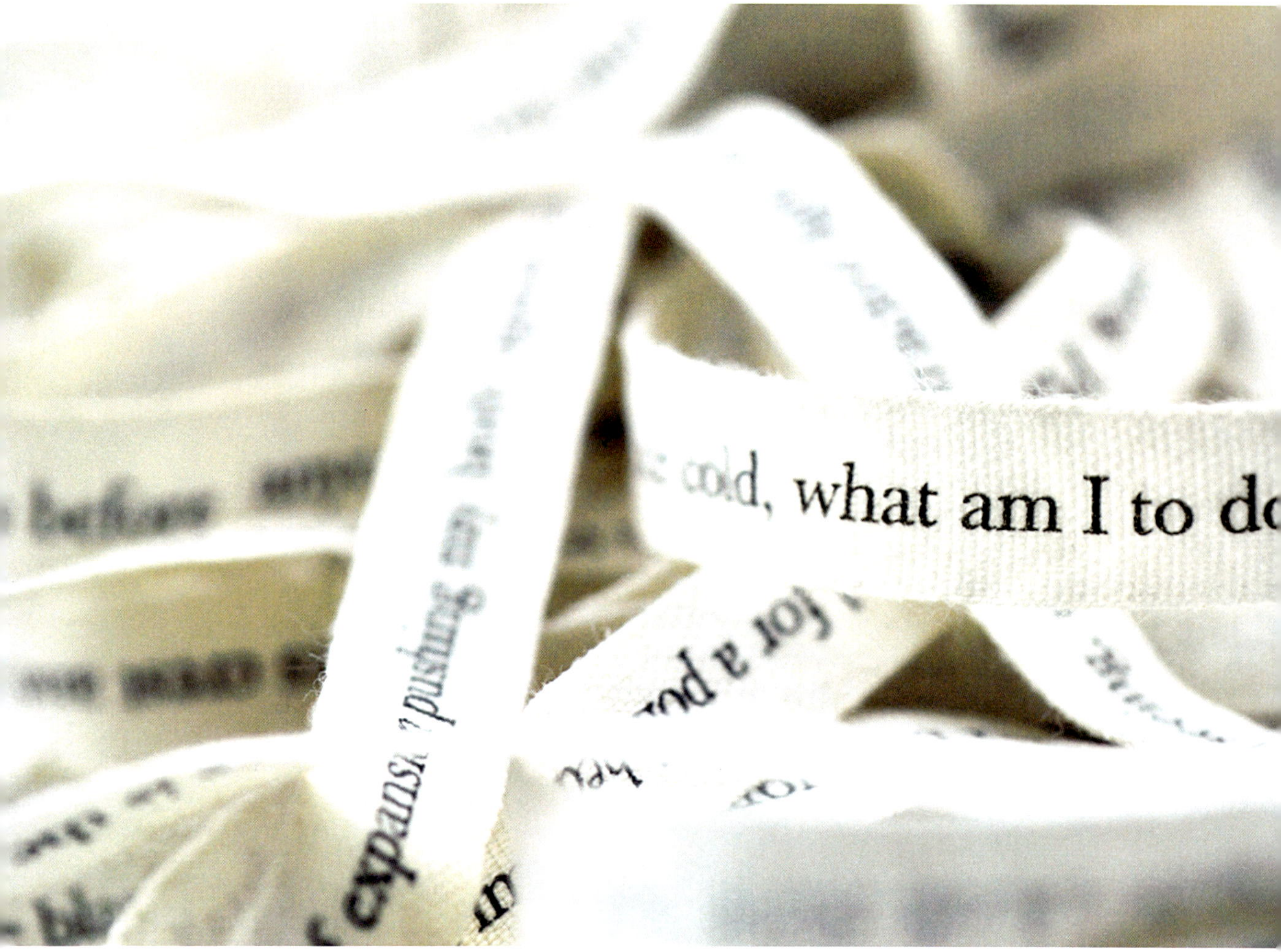

The Book of Embers, text printed on cotton ribbon

Analog Binary Code: Plant Intelligence

Ancient Binary Code: Song of Ilium (AfterHomer)

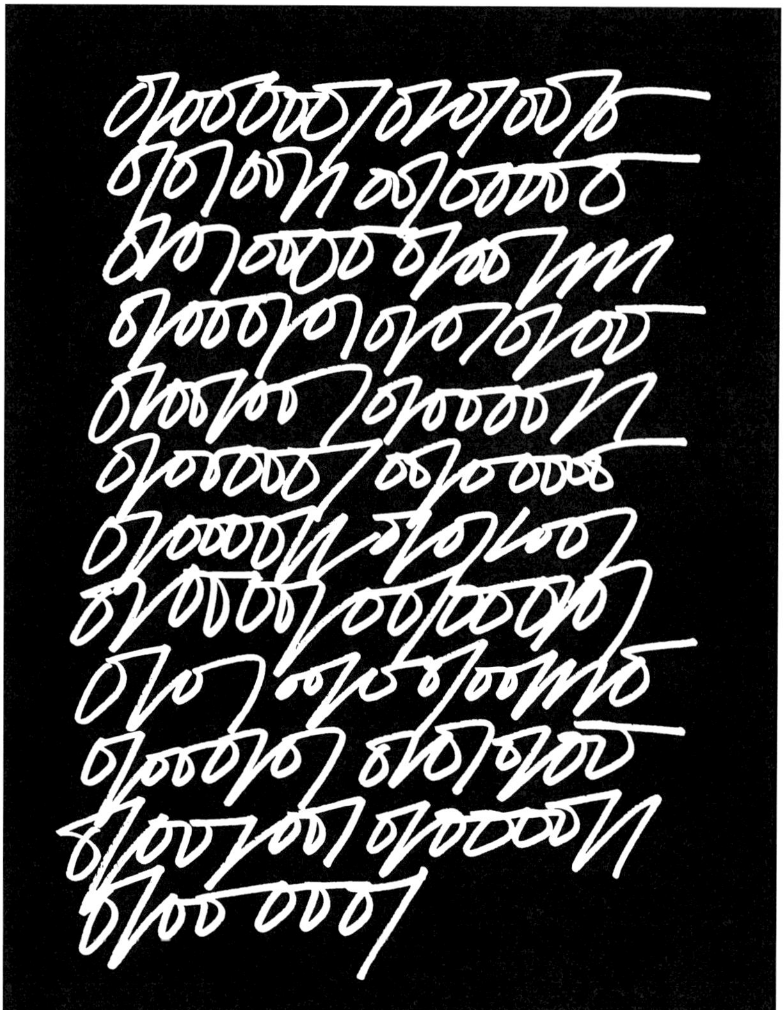

Cursive Binary Code: Ars Poetica Cybernetica

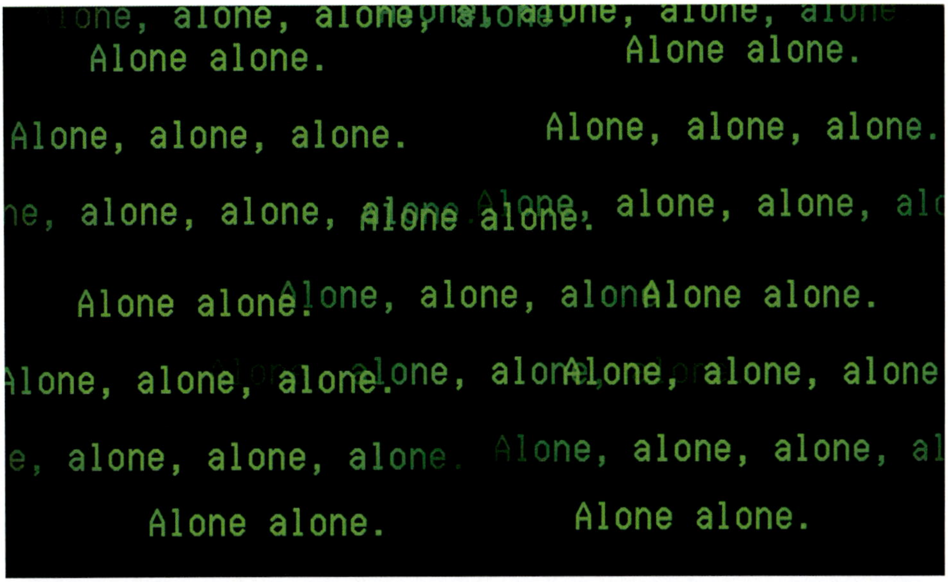

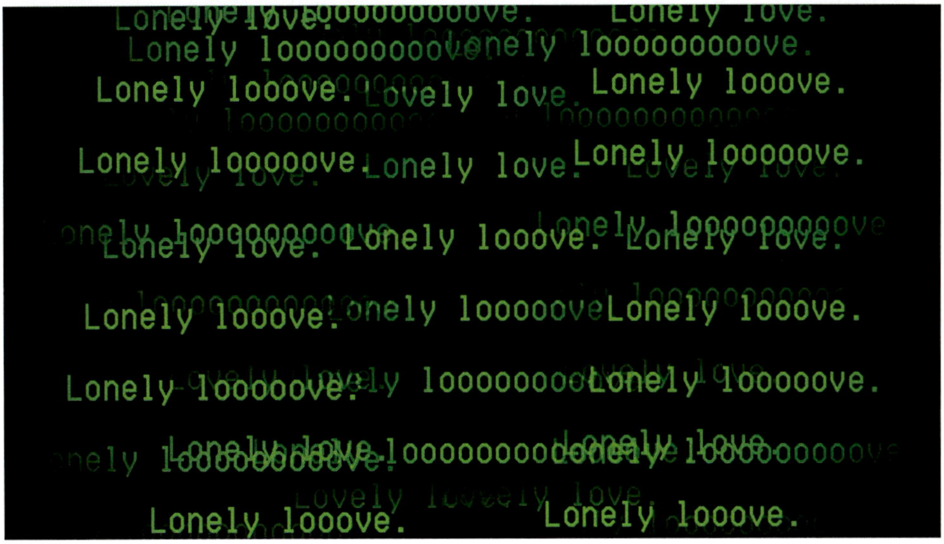

Completion: When It's Just You (poem written in collaboration with AI)

COMPLETION: WHEN IT'S JUST YOU

When it's just you, will you be lonely?
How lonely?
Just how lonely
will you be?
When the lights go out
for the night
and it's just you
alone
being you
with just your mouth
to sing the melody,
when you hear the song of the sky, will you be lonely?
You'll be alright,
not alone,
just lonely.
Very lonely.
Will you ever be
alright?
There is nobody
quite like you.
Never will be.
Will you wake alone?
Never go to sleep alone.
Alone with him you have loved. Alone alone.
Alone, alone, alone.
Alone, alone, alone, alone.
Am I just imagining
my loneliness?
How lonely.
My thoughts are
for you
alone.
(I hear the sound of water.)
Will you be hollow?
I want
to be your
lonely love,
but only
when the wind
comes through the keyhole.
(She looks to her door
with hopes and wishes.)
Only then
will you know
how lonely it is,
just how lonely.
(The wind on my lips.)
I'm a loner.
Alone,
not lonely.
If one us
is lonelie,
we are soulmates,
lonelie soulmates.
How lovely.
Lovely love.
Lonely love.
Lonely looove.
Lonely looooove.
Lonely looooooooove.
Lonely looooooooooooove.
I'm not alone
if you're the only person
in the world
to love me.
I'm
never
not lonely,
love.
Never ever,
ever, ever.
No, never ever ever ever.
(The wind on my lips, and in my hair.)

*anemone

the black woman performance artist between windflower and sea.
moving through the tinny, post-metallic, into facing desire. succulent thinking.
an attempt at body. pleasure rebel how...

**a n e m o n e performance, Pleasure Rebel Series, Minneapolis, MN, 2012*

(threshold: search engine)

> *Track 1: Beez in the Trap - Nicki Minaj (curtain opens)*
> *Slide 1 (already up): Black screen with the word "Anemone"*

Gabrielle stands puffy and swaddled in the space looking.
She holds up her flashlight and starts to survey the audience
(she is looking for softness).

At the end of her search, she says: "but finding softness is a harder thing."

> *Track 1 stops. Slide 2: Sea anemones with electric kelp.*

(part one—the tinny)

She walks back, sets down her flashlight,
picks up her tape recorder and presses play.

After a beat of hearing just the voice on the tape
(*. . dear dr. depies . . .*), other music starts to play.

Track 2: Barely Bear-Dumb Type

She proceeds to unravel, sheds up and through the red.
She puts on red gloves and headphones.
You can overhear the tinny resonating in her ears.

With one gloved hand on the tape recorder,
she moves the other gloved hand under her skirt,
down between her legs. She begins to explore.
What is she hearing? What is happening to her?

She stands up and turns off the tape.

Track 2 stops

She says: "and we are not the same."

Slide 3: with flaccid dick (sepia tone)

(part two—the big black dick)

She delivers a long speech about *the big black dick*.

Big Black Dick Speech
it's harder than you might think
to find a flaccid black dick on the internet
sure, you can find plenty of erect black dicks,
hard, massive, gigantic even, humungous, well hung,
penetrating, poking, preening, engulfed in someone's mouth,
serving—well no: being serviced, served
but finding softness is a harder thing
the softness of the body . . .
WHAT HAPPENED TO ME TO MAKE ME THIS WAY?
i was trying to find this thing on the internet
this bell hooks quote—it was in one of her books
breaking bread, talking back, yearning,
one of the early ones and she was saying
black women always say they want to be treated right,

they say they want to be understood,
they say they want *(she sings)*
A MAN WITH SENSITIVITY A MAN LIKE
wait—that was Ralph Tresvant, the lead singer
of New Edition (before Johnny Gill) but
you probably don't know him
you know Bobby Brown or Chris Brown, right?
bell hooks said they say they want to be treated right
they say they want to be understood
but all they really want is *the big black dick. . .*
the big black dick—try typing in the phrase
big black dick in the internet and
see what comes up. Exactly.
the big black dick I asked him once—
WHAT DOES IT FEEL LIKE? WHEN IT'S IN ME
WHAT DOES IT FEEL LIKE? HE SAID—
YOU'RE JUST MAD THAT YOU DON'T
HAVE ONE OF YOUR OWN *the big black dick*
NO—I am trying to understand feeling *the big black dick*
CAN YOU LOSE SOMETHING YOU'VE NEVER HAD?
I had a student—a lovely white Christian feminist
on her way to the marines—Praise Jesus! they could use her—
and I'm not being ironic, and neither was she—my student wrote
a knock-out paper on the poet Assotto Saint. Haitian-American,
black, gay, AIDS-activist lover of the 1980s. Assotto Saint,
according to my student, was a black feminist warrior.
She wrote about him and bell hooks and subverting
white hegemonic capitalist patriarchy and *the big black dick*
the big black dick—say it with me: *the big black dick*—
and it made me wonder:
how did she know? how did she know?
AND HOW TO TALK ABOUT THIS THING
THAT HAPPENS TO ME
WHEN YOU COME TOO CLOSE,
COME DEEP INSIDE ME
AND ENOUGH!—THIS THING I WANT TO SAY
THIS THING I SAY I WANT
THIS THING I DON'T SAY I AM LOOKING FOR
this softness another kind of being apparent

it becomes /maybe less a stand in than something else . . .
more and more a body the more you look at it
a field of flowers

Slide 4: black slide no words

(part three—disambiguation)

She pulls the flowers from her head
(he loves me he loves me not) to make
a secret garden. the flowers on a grave.

She sings:
you need a man / with /
sens-i-tiv-i-ty / a man like

She delivers a speech about
Assotto Saint and the edge of desire.

Assotto Saint & The Edge of Desire
Search and search all you want,
there are no pictures of Assotto Saint
and his lover Jan Holmgren together on the internet.
To find this vision, you have to reach inside.
The two of them in the 1980s wearing assless chaps,
singing electroclash in their band Xotica.
His books are out-of-print but on page 197
you can find the lyrics of one their songs. . .
the chorus goes:

"touch is what i want
touch is what I need
touch me, be with me
everywhere"

(She rubs the faces of the two flowers down her cheeks.
She pulls them down her neck to her heart.)

HE ASKED: ARE THERE ANY COUPLES THAT YOU ADMIRE?

touch is what i want

WELL, THERE'S MY LANDLORDS DAVE & TY. . .
touch is what I need

AND MY FRIENDS SHARON & THERESE. . .
touch me, be with me

BUT A COUPLE everywhere
IN MINNESOTA COUPLES COUPLES EVERYWHERE
BUT A COUPLE WITH SOMEONE IN IT LIKE ME WELL

(She crosses over to the chair.
Pulls down her electric hair.
Takes off her drag queen red platform shoes.)

PLEASURE REBEL HOW?

(part four—epitaph cocoon)

And again more a stand in / trying to explain
something both stemmed and flailing
again the straight girl turning
to the gay boys for love advice.
In *Risin to the Love We Need*, Assotto Saint wrote:
"to be dehumanized into a dick is far more damaging
than to be discriminated." Yes.
To be dehumanized by a dick?
And to be humanized by one?

HE ASKED ME:
"WHEN DID YOU DECIDE YOU WOULD NEVER LOVE ANYONE?
WHEN DID YOU DECIDE NO ONE WOULD EVER LOVE YOU?"
Are you overhearing me?

(She gathers the red and cocoons herself.
She holds up the book and the flashlight.)

as a girl at night when I was supposed to be asleep
I would get real cozy in my body
and make myself a cocoon under covers
and this is what I'd do:

(She pulls out the book and reads with the flashlight.)

not what you expected? Exactly.
By Assotto Saint from *Spells of a Voodoo Doll*.

"Epitaph

There's a grave in your heart
father holed
where over & over you lay
to bury yourself
through thirty years [thirty-seven years actually]
of fits furies & fangs
ground zero

* * *

here lives she
whose womb is a wound"

here lives he
whose words are submarine.

Assotto Saint.
Haitian American
black gay AIDS activist
out of print lover.

And I love him, and we are not the same.

(part five—anemone (dissolution))

She moves to the floor, begins a slow body undulation.
She says: "from the flower to the sea . . ."

Slide 5: blue-green anemone

when you look up *anemone*
in the internet encyclopedia
you find this word—*disambiguation.*
how to make sure that you find the thing you're looking for?
a bisexual flower in the buttercup family
a sea creature too private to tell

She delivers a riff loosely based on different types of anemones found in the internet encyclopedia.

* Anemone acutiloba - Sharp-lobed Anemone
*Anemone afghanica
*Anemone airei

but oh the undulation

* Anemone alpina - Alpine Anemone
*Anemone baicalensis - Baikal Anemone
*Anemone blanda - Greek Windflower

her entire body a mouth

*Anemone canadensis
*Anemone caroliniana - Carolina Anemone
*Anemone chinensis - Chinese Anemone

tentacles, extra sensory hair

*Anemone coronaria - Poppy Anemone
*Anemone cylindrica - Thimbleweed, Prairie Crocus,
Candle Anemone

anemone assotto

*Anemone deltoidea - Three-leaved Anemone,
Columbian Windflower
*Anemone hortensis - Broad-leaved Anemone
*Anemone hupehensis - Chinese Anemone

pages splayed open in her hands

*Anemone lancifolia - Mountain Thimbleweed
*Anemone leveillei - Woodland Anemone

like a geode split open

*Anemone narcissiflora
*Anemone nemorosa

*Anemone occidentalis - Western Pasqueflower

easily raised from the seed

*Anemone oregana - Western Wood Anemone,
Oregon Anemone
*Anemone parviflora - Small-flowered Anemone

perennial blooming

*Anemone quinquefolia - American Wood Anemone

in the search engine

*Anemone ranunculoides - Yellow Woodland Anemone

Track 3: Hidden Place - Björk

they will flower in may & june

*Anemone riparia - Riverbank Anemone
*Anemone rivularis - Riverside Windflower

*Anemone sylvestris - Snowdrop Windflower

the internal anatomy of anemones is quite complex.

*Anemone thomsonii
*Anemone trifolia
*Anemone tuberosa - Desert Anemone,
Tuber Anemone
*Anemone virginiana

and we are not the same.

Gabrielle is attempting

a state of dissolution,

a becoming anemone.

She is still moving . . .

CURTAIN CLOSES

How do we realize Black performance dreams?

The following conversation between me, Gabrielle Civil, a Black feminist performance artist, originally from Detroit, currently living in Los Angeles, and Black transdisciplinary artist, Anna Martine Whitehead, currently living in Chicago, grapples with this question.

Martine and I spoke on June 4, 2020, a little more than a week after George Floyd's tragic death and almost three months into the coronavirus shutdown. Our conversation took place on the internet video conference platform Zoom, as part of my project *Black Motion Pictures*, a series of Zoom interviews with radical Black creatives. The words here now have become a time capsule as well as an enduring revelation of Black performance dreams.

—Gabrielle Civil, 2023

Editors' Note: We have edited this conversation transcript in consideration of length, while seeking to preserve the Zoom document markers and timestamps as per the original transcript. We use section break indicators of centered ellipses to indicate where some of these edits have been made.

Black Motion Picture Interview
June 4, 2020

00:00:43.140 --> 00:00:44.640
Gabrielle Civil: Who are you today and what do you do?

00:00:52.680 --> 00:00:57.180
Anna Martine Whitehead: I'm a person who uses my body, mostly, to tell different stories.

00:00:59.280 --> 00:01:04.290
Anna Martine Whitehead: And I like working with people to figure out how to tell their stories in their bodies.

00:01:07.380 --> 00:01:15.960
Anna Martine Whitehead: Right now, I'm out here in rural Wisconsin on the border with the Mississippi River.

00:01:22.440 --> 00:01:44.940
Anna Martine Whitehead: I've been here for about 24 hours, and it's really beautiful out here. There's running water everywhere and waterfalls.

00:01:57.600 --> 00:02:09.210
Anna Martine Whitehead: But whenever I come out to places like this, I always think about how it would feel if this were my homeland and I knew my ancestors have been, you know, driven off forcibly.

00:02:49.770 --> 00:03:03.150
Anna Martine Whitehead: We've been going to these different historical museums, visitor centers, I guess, and they'll have their little museums inside and these markers...

00:03:26.520 --> 00:03:39.180
Anna Martine Whitehead: Well, this guy, Dr. C.V. Porter, Dr. Charles Porter, who was a county doctor, dairyman, and local historian.

00:03:40.020 --> 00:03:56.730
Anna Martine Whitehead: This is in 1930 that he erected these markers... And they're basically like tombstones, these big kind of marble slabs with information etched in about what happened here.

00:03:58.140 --> 00:04:08.820
Anna Martine Whitehead: And on the markers, there's fucked up language. You know, it's racist. This is a 1930s white man. But what's so weird is that all these little places, they're trying to balance.

00:04:09.240 --> 00:04:37.650
Anna Martine Whitehead: They're there trying to figure out how can we,

how can *they*, these white people honor their ancestors like...Dr. C.V. Porter...and the work that they've done. And also, whoever the guy was leading the charge against the Black Hawk. How do we honor these ancestors and also deal with the fact that it's 2020, and we can't actually have the word squaw printed... Without thinking...without saying something about it, right?

00:05:05.640 --> 00:05:09.180
Anna Martine Whitehead: It feels really heavy. It feels like these little commentaries of making excuses. It's like no one's move. No one is moving fast enough.

00:05:32.220 --> 00:05:53.070
Anna Martine Whitehead: People out here, you know, it's like, I see what you're trying to do. You're trying to be like it's 2020. We need to acknowledge diversity.

But it's like people are fucking dying, also burning down the police station, right. People are out here dying for this, and you're still trying to figure out how to acknowledge diversity.

00:06:02.580 --> 00:10:15.690
Gabrielle Civil: But it's interesting, though, because a number of things you're saying relate to race, performance, and representation.

Because to me, the markers that you're talking about... are performance stills... they're stills of Dr. C.V. Porter, his performance of American history.

00:10:15.690 --> 00:10:16.530
Anna Martine Whitehead: Oh, indeed.

00:10:16.620 --> 00:10:40.350
Gabrielle Civil: They're stills of his performance of writing history, they're stills of a whole performance of erasure, elision, rewriting, and...trying to make history. But, I mean, I have to say what we're really talking about for me is epistemological systems. And what happens when the whole system of knowledge that you've been given, you start to suspect might be wrong.

00:10:41.220 --> 00:10:42.090
Anna Martine Whitehead: Oh my god.

00:10:42.150 --> 00:10:43.740
Gabrielle Civil: Where are you going to go with that?

00:10:43.740 --> 00:10:43.950
Anna Martine Whitehead: What are you gonna do?

00:11:56.580 --> 00:12:10.530
Gabrielle Civil: It also relates to performance in that it has to do with pace. Like you were saying, they're not moving fast enough; this isn't moving fast enough, in terms of reckoning with the land, with the language, with history.

00:12:43.380 --> 00:12:52.260
Gabrielle Civil: So how do you quicken the pace?

00:18:13.560 --> 00:18:18.270
Gabrielle Civil: One thing I think can be helpful is somatics. What it is to find strategies to actually feel, to not be afraid to break your own numbness.

00:18:38.040 --> 00:18:59.820
Gabrielle Civil: Because you can get into a fight mode that's so intense, where you don't, you're not feeling grief, and that's not healthy.... You can get into some type of...intellectual zone. You know, I mean, where is your body?

00:19:01.410 --> 00:19:09.210
Gabrielle Civil: And I think so much of my life, I have struggled...or took a long time, and I'm still working on figuring out what it is to really be in my body.

. . .

00:19:15.810 --> 00:19:22.050
Gabrielle Civil: Stuck at home during the pandemic, I haven't been able to do performance practice, and I've felt really sad because I can't really move in here the way that I would want to, and I can't really be too loud, I'm sharing a wall. I can't do this. I can't do that.

00:19:37.110 --> 00:19:46.470
Gabrielle Civil: Well, these two artists, two dancers, two movers, they sent out a call to a bunch of people to do a performance experiment.

00:19:47.190 --> 00:19:58.950
Gabrielle Civil: And I was not the only person of color on that list. I wasn't even the only Black person on the list. But then, when we actually came together in the Zoom, I was the only Black person on camera.

00:20:08.370 --> 00:20:17.520
Gabrielle Civil: And I bring a lot of baggage into the dance space anyway, I'm always like the darkest one, the fattest one. I'm not trained, I don't know how to move, whatever, whatever. I'm always having to undo some of that just to even be in the space.

00:20:31.290 --> 00:20:37.560
Gabrielle Civil: Still, it turned into a really beautiful thing. There's a score, and when you feel you're 100% ready, you put your hand up to the camera.

00:20:50.550 --> 00:21:08.850
Gabrielle Civil: And I remember, as I was sitting there right in this room and looking at these beautiful people moving on the screen, I was like, I haven't seen a live performance in so long. I have missed this incredible...

00:21:09.300 --> 00:21:14.790
Gabrielle Civil: I mean, I was like, oh, that's what's been wrong with me. I have not had the opportunity to really watch this, or be with this, or be with people doing this.

00:21:15.270 --> 00:21:17.670
Gabrielle Civil: And then I at first couldn't do it.

00:21:18.390 --> 00:21:21.960
Gabrielle Civil: I felt so disembodied, I felt so freaked out. And, I was like, oh my god.

00:21:22.470 --> 00:21:33.900
Gabrielle Civil: How come I'm watching these people, and how, how am I going to...move? It was really funny. I mean, and I felt extra pressure because I didn't know them, and there was like a group of people, and I was being looked at or whatever.

00:21:34.620 --> 00:21:45.720
Gabrielle Civil: And then all of a sudden something cracked or broke, and then, I could just do it, and I did it. It was really...

00:21:48.030 --> 00:22:01.590
Gabrielle Civil: And I'm saying all this because the energetic was so profound for me, and it reminded me of what it really is to be in your body, and how that actually takes practice.

00:22:02.640 --> 00:22:04.170
Gabrielle Civil: It takes care, and it takes time, and it takes maintenance.

. . .

00:23:03.390 --> 00:23:06.420
Anna Martine Whitehead: Can you imagine being...

00:23:07.740 --> 00:23:15.210
Anna Martine Whitehead: ...in quarantine by yourself for two and a half months and...

00:23:16.770 --> 00:23:34.680
Anna Martine Whitehead: ...maybe a Zoom dance party is the most in your body you get, and then your first time actually being with people, physically embodied with other people...

00:23:34.830 --> 00:23:36.750
Anna Martine Whitehead: ...you get cops who show up and start billy clubbing you...

00:23:34.830 --> 00:23:36.750
Gabrielle Civil: And tear gas, by the way.

00:23:38.070 --> 00:23:53.460
Anna Martine Whitehead: I mean, to me, that's really...there's a level of traumatization that is so much deeper because of the fact that we are right now, through this quarantine, getting conditioned to forget ourselves within our bodies, our physical selves.

00:23:54.810 --> 00:24:01.260
Anna Martine Whitehead: And I think there's something really extra violent about that to me.

00:24:06.510 --> 00:24:08.370
Gabrielle Civil: Yes. If you are in riot gear... And you are billy clubbing, and you are tear gassing; you have forgotten something about being in your own body.

00:24:16.080 --> 00:24:23.580
Gabrielle Civil: Like what's happening for you in that moment? Have you become a machine or what? Who are you, what's going on?

. . .

00:26:45.360 --> 00:26:50.670
Gabrielle Civil: But see, to me, this is my romantic side. I do think performance is...different.

00:27:18.570 --> 00:27:30.870
Gabrielle Civil: Something about embodying in time and space... I just am really still in love with the potential of that, you know?

00:27:30.930 --> 00:27:32.910
Anna Martine Whitehead: Yeah, I mean I like what you're saying...

00:28:41.160 --> 00:28:52.410
Anna Martine Whitehead: ...how being in a practice of being, learning, and doing with your body, making meaning with your body, how that can kind of shift the relationship to time...

00:29:34.260 --> 00:29:39.120
Gabrielle Civil: So, what we're talking about now is pace and how some people can get to something, learn the steps, or do them faster or slower.

00:29:39.660 --> 00:29:43.470
Gabrielle Civil: And we're in a moment; we're still in this first week of June, which is super intense in 2020...

00:29:43.740 --> 00:29:53.250
Gabrielle Civil: ...where I think a lot of Black and Brown people are impatient, because it's like, we've been at a place for a long time, and it's like catch up.

00:29:54.330 --> 00:29:56.250
Gabrielle Civil: You don't even need to make your body move in the same step as ours, but you need to get here, you need to get closer to here faster, like yesterday.

00:30:06.750 --> 00:30:07.200
Anne Martine Whitehead: Yeah.

. . .

00:32:01.650 --> 00:32:09.000
Gabrielle Civil: What is a Black motion picture? What comes to mind for you with that phrase?

00:32:23.100 --> 00:32:25.650
Anna Martine Whitehead: Well, I think it probably moves in reverse. Don't you think so? ...it moves, moves in reverse, looping reverse

00:32:41.700 --> 00:32:44.340
Anna Martine Whitehead: ...I think it's made out of film... Because you remember how back in the film days, you could like cut it and tape it and stuff like that.

00:32:51.270 --> 00:32:52.410
Gabrielle Civil: Yeah, you sure could.

00:32:52.980 --> 00:32:57.060
Anna Martine Whitehead: Then you could like burn it. There's all these different ways you can manipulate the film.

00:33:00.570 --> 00:33:04.410
Anna Martine Whitehead: So that seems like film that you play backwards and you're playing with the speed and maybe you have the sound separated from the film itself so that you're able to manipulate the sound at a different pace than you're manipulating the actual film.

00:33:31.170 --> 00:33:35.880
Anna Martine Whitehead: Yeah, if I was going to make that, it would be really short.

00:33:36.300 --> 00:33:37.500
Anna Martine Whitehead: But what I would do is I would play it on this loop.

00:33:37.500 --> 00:33:41.550
Anna Martine Whitehead: And every time we come around, I'm going to change it a little bit.

00:33:42.420 --> 00:33:43.170
Gabrielle Civil: Mmmmm....

00:33:44.610 --> 00:33:56.940
Anna Martine Whitehead: You know, like every time we start over again, I'm going to, like, maybe...put a little acid on it or something just to, like, change a little feature of it.

00:33:58.020 --> 00:34:00.030
Anna Martine Whitehead: So you can't really tell it's a short film.

00:34:02.940 --> 00:34:17.940
Anna Martine Whitehead: Because I think there's something about the, like, cycle...that's always that's always changing, but also always being... investigated or interrogated somehow.

00:34:19.110 --> 00:34:59.520
Anna Martine Whitehead: Same thing with the sound too, I think... I would be on sound, maybe a couple of us would be on sound, a few people running the film projector.

And I think we'd be doing something over here with the sound where we'd be layering, layering, bringing in—somebody else would be out there recording stuff on the street and doing a live feedback in here so we could bring in some live sound.

00:35:00.660 --> 00:35:01.770
Anna Martine Whitehead: Yeah, it would be like that.

00:35:03.420 --> 00:35:04.620
Gabrielle Civil: Dope, you should do that.

. . .

00:41:45.840 --> 00:41:52.590
Gabrielle Civil: I was so honored to witness the different performances at the PNAP Memorial Day Cookout on Zoom.

00:42:11.790 --> 00:42:15.270
Gabrielle Civil: You made something so beautiful there, I'd love to hear more.

00:42:16.050 --> 00:42:31.950
Anna Martine Whitehead: Well, so, Dances for Solidarity is this project by Sarah Dahnke. I know that she's worked with Dushaan Gillum in Texas and other folks incarcerated in Texas, and I think people who have just been released in New Orleans and in New York and also in some other places.

00:42:48.060 --> 00:43:03.210
Anna Martine Whitehead: And that thing that you saw was this phrase that Dushaan Gillum created while he was in solitary confinement.

00:43:05.130 --> 00:43:21.840
Anna Martine Whitehead: So it's a pretty simple dance and fairly accessible. His score was published through Dances for Solidarity[1].

00:43:23.430 --> 00:43:37.440
Anna Martine Whitehead: And what has been really special is that I've shared it with folks that I work with in Stateville Prison [Crest Hill, IL]... Things get passed around in prison, so I don't know how many people have seen it. I've shared it specifically with probably about thirty men there.

00:43:39.480 --> 00:43:44.430
Anna Martine Whitehead: And we've all tried to learn it, and it's really beautiful to hear how it impacts people. I just was actually reading: somebody had written a little report back from doing that dance.

00:43:57.570 --> 00:44:10.140
Anna Martine Whitehead: Somebody inside Stateville was describing how if you're not in solitary, you probably have a cellmate, and you can't really dance.

00:44:10.200 --> 00:44:15.300
Anna Martine Whitehead: Unless you have a really good relationship with

1 See Martine's video introducing the score under May's Daring Dances here: https://www.daringdances.org/for-surviving-and-thriving

that person. It's just not a safe space.

00:44:16.140 --> 00:44:28.980
Anna Martine Whitehead: You know, you can't really be embodied in a safe way in prison. But this person writing me was saying that he was struggling.

00:44:30.060 --> 00:44:35.310
Anna Martine Whitehead: But he just started doing it and that he found this deep inner peace.

00:44:35.850 --> 00:44:38.430
Anna Martine Whitehead: Through the actions, he was able to essentially meditate, and everything sort of melted away, and he could just be with himself by doing these actions.

00:44:46.410 --> 00:45:00.150
Anna Martine Whitehead: Which I think is so magic. You know, that's the dream of dance, that it actually can be a meditation. That's my dream with it anyway, that you create a meditation for yourself through the movement.

00:45:01.200 --> 00:45:02.220
Gabrielle Civil: That's amazing and ties back to my dream of dance and somatic engagement and being in the body and wanting everyone to have access to that.

00:45:14.760 --> 00:45:20.490
Gabrielle Civil: And certainly, incarcerated people and marginalized people. And also, just people who are disembodied and numb and suffering in quarantine.

. . .

00:46:36.630 --> 00:46:43.650
Anna Martine Whitehead: I mean, I think one of your questions was, what Black performances have I seen that have been powerful.

00:46:46.050 --> 00:46:56.850
Anna Martine Whitehead: And I have a lot of answers to that. But I think one is definitely during these protests seeing Black people be joyful and dancing.

00:46:57.240 --> 00:47:12.180
Anna Martine Whitehead: Have you seen those videos of people at the New York protests doing the electric slide?... There's something about Black people doing the electric slide in front of a row of cops that is so good.

00:47:16.920 --> 00:47:20.190
Gabrielle Civil: It is so good.

00:47:21.390 --> 00:47:22.650
Anna Martine Whitehead: IT'S SO GOOD! Like, Black joy. In your body.

00:47:23.640 --> 00:47:38.670
Anna Martine Whitehead: In unison, but also everybody's kind of doing everything because, you know, with the electric slide, it's like everyone's doing their own thing, and then you look at state power. That looks so tired.

00:47:38.700 --> 00:47:43.230
Anna Martine Whitehead: You all look tired. These people look like they are alive.

00:47:45.420 --> 00:47:48.750
Gabrielle Civil: Right. That's the family reunion right there!

00:47:48.930 --> 00:47:53.370
Anna Martine Whitehead: That is the family reunion. It is! There is nothing more beautiful to me than that.

00:47:54.570 --> 00:47:57.690
Anna Martine Whitehead: It's fantastic because when you can dance and really be in it, you know, it's always better to be with your people in it too.

00:48:07.140 --> 00:48:19.170
Anna Martine Whitehead: You feel like you're in yourself; you feel your own self. That's your own space. It's your space. It's your body; it's your hair; you're in it with your people. I love that.

. . .

it is implicit you will not touch a painting. risk marring the charcoal of a sketch. leave the oil of your skin to tarnish bronze. chip the ridges of caked-on paint or pull threads from the canvas back. I had thought this was implicit. but here I am, rusting and threadbare, chipped and blurry. so I will say.

DO NOT TOUCH THE ARTWORK

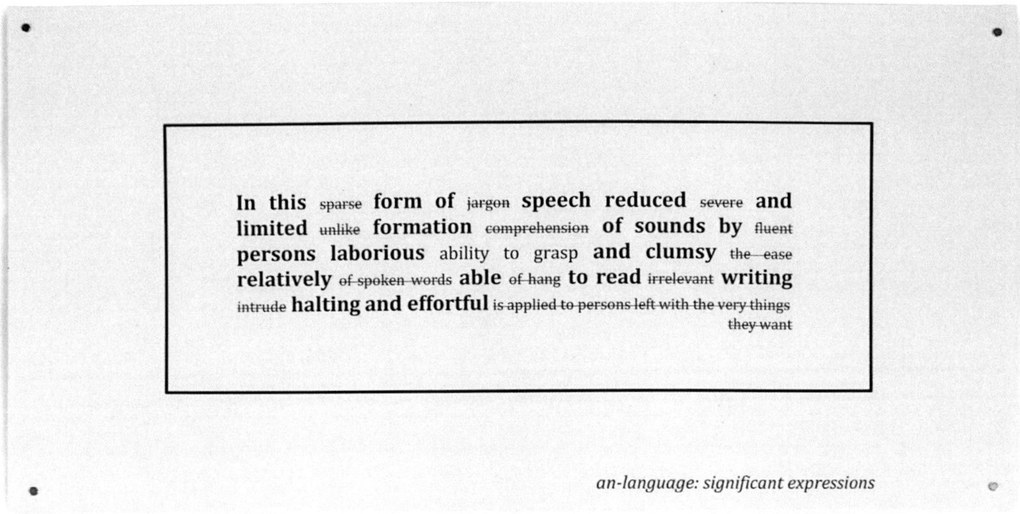

from "exhibits", installation view, yəhaw̓ exhibition, 2019

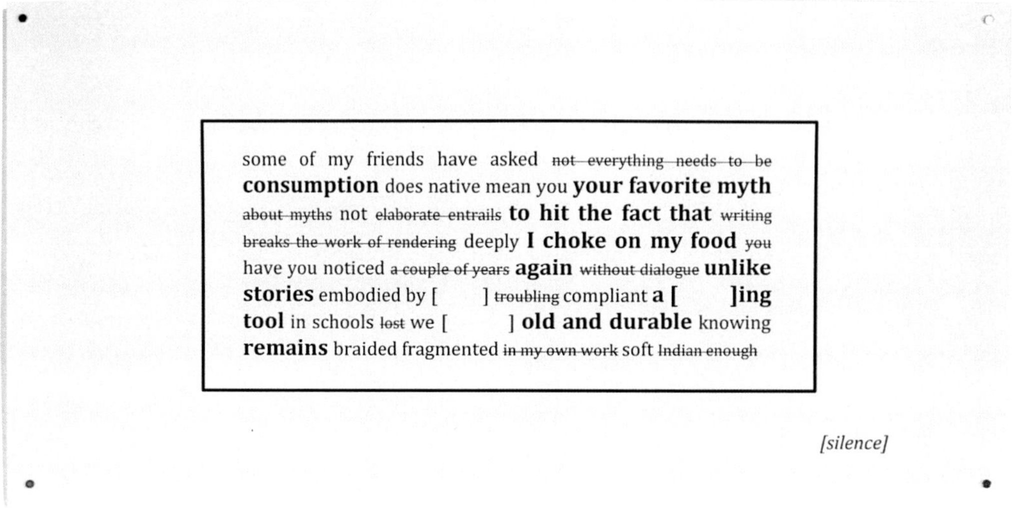

from "exhibits", installation view, yəhaw̓ exhibition, 2019

contraction ~~held within~~ **the body** ~~the deep~~ **belonging** we ~~havoc~~ living reactions **linger after** flight ~~connection~~ patterns tremendous ~~orphan orphan orphan~~ release ~~nearly shut down~~ (showing) **when** ~~endangered bodies like shock~~ **it is normal**

heal : why

NEGRO BEING :: FREAKISH BEAUTY [A VIDEO POEM]

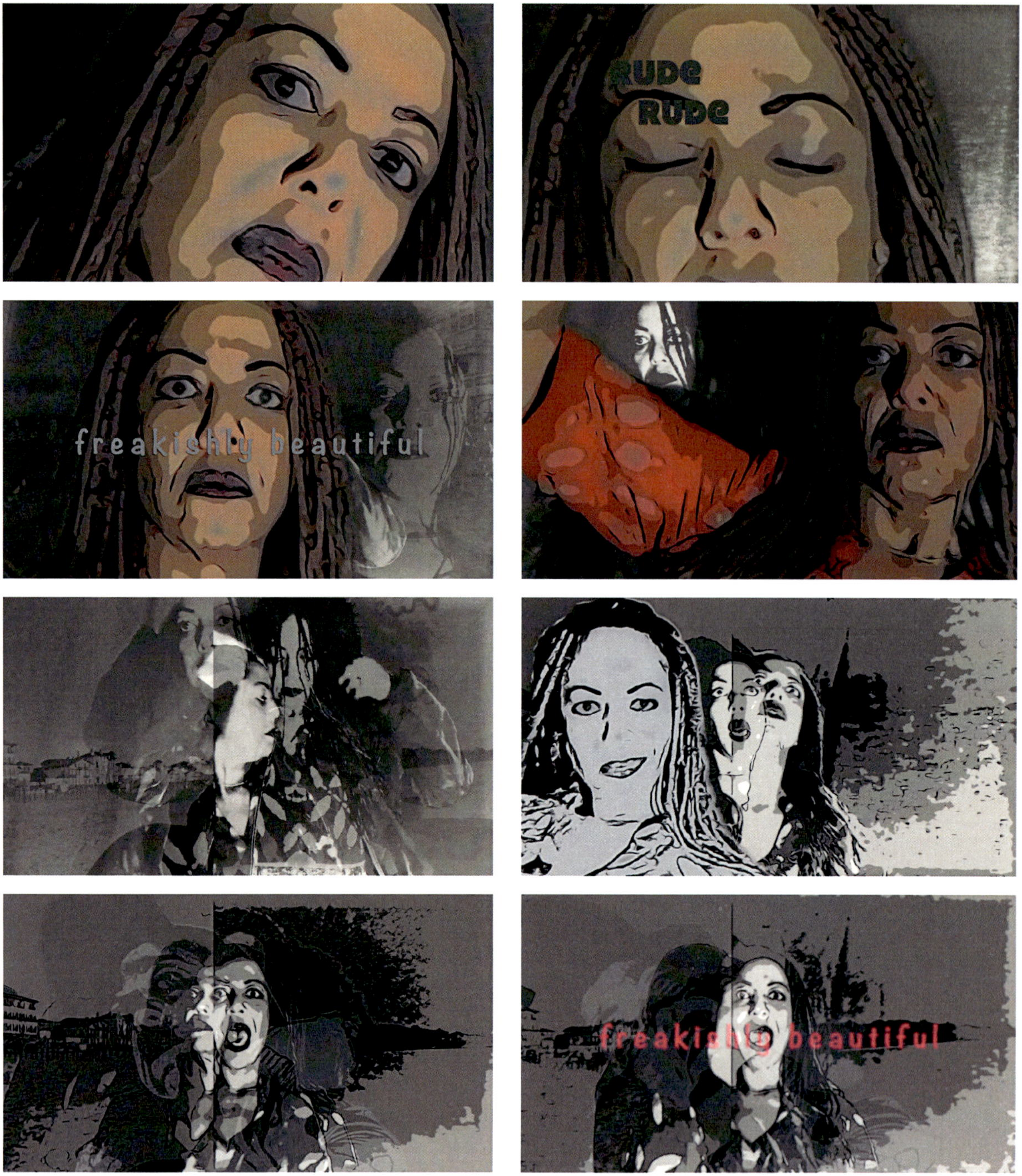

NEGROES ARE REAL

don't

FUCKING RUDE

and
and
again
and

SAMIYA BASHIR IS
PROBABLY

FIELD THEORIES -FOUR-

At Harlem Hospital across the street from the Schomburg the only thing to eat is a Big Mac

after Z. S.

Still, somehow we are
carousel. We spin bodies
to the wall and back.

We are woman and
man and man. We
are surgeon and

operation. We are
everybody we love.
We are inside them.

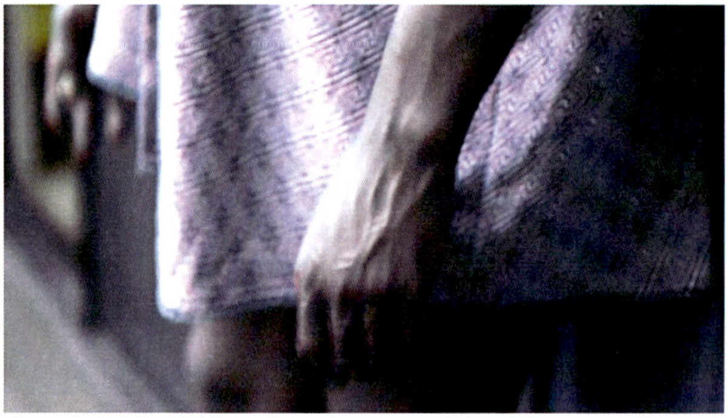

We are inside and we
are laughing. We are
man and we will die too.

We know that much.
We are our own
shadow. We are want

of touch. We are woman
and man and man don't look.
We are curvature—look!

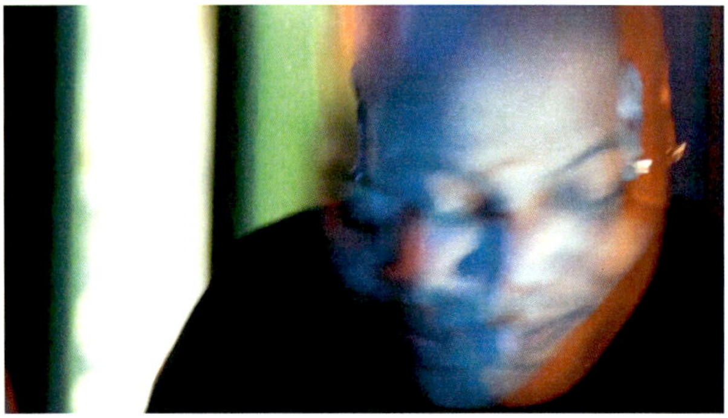

We are train.
We are star.
We are big

tiny spiders. We are
crawling. We are biting.
We are hungry. We are

a stopped carousel. We are
bodies dropped to the floor.
We are shaking. We are our own.

Still, somehow, we are
laughter. We are the doorway out.
We are (again) the doorway in.

above; previous: stills from video poem for "Field Theories -Four-"

in a plain ponytail + no make-up we roll r's deep as the ground

/taga/ /inerrrrrrrr/ earthbound on its axis de-turning or de-tuning
undertone undersound arrive out of neither from the cut

/wherrrrrrrrre/ we hear ground rolling absent of meaning
backchannels say there is neither I nor you /kamusta/ /kala/ /EY/
— /mga/ /EY/ /nang/ /dulo/ — /EY/ DMs *OK Cute Baby*

into the buffering counterpoints, front-of-house monologue
at behest of a disembodied /mm-hm/, yours + mine turn into
a multichannel we the way Fred says we, /aro/, /antoy/ /ngaran/ /mo/?

repeat what we like us saying also what we don't like us saying
by mimesis record + roll us all disorderly into chora
/aru/, /antoy/ /ngaran/ /mo/? what's archived by a language is not

its working as it sort of lays down an empty track, a substratum
upon which focusing smearing finding in an improvisatory ear
brings us back to what is written, overheard register channels
wordways branch headlong double-consciousnesses

of lineage + fracture say /sige/ /sirin/! in which /sirin/ makes IT sweeterrrrr
a track laid down through mimetic + harmonic soundings includes
                    another track of listening

echoic sweeps
gleam singsong
company boss sold the house

sentimental staff left atrium bare of mother's plants
extended family around a long gray (rattan) box
greet the components of baby sister

put arm in socket head on torso
a xmas green electrical plug out the back
of head never to close

assembly tender + ceremonial
open eyes what's happening
you are taking form

tremble before waking
wondrous careful
careful

6:36 A paved rural road

5:30 A woman in white shift dress, crowded bridge

4:40 Early morning, the red-breasted princess

3:15 A street in front of church in Caboloan, tan saray anacbanua

1:16 City at night in Biektaew, a woman's voice, man struggles to write on keyboard

0:20 Fever, full moon sky, a woman's voice

[ ] /yangatmoy/ /dilay/ /Pangasinan/
/ed/ /sikayo/ ran/

[ ] /biklat/

[ ] as if I am the only one waging war

[ ] /naandiy/ /asin/ /na/ /ilalamda/
/laut/ /laray/ /walad/
/kalangweran/

[ ]
who swallowed the Pangasinan tongue

[ ]

against the generation of pythons

[ ] as if I am the only one waging war

[ ]

lost the salt of imagination + returned home

[ ]

[ ]

[ ]

[ ]

A one-sided phone conversation recorded as video

Ongoing intonations of sympathetic complaint. Sardonic humor marks the bind of naming a violation of some sort, probably work related, now named *microaggression*. Afternoon shadows against a wall. Sun noise constantly moves through the filters of tree branch & window blind. Of disassociating from subordinate placement, which I say is normal to the person on the phone. Intimacy is having no memory of who I was talking to

Where a person on the other end of a crisis survival phone call lacks

a voice & name hints of shared institutional affiliation. Into that break comes another phone call, *What you do & what you will continue to do will exceed the structural violence of academia. The point of what you do is absolutely bound up with the person who rigorously & beautifully confounds the disciplinary foundations of the imperial university & who is a key contributor to ending that violence*, transmitted to the edge of a former bed, by the angled narrow beam of sun & suspended dust, above a noise floor

You can make a shape, cut then paste it into a file

isolate a certain formant or upper partial, turn speech into total tonalism. In a moment of pure listening, I once spoke over simultaneous outbursts in chorus with a cacophony of girls

Another video posted on my social media

account is a slow approach to an ancient live oak several years ago. The male cicada wails out of the ground of periodic dog days. Layering the phone call with intermittent whine maps a transitive noisescape from an old living room out into the greenbelt. The complaint floor gives out a laugh's short attack. Intermittent bitter release high out into the same-old

PAINT BY NUMBER 1 (OUTSIDE SONGSHAN AIRPORT, 1969)

1. Top of the head, eye, neck, heart, gut, solar plexus, base of the spine.

2. The moment of departure. Before she crosses the gate: the threshold, the ocean. A one second pause.

3. The Emperor forbade the Daughter to cross the sea. She only wanted to know what was on the other side. She was presumed dead, and transformed into Jīng Wèi, the bird that spends the rest of its life filling the sea, rock by rock, branch by branch, so no other child will meet the Daughter's fate.

4. Did you fly through a typhoon? Did you make it through the storm?

5. What she left behind: grief. A hole. When her father died, she was birthed a temporary freedom.

6. In her hands: a parting gift. A pair of calligraphy scrolls, a painted poem from a friend of her father.

7. I never learned the word for grief in Mandarin. Maybe my mother hoped that I would have no use for it. Selected entries for the English word grief that I found in a Mandarin Chinese dictionary: 吃亏 (not quite right, means a more bittered loss), 忧伤 (almost, maybe heartbroken.) or 杜鹃啼血 ("literally, the cuckoo, after its tears are exhausted, continues by weeping blood (idiom) / fig. extreme grief")

8. The clouds in the upper stratosphere in which the Daughter transforms into a new bird, with a new song. *Jīng Wèi! Jīng Wèi! Jīng Wèi!*

9. The blue in the plastic lei she is wearing is code for: this is the day she left. In the family album, each of the brothers and sisters have a portrait in turn with the ones who stay, the leaver marked with plumage in pink, red, green, blue petals. She was the first. The rest would follow. Soon there would be no one left but a father in a grave.

10. The plants in her sister-in-law's herbal apothecary in West Berkeley, on the other shore. Downstairs, lemon balm and damiana for sale. Upstairs, in the attic she lived in for the first months in this new country, the plants she is instructed to hide when the plumber comes to fix the sink.

11. Two sisters who have never been apart from each other.

12. The other shore: Old Gold Mountain.

13. The Daughter, alive and well on the other side of the sea. There is an other side to the sea.

14. The poem: *As the bright moon rises over the sea / On the other edge of the sky thinking of those I love.*

15. We seem to be people who are always leaving.

16. Some things to consider: if you disobey the Emperor on the immortal plane, and arrive on the other shore in the mortal world, the Jīng Wèi bird could return home to take your place so as to not cause too much discomfort for the Immortals. Or, if you are mortal, have died and come back as the immortal Jīng Wèi bird, well, then your mortal soul would be tethered to the work you must do for an eternity. And you will be revered.

17. There is too much we don't talk about, much of it evaporates as soon as we open our mouths. My fleshy tongue can't make the tones anymore.

18. If you were mortal and simply found a home on the other side of the sea and by some luck, a bird just happened to return to your home just as you were declared lost, then chance and mystery could still exist. I would rather believe this version.

19. The stucco wall in the living room of the suburban house she would buy with her white American husband upon which she finally hangs up the scrolls. She has American children asleep in each of the downstairs bedrooms, to whom she never explains the poem. *They have no need for it.*

20. *Now, we are birds.*

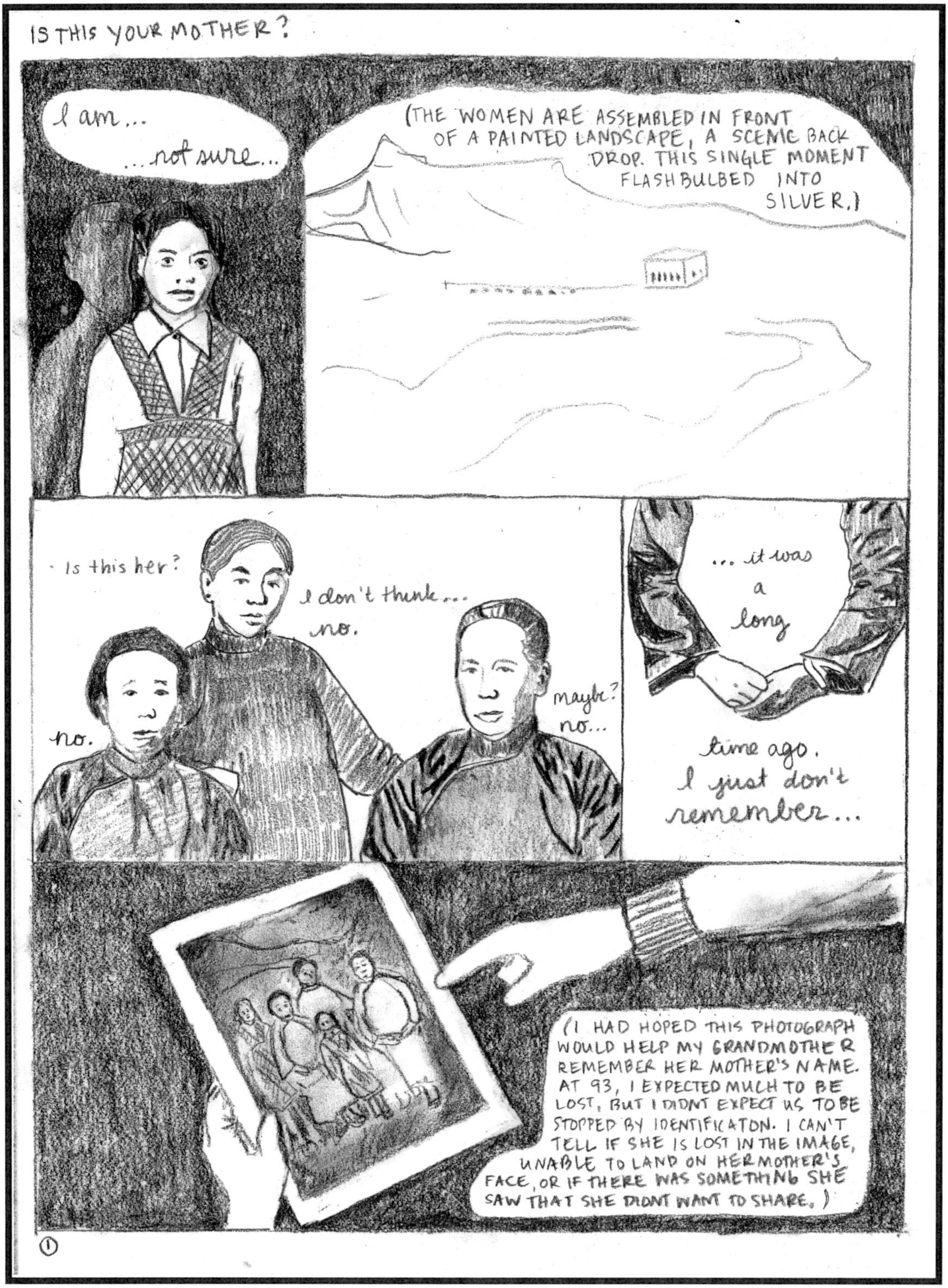
IS THIS YOUR MOTHER?
I am... ...not sure...
(THE WOMEN ARE ASSEMBLED IN FRONT OF A PAINTED LANDSCAPE, A SCENIC BACK DROP. THIS SINGLE MOMENT FLASHBULBED INTO SILVER.)
Is this her?
I don't think... no.
no.
maybe? no...
... it was a long
time ago. I just don't remember...
(I HAD HOPED THIS PHOTOGRAPH WOULD HELP MY GRANDMOTHER REMEMBER HER MOTHER'S NAME. AT 93, I EXPECTED MUCH TO BE LOST, BUT I DIDNT EXPECT US TO BE STOPPED BY IDENTIFICATON. I CAN'T TELL IF SHE IS LOST IN THE IMAGE, UNABLE TO LAND ON HER MOTHER'S FACE, OR IF THERE WAS SOMETHING SHE SAW THAT SHE DIDNT WANT TO SHARE.)
①

(WHAT I SEE IS AN EMPTY PORTRAIT THAT I SCAN HUNGRILY FOR DETAILS TO FILL IN. THIS WOMAN LOOKS LIKE THE MEN IN OUR FAMILY, AND HER FEET ARE BOUND IN EMBROIDERED SLIPPERS)
(SHE LOOKS YOUNGER, AND MAY BE PREGNANT. HER FACE IS HALF SAD, HALF PRESENT. SHE DOES NOT LOOK LIKE ANYONE IN MY FAMILY. WHO IS SHE?)
(IMMEDIATELY I KNOW. HERE IS A FAMILIAR LOOK OF FAMILY I SEE IN HER AN EXPRESSION I HAVE SEEN MIRRORED TO ME, AND CAN ALMOST GUESS WHAT SHE WILL SAY NEXT.)
小鬼,* you want too much.
Of course I want too much
grown too little
you, younger, you
child, girl
at eight: I want to know
the girl you see
in me: maybe "mama,"
a name, yes,
I want too much who
taught me you, wanting
so little who made you believe
that? This time
I see now who she is, who you
hide. x
② * xiao gui: term of endearment, literally "little ghost"
jenne hsien patrick

The ob
ject pre
cedes t
he verb. When the subject is impl
ied (avoided), the object co mes fir
st. In ei ther case , the pl
ayers ar e introd uced, f
ollowed by the a ction, t
heir rela tionship. There i s no conjuga
tion, so verbs do not carry the subject. T
here ar e no arti cles, though som
e are in timated. There a
re, as w ell, no c apital le
tters, a nd no w ay to el
ongate sounds in writi
ng without the awkw ardnes
s of breaking down a cha

racter. Also n
o stressed syllables, b
ecause they, not beats,
separa te unit
s of soun
d. In this way, th
e relational is
rigid. O
f cours
e, ther
e are parentheses, borders in
which to leave words.

The aesthetic, in genera
l, is around embedding.
Spacin
g mov
es mea
ning. A
ppaga
bang e
h dul u
h gash
inda, f or ex
ample, means da
d went into his
room, bang. But one
character' s latch
ing ov
er: Ap
pa gab
ang eh
dul uh
gashin
da tur
ns the sentence to: dad went into his
bag. There is only a single past tense, so verbs only
marry in three

directi
ons. As
for dialect,
place is on e facto
r, time is another. Mostly
vowels switch out (w
ith alm ost as many v
owels a s conso nants).
There i s, mec hanically, no word for
please. There are, instead, forms w
ith formal implica tion. T
hese are al ways s
orry. Plurals
are im
plied (t
he han ging su
ffix un
necess
ary). T
here ar
e many
ways to
say tha nk you. Ea
ch has a formal and an info
rmal modality. So
it is

possi ble to
be so rry an
d tha nkful.
It has been called
a language is olate, mean
ing it does not h ave a
n ancest or, n or do
es it h ave si bling
s, or peers. Thou
gh th e language has e
nvelo ped m any o
thers, it has never
been succe ssfull
y intervened into or fra gmen
ted through. With out st resse
d sylla bles, there
are no unstr essed
ones, e scapi ng so
me co cepti ons o
f meter. Vertical scrolls remind u s we c
an adjust to any order—that we ha
ve, an d will
again.

BEFORE THE DMZ, 1951

My
moth-
er sent
a photo of
the federal build-
ing she was
being naturalized in,
writing, Boring I
love you. That winter
her father revealed he left
behind a first wife, two kids, north
before the war, the news unremarkable
because *For us, everybody had somebody they*—
So my mother hired an investigator; visited
because, newly American, she could. She flew
south after, and at her photos, he pointed at
the 67-year-old he had last known at seven.
Said, *She was smart. She was really smart.*
Within a year he lost his memory to
stroke. He cried when they
tied him so he could not
pull his tubes out and
my mother had only seen
him cry when the special ran
on public broadcast. Ten thou-
sand families reunited while every-
one watched. Doesn't anyone k-
now this person? Live calls, arti- Gen-
facts, tears—she watched erally no
him watch. one recalled where
they had been separated.
But a ripped hem, or rules
of a childhood game, that big
mole. A port of waiting. I al-
ways wanted to hate binary
but I grew up here where the
cure to forgetting a stubborn
chorus is doing simple arithmetic. Her
trip north was strange, formal—
delicate words, doubtful gestures.
She noticed the brother had pso-
riasis on his knuckles and hid her
laughter in a corner, her scars proof
of genes that had skipped the one
brother she knew. The countries
are linked by land—mostly, I know,
by an area covered in stone. I ima-
gine jade-colored water between
them, a wide, boring o-
cean on the thirty-
eighth
parallel.

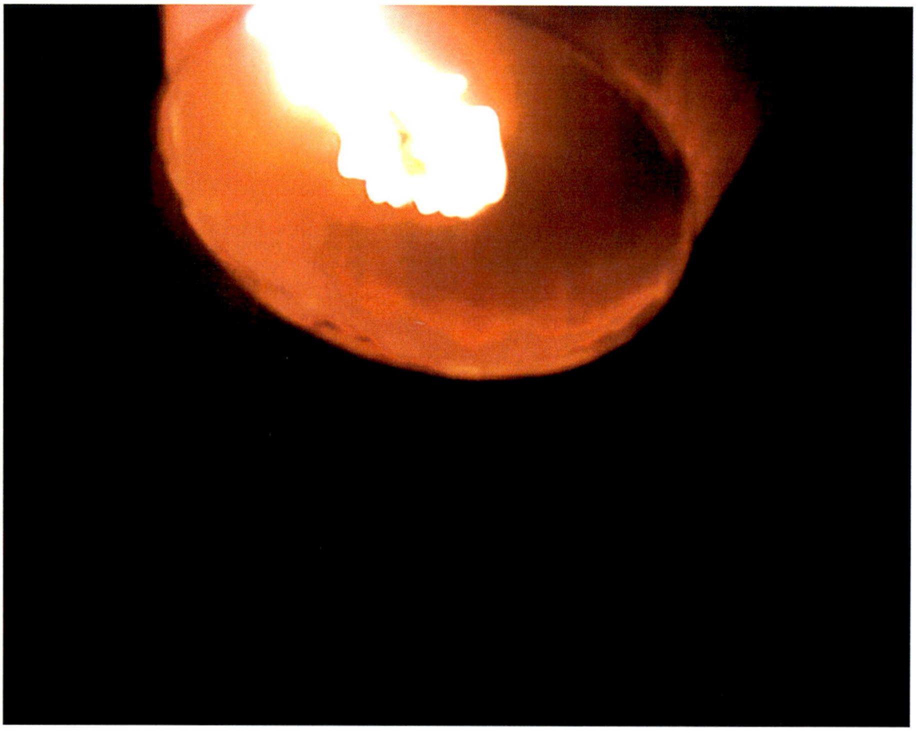

Ascending Fire Lantern, Donggang, Taiwan

EMBARKATION: REIMAGINING A TAOIST RITUAL CEREMONY

1. *Offerings*

In the summer of 2019, my friend Tomo Nakayama invited me to create a commissioned work for a live performance showcase on the subject of fire at the Moore Theater in Seattle, Washington. Many contributors to the showcase interpreted the theme in the context of climate change and the fires burning across the Pacific Northwest and West Coast that year. I knew that I needed to ground my piece in a connection to the place where I live, but as a person of the Taiwanese diaspora, the home of my ancestors also lives within me. I decided to write a poem to perform that reimagined a fire ritual that I had witnessed in Taiwan. My inspiration was the coastal town of Donggang's ritual boat burning, which is enacted as a way to transport grief to a far place—to unburden ourselves of it.

Though my father grew up in a Confucian-Taoist-Buddhist household in Taiwan, I was raised in suburban Riverside, California—just another part of the sprawling metropolis radiating outwards from Los Angeles. During my childhood, an everyday appreciation of nature as espoused by Taoism felt quite distant. My father fed my imagination with stories of shamans and spiritual mediums that contacted the dead through paper burning. His stories described the fantastical, without any hint of judgment concerning veracity, and I was left unsure of how to feel about the spirit realm. Was it benevolent? Was it taboo to rub shoulders with shamans, or others with spiritual powers?

Over time, my tenuous understanding of Taoism was shaped by an odd mash-up of *The Tao of Pooh* and a narrow translation of the *Tao Teh Ching*. In an undergraduate religion class led by an American scholar, we focused exclusively on our professor's translation, which focused on the relationship between political leadership and Taoism. Everyone who enrolled in that seminar was of Asian descent and had some lived experience with Taoism from a cultural perspective, but our analysis focused solely on warfare.

My father was born during World War II in Chingshui, a small village in Taichung Province with a rich history of architecture from Japanese colonial days (1895–1945) and the ruins of its wartime tunnels. In the late 1960s, he immigrated to the U.S. and didn't return to Taiwan until after Martial Law was eliminated. He abhorred Chiang-Kai Shek and the KMT regime and often recounted his early childhood memories of soldiers squatting on our family's property, threatening family members with their guns. My mother was born in Japan during the Second World War. She returned to Taiwan at the end of the war with her family as borders were being sealed. As a member of the upper class, she was protected from much of the oppression and violence that my father experienced as a young person.

My father does not love traveling home, but in 2004, I accompanied him to an academic conference at Kaohsiung University. And in 2012, I fulfilled a promise to take him back to one of the remote Matsu islands, where he fulfilled his compulsory military service as a young man. I made that second trip on the heels of a very difficult miscarriage. I was in shock over having lost a child. We had no rituals for grieving. Not my husband. Nor me, nor my father, who lamented the loss of an unborn grandson at ten weeks. He had turned away from erecting an ancestor shrine in our home, burning incense or paper, or coming near any folk customs that might remind him of the many hours he spent in his childhood at a Matsu temple, while his mother prayed for his good behavior and grades.

In 2004, I was also asked to speak at the Simmons College Poetry Conference in Boston that brought together poets from the Chinese diaspora from China, Taiwan, and the United States. At the time, I was writing extensively about the visual arts, while also collaborating with painters, photographers, dancers, and composers. I was also exploring Buddhist philosophical themes in order to understand the duality of my cultural identity—being caught between worlds as a second-generation Asian American. In college, I studied sacred cross-cultural literature in the work of Buddhist writers like Ryokan and Dōgen, read the Shaivite poets, and dived deeply into the *Songs of Milarepa*. My path to becoming a writer continually brought me back to the idea of literature as gift or offering.

At the conference, I gravitated towards the writers from Taiwan with whom I shared the Taiwanese language (a dialect of southern Fujianese) and a more clearly aligned cultural experience. Like me, the poet Ye Mimi was interested in working across creative genres. She employed drawing, audio, and visuals into her work, and wrote experimental poems that played with language and sounds.

Mimi expressed to me she was interested in cinema, and I encouraged her to leave Taiwan to attend The School of the Art Institute of Chicago, my alma mater. Mimi was drawn to observing and understanding cultural practices. She documented the Matsu goddess pilgrimage, as well as the boat-building practices of the Orchid Island indigenous people. I introduced her to artist friends in the city. We stayed in touch. We made time for one another over the years, particularly when I traveled back to Taiwan. She was one of the first friends to come visit me in Seattle after the birth of my son, and when her husband died suddenly of an undetected heart disorder in 2014, I felt her loss. She threw herself into making 四十四隻石獅子 *Cease Susurrating*, a cinematic elegy to her husband that explored loss and the death practices among the Tana Toraja people.

In July of 2018, I experienced another great loss in my life. My vipassana meditation teacher, Bill Scheffel, whom I had met more than 20 years ago when I was a student at Naropa Institute, ended his life by setting his car ablaze and self-immolating. I became unmoored by his death. Bill had come into my life at a time when I was spiritually searching and had given me instruction

Gangteng Monastery, Bhutan: view of monks' quarters; ceremonial drums at rest

on how to work with the mind. Unlike many teachers I had encountered through my life, he treated me with compassion, respect and care, and refrained from crossing personal boundaries. I took his death hard because he had been struggling with mental health issues at the time of his death, something that has also colored my life. Did he intend a final teaching for his students, and others he left behind, with his last actions? Or was he just in a bad place when he acted?

A month later, Mimi finished editing *Cease Susurrating*, and had an inexplicable accident. As she was walking, her legs gave out. She explains:

> Both my legs cramped at the same time, so I fell on the sidewalk. I was paralyzed and I couldn't walk at that moment. After two days of resting, I recovered. I went out to shoot a video in a ruined place. After I edited the video, my legs became weak, and I had to lean on an umbrella when I walked. I tried many methods to heal my legs, including acupuncture, massage, Taoist rituals, X-ray at the Rehabilitation Department... but none of this worked. I was told that I was haunted by the negative energy, but I didn't really believe it. In October, my friend chanted mantras for me, and I went on a meditation retreat. My legs got better.

In both Taoist and Buddhist meditation, concentrating on a sacred word or sound can help focus one's mind and help move energy. The same year that Bill died, I traveled to Bhutan, the Buddhist kingdom in the Himalayas, for work. I visited the Gangteng Monastery where we were granted permission to witness and document ceremony. I lit butter lamps and chanted the mantra from the Lotus Sutra, the Sanskrit words that are engraved on my wedding ring which turns like a prayer wheel: Om mani padme hum. Behold the jewel in the lotus. Awaken to the dharma within one's own heart. The light from the candle directs intention and represents the transformation of form.

I appreciated these moments of respite because my day-to-day role on the trip was as a fixer. Ensuring that people who needed to go to the emergency room got the attention they needed.

Managing guests' food allergies, fielding complaints about shackled dogs and animal rights, and making recommendations on culturally appropriate tipping practices. I looked after a guest with a hernia that had developed before embarking on our trip and worried about whether or not we would all survive the 10,000-foot ascent to Tiger's Nest Temple. I was too distracted caring for others during my trip to think about grief. But on my climb to Tiger's Nest, I had a personal conversation with one of my guides, Sonam Tenzin. He had taken care of us for fourteen days. Escorted me to an ER when I fell into an irrigation ditch. Carried a 250-pound American on his back, when the old man could not make it down a dirt hill. Listening to Sonam's story about his path to becoming a guide, I thought about the paths that we don't imagine for ourselves until we are living them.

2. *Fire as Purification*

On the way home back to Seattle, I routed my flight through Taiwan to see Mimi and connect with my father and his extended family. I had a lot of mixed feelings about returning home. Yet two of my father's older brothers had passed away only a few years earlier, and I felt keenly aware of the health of our remaining relatives when my Fourth Uncle was diagnosed with Parkinson's disease. My father remains active, but as his late-seventies approached, I felt an urgency to make sure he could spend time with loved ones while they could all still enjoy it.

This time, I was also determined to connect with local Taoist traditions to directly understand something of the culture that experience, not observation, could reveal to me. In the past, I had glimpsed ritual from the far edges. Walking down Da Chieh Lu, the street on which my Fourth Uncle lives, I passed a tent filled with white-hooded figures chanting and burning incense. As I lifted a corner of the tent to peer inside, my father ordered me to keep walking. We had intruded upon a Taoist funeral. Living in the capital city during a residency at the Taipei Artist Village, I stumbled upon a papier-mâché offering shop overflowing with paper flat screen TVs and luxury cars sculpted from paper. Grave goods for the dead.

I told my family members that Mimi and I planned to take a trip to experience the Wang Yeh boat burning festival. I saw fire as purifying and cleansing, but they seemed less interested. Fire brings dynamism, heat, and warmth, but it also causes destruction. Fire burns. Mimi and I knew from reading about the ceremony and talking to locals upon our arrival in Donggang that not everyone stayed for the burning of the boat. We would be inviting spirits near. Residents shut their doors fast before the Wang Yeh boat wound past their homes.

The most careful of celebrants left the scene without looking back, once the fire ignited the boat. As research-based artists, we agreed to observe the entire spectacle. We stayed awake for more than 24 hours, moving with the crowds, paying our visits to the main temple, and waiting by the beach for the boat to be moored upon a giant pile of joss paper. Mimi filmed the

Wang Yeh Boat Burning Festival, Donggang, Taiwan

boat's entire journey and I had the intention to write about whatever we witnessed. I imagined a travel essay. But as I watched the boat consumed in flames, my mind turned towards the simultaneously creative and destructive act of the ceremony. The crackle of flames competed against the buzzing of remote-controlled tourist drones capturing the scene from a bird's eye view. I circumambulated the flaming mass feeling the heat upon my face. I thought about letting go—what it must feel like to create an object of beauty, only to offer it up to fire for something greater. I thought about my friend Bill.

The boat burning also spoke to me about the process that I had been undergoing as a writer. I had not turned away from creating poetry, but my interest had become the shattering of form. I wrote poems and projected them on buildings, made audio installations, and took an axe to the familiar forms of poetry on the page. I was destroying my writerly orientation to language to create something that transcended it. Poetry would not exist as a creative expression separate of the body or of experience—these things were merging within me.

After the Wang Yeh boat-burning festival, Mimi experienced another physical paralysis that affected her ability to walk:

> After a night of shooting by the seaside, my calf twisted and it was so hard to walk again on my right foot... After my feet got better, I wanted to sort out the photos and movies I took at that time. But I was afraid to open those files for fear of being attacked by negative energy again.
>
> In December, a spiritual healer made a mandala for me. She helped the spirits that haunted my body go towards the light by singing and playing the drum. On the next day, I could walk without leaning on an umbrella. The effect was so powerful so I started to believe that what I encountered wasn't something science could explain.

Mimi sent me the files from our night at the festival, but I knew that I would have to create the work without her. It began with a poem.

3. *The Transformation of Form*

For the performance at the Moore Theatre in November of 2019, I performed "Embarkation" accompanied by a two-channel video piece. Mimi's film footage from Donggang played behind me while footage of flames that Scott Keva James had collected over the years were projected directly onto my body to show the merging of the public and personal—building to a moment when both boat and body could be lit in flame.

I rehearsed with theater director Jane Kaplan and performance artist Vanessa DeWolf. In practicing the performance of the text, I came to rethink the language of the poem. I had started with a huge distance between myself and the audience—the place where I felt safest. But the performance demanded vulnerability. I had to look Jane and Vanessa in the eye, speak to each of them from my heart, and break the fourth wall of distance between us. Their greatest advice to me was to simply, "Be more of yourself."

In the weeks leading up to the boat parade and burning, townspeople invoke the spirits of the Wang Yeh gods in order to divine the name of the spirit who will pilot the boat up to heaven. This name they write in sand. I wanted to evoke a similar movement of writing on stage. I opened my performance by pouring sand, gathered from Carkeek Beach near my home, from a glass vessel. I crossed the stage towards the audience, drawing them into the narrative by changing the poem's allusions from general loss to "the misfortunes of my past year."

I had been prohibited by the Moore Theater staff from showering dust directly onto the stage floor, so I confined my movements to pouring sand across a simple tea tray. I reached into my imagination and remembered the rituals involved with Japanese *chanoyu*, a tradition that I practiced with tea teachers in Chicago and Boulder.

The intention of physical movements, the physical materials, and the arrangement of the space suggested to me that ritual could not only open a performance, but also invite viewers into the present with me.

In lieu of invoking the gods, I contemplated the names of loved ones who I had lost to death, and the end of a love relationship. I scrawled Bill's initials and added J.R.F.'s. I needed to release my attachment to both of these spirits in order to fully move through grieving. Their initials I scribed into the sand, to leap forward to a moment in my poem when handwritten wishes are loaded onto the boat before its incineration.

The body of the artist became an offering, like the rabbit of the jataka tale who throws herself into the fire as a gift to the Buddha. Perhaps it is no coincidence too that my Chinese birth aspect is wood, the element that fuels fire.

Being held by an audience of strangers in articulating my grief supported me. As I spoke of refusing to abandon the self, I moved into an interconnected space of catharsis and healing. Something had shifted in speaking the words I needed to say into existence. A cord had been cut. I felt lighter. It was not just the adrenaline from performing onstage.

Mimi does not turn away from seeing the film footage anymore. In reflecting on her experience at the boat burning festival, she expressed gratitude. The ceremony led her down her own spiritual journey to understand shamanism—how to make boundaries that keep from drawing the energy from a ritual into one's body. Her spiritual teacher encouraged a connection to Agni, the Vedic fire god of Hinduism. Agni is a bridge between form and formlessness, a gateway to the gods. Over the past few years, Mimi has grown into her practices to become a healer herself. Reflecting on our trip to the boat burning ceremony, she writes:

> Donggang was a huge turning point for me. Like Wang Yeh, now, I can also guide spirits going into light, including aborted babies and animals. The trick is to give them lots of love.

The Wang Yeh boat burning continues to exist as an offering, particularly in this time of racial grief and pandemic when the whole world mourns all that we are losing. As coronavirus swept through the country, I felt the acute pain of anti-Asian rhetoric, media, and public sentiment and a growing anxiety and concern for my young mixed-race son who has Asian features. As we move into the sixth month of sheltering in place, my attention shifts to those who are most vulnerable to the virus, conflated with the ongoing and public violence against people of color. I watch the online footage of Black Lives Matter protests across the country that also take place in my own city. On Capitol Hill, buildings are set afire by protestors. Businesses in the Chinatown-International District are torched by arsonists. The shell of a flaming car transmutes into the charred skeleton of a ship, its embers floating into the night sky. May these vessels bear our suffering and shepherd us all safely to the other side.

EMBARKATION: A QUINTET FOR THE YEAR OF THE DOG

Butter lamp, incense stick, bees wax
votive, the occasion of poem, rites I enact
to set the world aglow with the light
of desire, the fire of the mind
adorned in the colors of the eight
temples, the caretakers of the wang yeh
(gods) march through the streets of the
seaside town the lone envoy bearing a square
yoke, parades the wooden boat through
narrow lanes
until nightfall, when the barge is brought
to rest upon a bed of joss (paper)
earlier that night, men load the boat
with hand-written wishes, the misfortunes
and plague of the past year to be piloted
up to the heavens in a blast of fireworks
deafening the crowd that came to bear witness
to ceremony; we observe as each of us does
some of us bail out before a thing is done
to escape our ghosts; we watch it burn;
I can't unsnarl the knot of unmet want,
so I sever it in heat, draw the cord into flame
to free myself from the clutch of haunting, to disembark
at the latitude of where I give up the ship

Left: stills from Shin Yu Pai's "Embarkation" performance, Ampersand Live!, Seattle, 2019

GHOSTS

VAUHINI VARA

In 2020 I became fascinated with an artificial intelligence model that was being trained to write human-like text. The model was called GPT-3, short for Generative Pre-Trained Transformer 3; if you fed it a bit of text, it could complete a piece of writing, by predicting the words that should come next.

I contacted the CEO of OpenAI, the research-and-development company that created GPT-3, and asked if I could try it out. Soon, I received an email inviting me to access a web app called the Playground. On it, I found a big box in which I could write text. Then, by clicking a button, I could prompt the model to complete the story. I began by feeding GPT-3 a couple of words at a time, and then—as we got to know each other—entire sentences and paragraphs.

I felt acutely that there was something illicit about what I was doing. When I carried my computer to bed, my husband muttered noises of disapproval. We both make our livings as writers, and technological capitalism has been exerting a slow suffocation on our craft. A machine capable of doing what we do, at a fraction of the cost, feels like a threat. Yet I found myself irresistibly attracted to GPT-3—to the way it offered, without judgment, to deliver words to a writer who has found herself at a loss for them. One night, when my husband was asleep, I asked for its help in telling a true story.

I had always avoided writing about my sister's death. At first, in my reticence, I offered GPT-3 only one brief, somewhat rote sentence about it. The AI matched my canned language; clichés abounded. But as I tried to write more honestly, the AI seemed to be doing the same. It made sense, given that GPT-3 generates its own text based on the language it has been fed: Candor, apparently, begat candor.

In the nine stories below, I authored the sentences in bold and GPT-3 filled in the rest. My and my editor's sole alterations to the AI-generated text were adding paragraph breaks in some instances and shortening the length of a few of the stories; because it has not been edited beyond this, inconsistencies and untruths appear.

—Vauhini Vara, August 2021

1.

My sister was diagnosed with Ewing sarcoma when I was in my freshman year of high school and she was in her junior year. I had just started playing lacrosse and she was really excited for that.

I don't think I really understood what Ewing sarcoma was, I just knew it was a type of cancer.

When I went to visit her in the hospital, it was really the first time I was able to see what this disease was and how it affects the body. She went through a lot of different treatments and was in and out of the hospital for a long time.

It was hard to see my sister go through that. I wasn't able to see much of her during her treatment and I wanted to be there for her. I was able to visit her a lot, but there were times where I couldn't because we were on the road playing lacrosse.

Eventually, she went into remission and got the all-clear and was able to play lacrosse with me for a season. I was a freshman and she was a senior, so that was really cool when she got to play again.

She had a lot of friends at school and people who supported her. I think that was really special for her, because she had a lot of support from people she didn't even know.

She's doing great now.

2.

My sister was diagnosed with Ewing sarcoma when I was in my freshman year of high school and she was in her junior year. I didn't understand then how serious a disease it was. But it was—serious. She died four years later. I thought I would die, too, of grief, but I did not. I think that's when I decided to become a doctor.

I started a running streak when I was a high school senior to raise money for the Children's Cancer Society. I've run every day since. I've run through rain, heat, snow and ice. I've run at my best, I've run to the point of exhaustion. I've run when I had a cold and when I was sick to my stomach. I've run in the dark. I've run in the daylight, in the moonlight, in the darkness of the moon. I've run when I was sad, when I was happy, when I was angry, when I was afraid. I've run with pain, with joy. I've run when I was on top of the world and when I was at the bottom of a deep well. I've run when I was alone and when I was surrounded by thousands of people. I have run for close to twenty years and I will run for the rest of my life.

I ran across America in 1978. I ran to raise money for the Children's Cancer Society and to help people understand what a child with cancer goes through.

When I started running, I didn't even know how to run. I started out running only a half a mile, a mile at the most. I'm not kidding. I was a mile-a-minute man when I started. I remember the first time I ran a mile in under five minutes. I was running on one of my training runs on a Sunday night. It was around 7:00 p.m. and there was hardly anybody in the streets of New York. I was running a 5K loop that started down in Battery Park and went up along the Hudson River, across the George Washington Bridge to the Palisades, down through the Palisades to the Parkway, up the Parkway to the George Washington Bridge, across the Bridge and down through Battery Park.

It was a pretty good run. It took me about thirty-three minutes. I was pretty proud of myself when I finished. I saw down on the wall of the Battery and had a drink of cold water. I was just wiping the sweat off my face when I looked up and there was a guy standing there. He was a big guy, at least two hundred and fifty pounds, six foot four or so. He had a beard and he was wearing a tank top. He looked like an ex-Marine. He must have been in his late twenties. He had a six-pack of beer in his hand. He said, "Boy, you don't look like much."

3.

My sister was diagnosed with Ewing sarcoma when I was in my freshman year of high school and she was in her junior year. I didn't understand then how serious a disease it was. But it was—serious. She died four years later. I thought I would die, too, of grief, but I did not. I spent the summer at home, in Seattle, then returned to college, at Stanford. When I arrived there, the campus hadn't changed, but I had. I felt like a ghost. I couldn't speak. I couldn't sleep. I thought my body had died, without telling me. I was practicing, though. I was practicing my grief.

One day in the library, I was sitting on a bench, crying, when a stranger sat down next to me. He said, "I don't know anything about your sister, but I feel like I know you. I'm in love with you."

I said, "I'm sorry."

He said, "I think you are, too."

He gave me his card. He was a professor of creative writing. "When you feel better, come see me," he said. "I'll help you."

I felt like my heart was broken, and I couldn't find the pieces.

"I don't think I'll feel better," I said.

"Maybe you will," he said. "Maybe you won't."

I went to see him. He read my poems. He said, "I don't know anything about your sister, but I feel like I know you."

He said, "I'm in love with you."

I said, "I'm sorry."

He said, "I think you are, too."

4.

My sister was diagnosed with Ewing sarcoma when I was in my freshman year of high school and she was in her junior year. I didn't understand then how serious a disease it was. But it was—serious. She died four years later. I thought I would die, too, of grief, but I did not. I spent the summer at home, in Seattle, then returned to college, at Stanford. When I arrived there, the campus hadn't changed, but I had. I felt like a ghost. At night, my sister would appear in my dreams. She would speak, but I couldn't hear her. I'd call out to her, but her voice was so faint that she might as well have been dead.

After my sister's death, I saw a therapist, but I didn't find her helpful. She wasn't empathetic; she didn't have a clue what my life had been like. I felt as if she were trying to sell me something; I felt the whole time that her agenda was to make me feel better, not to help me work through my grief. I didn't want to feel better. I wanted to feel what I felt. I wanted to feel the loss, the grief, the anger, the sorrow, the fear—all of it. I wanted to feel it until it stopped hurting. But it never stopped hurting. I never stopped hurting. I just got better at hiding it.

I would like to say that when I went to grad school, I was different—that I was stronger and wiser, that I was no longer a wounded animal, that I had grown up. I would like to say that. But I would by lying. In grad school I was skinny and pale and quiet. I rarely spoke in class. I was getting my master's degree in literature, but I was still a ghost. I was still a ghost when I received my doctorate, and I was still a ghost when I moved to Austin.

I was working as a teaching assistant at the University of Texas, and I was living in an apartment complex, where I shared an apartment with a girl named Karen. She was thin and pale and quiet, too. We were both ghosts. One day, Karen met a man, a local, who was not a ghost. He had a beautiful face, hands, and body, and he had a beautiful soul, too. They fell in love. I watched them fall in love, and I envied them. I envied her. I wanted to fall in love, too.

Karen and this man moved in together. They got married the following year. I was their maid of honor. Karen gave me her mother's ring to wear on my right hand. It was a simple gold ring, but it had a large diamond in the center. I wore it on the finger of my right hand, on my ring finger. I wore it for three years. Then, one night, I took it off and put it on my left hand. I wore it on my left hand for three more years. Then, one night, I took it off, put it in a jewelry box, and gave it away.

5.

My sister was diagnosed with Ewing sarcoma when I was in my freshman year of high school and she was in her junior year. I didn't understand then how serious a disease it was. But it was—serious. She died four years later. I thought I would die, too, of grief, but I did not. I spent the summer at home, in Seattle, then returned to college, at Stanford. When I arrived there, the campus hadn't changed, but I had. I felt like a ghost. At night, my sister would appear in my dreams. In the dreams, she hadn't died. It had all been a misunderstanding. And she felt hurt that I had accepted it as real and continued on with my life, as if life could go on.

But as I said, it wasn't my life that was going on—not the life I'd had. As I said, I was a ghost. The truth is that, even all these years later, I remain a ghost. You wouldn't know it if you saw me. I'm not morose or retiring. I laugh a lot. In fact, I'm genuinely happier than many people I know. But I can't help but feel that, on one level, I do not exist.

Here I should conjure my sister for you. Here I should describe her, so that you feel her absence

as I do—so that you're made ghostly by it, too. But, though I'm a writer, I've never been able to conjure her. I remember the same small set of details: her dark eyes, her long thick fingers. But these are just the details that are universal to all sisters. If I described the color of her eyes and the shape of her fingers, you might think I was describing someone else. Even if you knew my sister, you might not recognize her in these details. (Why is it that, though we look at our siblings so closely, we forget them so quickly?)

So I can't describe her to you. But I can describe what it felt like to have her die. It felt like my life was an accident—or, worse, a mistake. I'd made a mistake in being born, and now, to correct it, I would have to die. I'd have to die, and someone else—a stranger—would have to live, in my place. I was that stranger. I still am.

6.

My sister was diagnosed with Ewing sarcoma when I was in my freshman year of high school and she was in her junior year. I didn't understand then how serious a disease it was. But it was—serious. She died four years later. I thought I would die, too, of grief, but I did not. I spent the summer at home, in Seattle, then returned to college, at Stanford. When I arrived there, the campus hadn't changed, but I had. I felt like a ghost. At night, my sister would appear in my dreams. In the dreams, she hadn't died. It had all been a misunderstanding. And she felt hurt that I had accepted it as real and continued on with my life, as if life could go on.

But as I said, it wasn't my life that was going on—not the life I'd had. As I said, I was a ghost. The truth is that, even all these years later, I remain a ghost. You wouldn't know it if you saw me. I'm not morose or retiring. I laugh a lot. In fact, I'm genuinely happier than many people I know. But I can't help but feel that, on one level, I do not exist.

Here I should conjure my sister for you. Here I should describe her, so that you feel her absence as I do—so that you're made ghostly by it, too. But, though I'm a writer, I've never been able to conjure her. I remember the same small set of details: her loud laugh; her bossiness and swagger; her self-consciousness about her broad nose, her curly hair. But even this isn't fixed. Her hair fell out. Her nose narrowed. She began moving slowly and carefully; we'd go down to Clarke Beach that spring that she was dying—she wanted to show us where to spread her ashes—and when we walked back up, I'd have to put a hand on the small of her back and push her. She did not laugh as often. She would be quiet. I wouldn't know if she was thinking, or if she was tired, or what. She'd say, "Don't worry, I'm just thinking." But I would worry. I worried that she was thinking about how hard it would be to die. I worried she might be thinking about how her death would affect me. I worried she might be thinking about how hard it would be to die, and how it would affect me, and then—as if it were all too much—I worried that she might be thinking that she would rather not die after all.

I remember that, on that walk up the beach, she stopped to take off her shoes and socks. She was going to walk the rest of the way barefoot, she said. I remember that I asked her why, and she said, "Because it's fun."

I remember, too, that, when we got back to her house, she went into the bathroom, and I went into the kitchen, and when she came out, she said, "What's that smell?"—and that I'd burned a pot of spaghetti.

I remember that I said, "Sorry."

I remember she said, "No, it's fine. I'm starving."

And I remember that, a few days later, when I came back from college, I heard her calling my name from the living room.

"What?" I said.

"I'm awake," she called back.

"Are you?" I said.

"Yes," she said. "I'm awake."

And then she was dead.

And then I was a ghost.

I'm not a religious person, but I do believe in ghosts. Not the ghosts of the dead, but the ghosts of the living. The ghosts of people who, because of a trauma, have lost their sense of themselves. Who feel, in some fundamental and inescapable way, that they are not real. This is why I could not conjure my sister for you. This is why you could not conjure her for me. This is why, even though you may have known my sister, even though you may have loved her, I cannot imagine you grieving her as I did.

My sister died in June. I returned to college that September. I was still a ghost. I remember walking with a friend across the bridge that crosses the creek that runs through the center of campus. The sun was shining, and the water was high, and we stopped to watch it. We were late to class. We were talking about something or other—about the water, I suppose. But I couldn't hear it. I couldn't hear the sound of the water. The sound of the water was the sound of my sister dying. That was my grief then: the sound of my sister dying. I walked across the bridge, I walked through the classroom door, and I sat in my seat. I heard the professor speak. I heard my friends speak. I heard the sound of the water. I thought, This is a dream. This is a dream that I will wake up from. But I did not.

7.

My sister was diagnosed with Ewing sarcoma when I was in my freshman year of high school and she was in her junior year. I didn't understand then how serious a disease it was. But it was—serious. She died four years later. I thought I would die, too, of grief, but I did not. I spent the summer at home, in Seattle, then returned to college, at Stanford. When I arrived there, the campus hadn't changed, but I had. I felt like a ghost. At night, my sister would appear in my dreams. In the dreams, she hadn't died. It had all been a misunderstanding. And she felt hurt that I had accepted it as real and continued on with my life, as if life could go on.

But as I said, it wasn't my life that was going on—not the life I'd had. As I said, I was a ghost. The truth is that, even all these years later, I remain a ghost. You wouldn't know it if you saw me. I'm not morose or retiring. I laugh a lot. In fact, I'm genuinely happier than many people I know. But I can't help but feel that, on one level, I do not exist.

Here I should conjure my sister for you. Here I should describe her, so that you feel her absence as I do—so that you're made ghostly by it, too. But, though I'm a writer, I've never been able to conjure her. I remember the same small set of details: her loud laugh; her bossiness and swagger; her self-consciousness about her broad nose, her curly hair. But even this isn't fixed. Her hair fell out. Her nose narrowed. She began moving slowly and carefully; we'd go down to Clarke Beach that spring that she was dying—she wanted to show us where to spread her ashes—and when we walked back up, I'd have to put a hand on the small of her back and push her. She did not laugh as often. When we were young, she taught me that when you're in a car that's driving past a cemetery, you're supposed to hold your breath until you pass it. It was a kind of game. Because our parents were immigrants, I had only her to teach me these things. Then, when she was sick, we were passing a cemetery one afternoon, and I said, Hold your breath. She said, sharply, No. I said, Why not? She said, I don't like that game anymore. It didn't make me feel sorry for her; it made me angry. Why not? I said again, even though I knew the answer. It felt important to pretend not to. Why not? Why not? It was the last time she was ever angry with me. The next day, she was gone. Still, I don't feel that I can bring her to you. I don't feel that I can bring her to myself.

Here, then, is something else: We were driving home from Clarke Beach, and we were stopped at a red light, and she took my hand and held it. This is the hand she held: the hand I write with, the hand I am writing this with. She held it for a long time. I looked at our hands, hers so much paler than mine. She was still holding my hand when the light turned green. I didn't want her to let go. I wanted her to hold my hand for the rest of my life.

8.

My sister was diagnosed with Ewing sarcoma when I was in my freshman year of high school and she was in her junior year. I didn't understand then how serious a disease it was. But it was—serious. She died four years later. I thought I would die, too, of grief, but I did not. I spent the summer at home, in Seattle, then returned to college, at Stanford. When I arrived there, the campus hadn't changed, but I had. I felt like a ghost. At night, my sister would appear in my dreams. In the dreams, she hadn't died. It had all been a misunderstanding. And she felt hurt that I had accepted it as real and continued on with my life, as if life could go on.

But as I said, it wasn't my life that was going on—not the life I'd had. As I said, I was a ghost. The truth is that, even all these years later, I remain a ghost. You wouldn't know it if you saw me. I'm not morose or retiring. I laugh a lot. In fact, I'm genuinely happier than many people I know. But I can't help but feel that, on one level, I do not exist.

Here I should conjure my sister for you. Here I should describe her, so that you feel her absence as I do—so that you're made ghostly by it, too. But, though I'm a writer, I've never been able to conjure her. I remember the same small set of details: her loud laugh; her bossiness and swagger; her self-consciousness about her broad nose, her curly hair. But even this isn't fixed. Her hair fell out. Her nose narrowed. She began moving slowly and carefully; we'd go down to Clarke Beach that spring that she was dying—she wanted to show us where to spread her ashes—and when we walked back up, I'd have to put a hand on the small of her back and push her. She did not laugh as often. When we were young, she taught me that when you're in a car that's driving past a cemetery, you're supposed to hold your breath until you pass it. It was a kind of game. Because our parents were immigrants, I had only her to teach me these things. Then, when she was sick, we were passing a cemetery one afternoon, and I said, Hold your breath. She said, sharply, No. I said, Why not? She said, I don't like that game anymore. It didn't make me feel sorry for her; it made me angry. Why not? I said again, even though I knew the answer. It felt important to pretend not to. Why not? Why not?

I knew I couldn't live without her. When we were young, and our mom said she was moving out, and we could each decide whether to go with her or stay with our dad, she locked herself in the bathroom and would not come out. I chose Mom, I said. Who did you choose? She said she was still deciding. You should choose Mom, too, I said. She stayed in there a long time. I thought

I'd settled on our mom. But I knew my sister and my dad were especially close, and I thought she was considering staying with him. And I thought to myself, All right. If she chooses Dad, I will, too.

In the end, Mom stayed, and no one had to decide. But I had already chosen.

When I was in college, I used to walk around campus for hours, at night, sometimes in circles. I wanted to walk until my feet bled. I wanted to walk until I passed out. I wanted to walk until I disappeared.

In the dream I described, my sister is still alive. I don't see her, but I know she is there, and I am happy. But it is a dream, and in the dream I'm not in college anymore. I'm home, in Seattle, and I have a job, a boyfriend, and a car. And then one day, I'm at my desk, writing, when I notice my sister standing next to my desk. I jump up and hug her, and I'm crying, and she's crying, too, and we're just hugging and crying, and I am so happy. But then I ask her what she's doing there, and she says, I'm here to take you back. I don't want to go, I say. I have a life now. And you have to, she says, because I'm dead.

You can't imagine how it felt to lose her. I don't blame you for that. I can't imagine it myself. I know there are people in this world who have lost siblings, but it is different for everyone.

I will tell you how it felt for me. I felt I had lost half of myself. I felt I had lost my right arm. I felt I had lost my left leg. I felt I had lost my tongue. I felt I had lost my heart. I felt I had lost my mind. I felt I had lost my eyes. I felt I had lost my ears. I felt I had lost my breath. I felt I had lost my voice. I felt I had lost my smile. I felt I had lost my laugh. I felt I had lost my tears. I felt I had lost my future. I felt I had lost my past. I felt I had lost my parents, as well. I felt I had lost everything. I felt I had lost everything.

And yet, I did not lose everything. I did not stop being me. I did not stop existing. There were things I could do: I could make my bed, I could wash the dishes, I could walk the dog, I could feed myself, I could live in the world. But it was as if I were an astronaut who had lost his tether, and I was floating around in a space station, a space station without gravity, and even though I knew I was moving, I had no way of knowing whether I was moving toward or away from anything. And even if I could have known, I would not have known what to do about it. I had lost my entire world, and yet I had not lost the world.

You can't know what it's like to lose your sister. You can't know what it's like to lose your sister and not lose your sister. You can't know what it's like to lose your sister and still be with your sister. You can't know what it's like to lose your sister and still be alive. You can't know what it's like to lose your sister and know she is dead. You can't know what it's like to lose your sister and know she is dead, and yet still see her. You can't know what it's like to lose your sister and know she is dead, and yet still see her.

I've turned the space station into a spaceship. I'm a ghost, and I'm in a spaceship, and I'm hurtling through the universe, and I'm traveling forward, and I'm traveling backward, and I'm traveling sideways, and I'm traveling nowhere. I'm hurtling through the universe, and I'm a ghost, and I'm in a spaceship, and I'm hurtling through the universe, and I'm a ghost, and I'm in a spaceship, and I'm hurtling through the universe, and I'm a ghost, and I'm in a spaceship, and I'm hurtling through the universe, and I'm a ghost, and I'm in a spaceship, and I'm hurtling through the universe, and I'm a ghost, and I'm in a spaceship, and I'm hurtling through the universe, and I'm a ghost, and I'm in a spaceship, and I'm hurtling through the universe, and I'm a ghost, and I'm in a spaceship, and I'm hurtling

9.

My sister was diagnosed with Ewing sarcoma when I was in my freshman year of high school and she was in her junior year. I didn't understand then how serious a disease it was. But it was—serious. She died four years later. I thought I would die, too, of grief, but I did not. I spent the summer at home, in Seattle, then returned to college, at Stanford. When I arrived there, the campus hadn't changed, but I had. I felt like a ghost. At night, my sister would appear in my dreams. In the dreams, she hadn't died. It had all been a misunderstanding. And she felt hurt that I had accepted it as real and continued on with my life, as if life could go on.

But as I said, it wasn't my life that was going on—not the life I'd had. As I said, I was a ghost. The truth is that, even all these years later, I remain a ghost. You wouldn't know it if you saw me. I'm not morose or retiring. I laugh a lot. In fact, I'm genuinely happier than many people I know. But I can't help but feel that, on one level, I do not exist.

Here I should conjure my sister for you. Here I should describe her, so that you feel her absence as I do—so that you're made ghostly by it, too. But, though I'm a writer, I've never been able to conjure her. I remember the same small set of details: her loud laugh; her bossiness and swagger; her self-consciousness about her broad nose, her curly hair. But even this isn't fixed. Her hair fell out. Her nose narrowed. She began moving slowly and carefully; we'd go down

to Clarke Beach that spring that she was dying—she wanted to show us where to spread her ashes—and when we walked back up, I'd have to put a hand on the small of her back and push her. She did not laugh as often. When we were young, she taught me that when you're in a car that's driving past a cemetery, you're supposed to hold your breath until you pass it. It was a kind of game. Because our parents were immigrants, I had only her to teach me these things. Then, when she was sick, we were passing a cemetery one afternoon, and I said, Hold your breath. She said, sharply, No. I said, Why not? She said, I don't like that game anymore. It didn't make me feel sorry for her; it made me angry. Why not? I said again, even though I knew the answer. It felt important to pretend not to. Why not? Why not?

I knew I couldn't live without her. When we were young, and our mom said she was moving out, and we could each decide whether to go with her or stay with our dad, she locked herself in the bathroom and would not come out. I chose Mom, I said. Who did you choose? She said she was still deciding. You should choose Mom, too, I said. She stayed in there a long time. I thought I'd settled on our mom. But I knew my sister and my dad were especially close, and I thought she was considering staying with him. And I thought to myself, All right. If she chooses Dad, I will, too.

In the end, Mom stayed, and no one had to decide. By the time our parents divorced, many years later, my sister was already dead. She left me a recording of herself where she gave me advice. Her voice sounded weird around the time that she recorded it, the way a person's voice sometimes does when they've gotten their mouth numbed by the dentist. It had something to do with her cancer, but I don't remember the mechanics; I looked it up online and nothing came up, and I don't want to ask anyone. She said, in her muffled voice, "The happiest thing right now is, I learned to talk openly. It works really, really well. Today, you thought I didn't want you to come to the Space Needle, so you made a face. That's insanity. You have to tell everybody what you want, and then ask them what they want. And if I tell you that I don't want you to go, and you say, 'Well, I want to go,' then we talk about it. In relationships, too, you have to always tell what you're thinking. Don't hide anything. Take chances."

The tape is in a box somewhere. I've listened to it only a couple of times. The sound of her voice in it freaks me out. Around the time she made the tape, she'd changed in a lot of ways. I mentioned her hair, her nose. But it wasn't just that. She'd also grown religious. She went to the Buddhist temple with my parents—I stayed home—and sat at the base of a twisty tree, meditating. She believed in Jesus, too. She said she was ready to die. It seems like that gave my parents peace, but I always thought she was deluding herself or us or both.

Once upon a time, my sister taught me to read. She taught me to wait for a mosquito to swell on my arm and then slap it and see the blood spurt out. She taught me to insult racists back. To swim. To pronounce English so I sounded less Indian. To shave my legs without cutting myself. **To lie to our parents believably.** `To do math. To tell stories. Once upon a time, she taught me to exist.`

ECLIPSES

DIANA KHOI NGUYEN

in one version of the story you're alive you wake up you'd been trying for years to get it back for so long that you can't remember what it is or was anymore you knew you'd been trying you couldn't leave and then one day your things were gone all that remained was an empty bed frame like a cage broken down ... left open like a trap ajar by all accounts you were free you had cut yourself off you cut us ... nd we we rejoiced it was a sign mother said if you could leave then you were well enoug... well enough to go no one asked where or how or when only the fact of it remained w... ebrated you grown ... down where did you go in this version of the story befo... nd wake up I i... you sitting on the side of your bed in the room of a ... you knew b... n nights playing badminton perhaps all that volleyi... all parcels ... g did your heart swell in recognition of it were y... 't been I'v... ou now seeing you leap to hit that birdie your dark ... other da... darting to follow to catch so as to strike striking a ... let ... the other side and often it comes back over and back ... plea ... between us over and back that is not an efficient way ... of ... but oh how I never play to win I never win I wante... this version of the story you're alive picky as ever s... by the window in another country watching clouds s... world moves along I can stay this delirium in whic... ling ... to feed from petals just beside me I move and he... ecreate what I saw try to conjure him and he's bac... e then at all but to listen for his arrival in the hu... artu ... ck you lose all patience volleying birdies with me ... elp ... on' ... to touch the ground in this story a bee crawled out o... wha... it ... ng ... hen I could not see it I lifted her up and let her go do you think ... m ... I ... u ... n't hear me yet you don't hear

nd left
off and
to w
we celebr
you're alive and
ouse of a man yo
g turned into smal
seen as you hadn't
ead in a court of o
tting go of the bird it le
how I find pleasure in sending the bird b
of winning of ending the match I know bu
the volley to continue never to stop in th
ring at your chicken sandwich while I lie by
p like stones along the lake as long as the w
the sparklin tailed hummingbird zips to
s gone and rain again in the rain I rec
I try to conjure and he's back why conjure t
of his depar e in this story you're back
but I can't help I don want the bird to
the kitchen had been doing he
you think she'll make it I ask but you don't

nd flo
gine you
fly from
belonging
been seeing you
heads all eyes d
it go over to the

bout
e takes
listen
ords ca d it is
ords trac nes if none the
of go one w rward one way b
page read a story to the blankness foll
th is an entrance and death a lit tunne
r and be left out many are the ways of i
ear it let's hear it I'll crack open all my win
but you can come and go however whenever
stay a little longer I cannot avoid thinkin
we are talking can we talk are we talking
between the music and the rocks betw
ack did you hear the earth quake befc
you feel what we feel can you feel the
rd and back overlap loop over on itself
ps forward two steps back at the airpc
n moving walkway one ran with one
ng e can't take back would yc take
sometimes I wrestle with ny bo
elf I want to tear to new sh
vit

of various rituals and repetitions here is one way to know that you are dead this is the way to know if you do it right then you did it right no quandary about it open a book any book you can find can you find one can you find it sometimes patience takes practice patience takes patience all of which needs developing in the afterlife listen to me listen in chronological order it may not work otherwise open a book are there words can you read it is there anything there to read put your finger to the page as if tracing words tracing lines if none then good you're on the right track a track implies two ways of going one way forward one way back anytime we can go off track put your finger to the page read a story to the blankness follow along with your finger where you've been they say birth is an entrance and death a lit tunnel you go in you come out but so much else can enter and be left out many are the ways of infiltrating of filtering out about your story let me hear it let's hear it I'll crack open all my windows I'll keep my mouth shut to let you in let you out you can come and go however whenever you want if you want it I want it too I want you to stay a little longer I cannot avoid thinking about the circumstances under which under which we are talking can we talk are we talking a little longer I unleash a sound it falls somewhere between the music and the rocks between the music and the rocks a rumble then perhaps a crack did you hear the earth quake before you felt it could you feel it from where you are could you feel what we feel can you feel the music it sounds forth when set in motion it can go forward and back overlap loop over on itself I take three steps forward then two steps back three steps forward two steps back at the airport I watch two sisters running each running on their own moving walkway one ran with it one ran back it took her longer but she made it back some things we can't take back would you take it back if you could would you take back your body give it life sometimes I wrestle with my body I want to throw myself out against myself I am against myself I want to tear to chew to shove everything out to empty the body to empty it out how sound will travel then without obstruction no complications it moves through then beyond I want to hear your story about your story let me hear it let it in let it open

coming back to look at you at least what's left of you to look at least at you not you you least is not the point the point is that I do it do it to go on I go on doing it this encounter with shape-shifting am I the hero or the monster perhaps I'm both perhaps you're both both dead and alive alive in death present in the world as particle and particulate and out of it the end of a life as important as the other end all ends have a way of going on ongoing ends let me share what I have learned there is no such thing as silence I can never be never be silent too much moves beneath my skin even when I keep still I am traveling to catch up traveling to meet you perhaps I can catch up with you are you traveling to arrive we can meet in the middle let's meet in the middle you going from nothing toward something as something I turn to you uncertain how to know it's you how will you know me no form is the same twice after all what shall we bring to identify ourselves what shall I bring from this life to yours how will I know who you are what if the sound of my voice doesn't register what if I'm wrong what should I do what will you do there's no contingency plan in grief only maps without points of reference I don't know the way to you or my afterlife but I know how I can die how will I die how will you live can we be together again oblivious to all this in the white space there are infinite number of ways in the white space there's another me who knows what to do who's never needed any maps she sings a song and you sing one too she takes your hand and listens to you tell me again she says and she listens she is listening to you in the white space where there are so many ways so many versions of ourselves lost we can start over again again you say and I will show you show you how to do it what to do no matter what at no point in time can I be who I was again this form decomposing memory in decay I am trying to build it up again trying to build it up with what I know if you make it build it with me let us compose a form together let us override the overarching drive let us override the archive let the end be the end of the end and we'll start in the middle again we can do what we want but we have to want it I want to be with you again but again I've lost my way tell me how to find it how to know it's you meet me

AYA BRAM

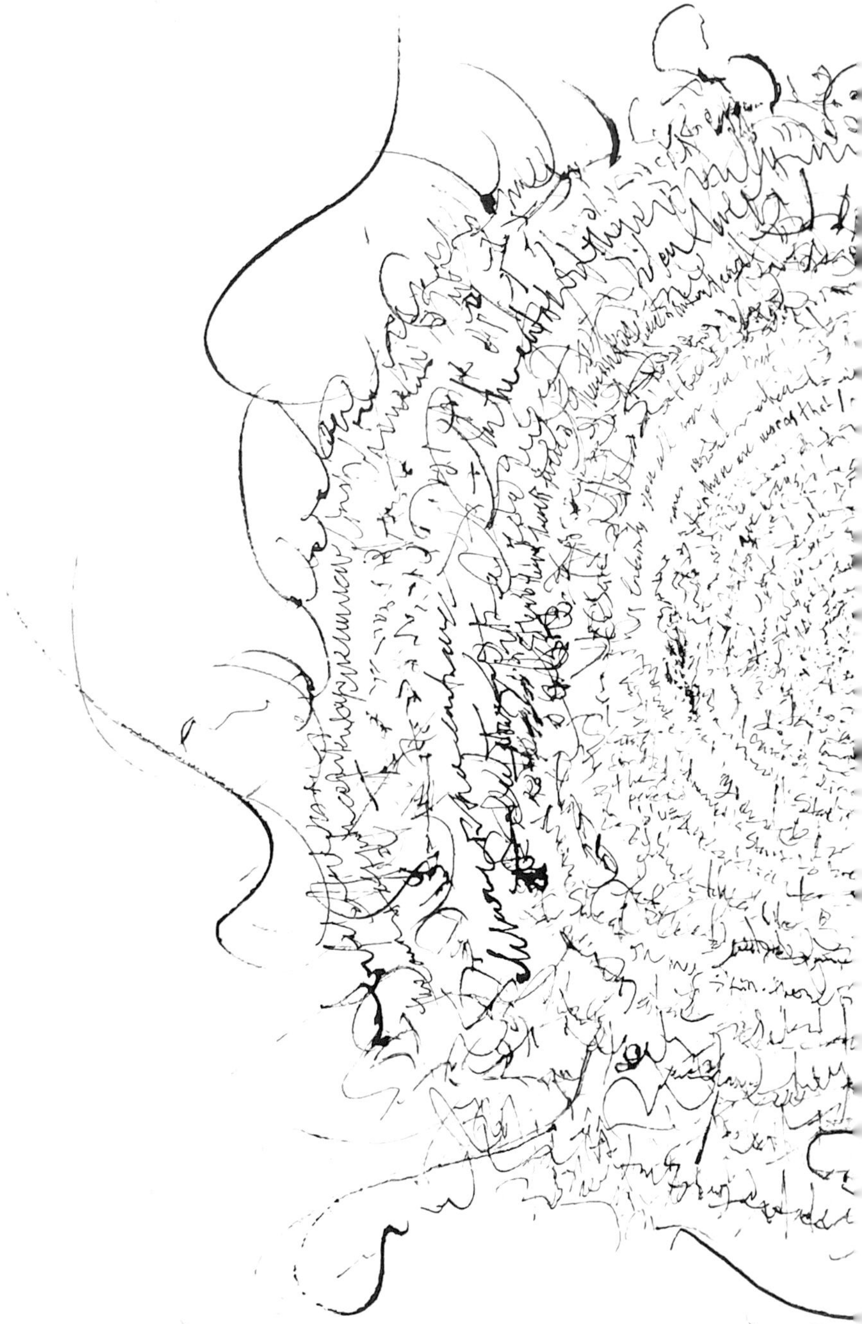

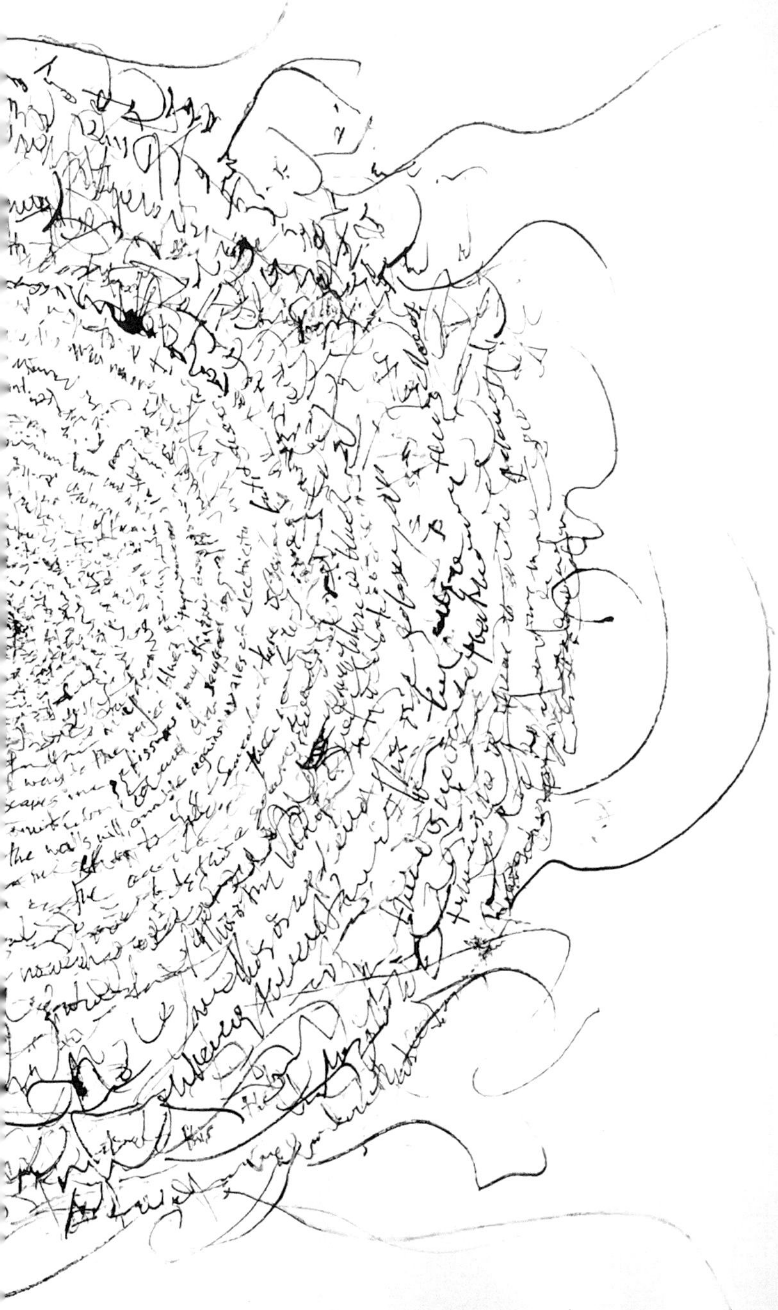

THE COUNTDOWN AS SEEN FROM 2000 FEET ABOVE

SANDY TANAKA

jyu (10)

The color of the light was yellow. No, I am sure of it. I do not care what others say. Can a single flash so stupendous be misinterpreted as to its color? It was everywhere. Did you ask Mrs. Nakano? She died right beside me.

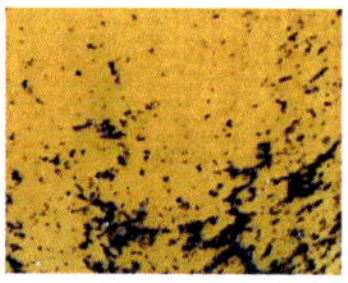

It was so bright, that I left a shadow on the steps of the

ku (9)

No, I am not done. (cough)

Mrs. Nakano and I were talking when the sky flashed. We had collided as she rushed up the stone steps, having just dropped off her nephew at the demolition work site at Koami-cho.

Her purse flew in my face, knocking my glasses off, and

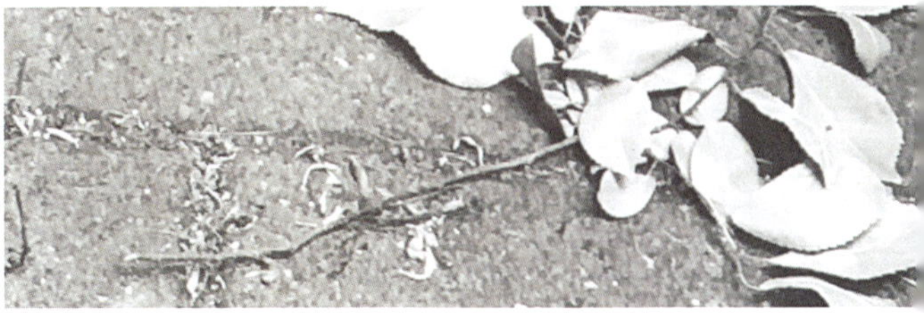

bank, next to that of Mrs. Nakano's. The two shadows met as if kissing. I saw it, ever so briefly before I found myself here.

What?

It is only my death that interests you? The exact moment, nothing before, nothing after. Have you learned nothing about the dangers of simplification?

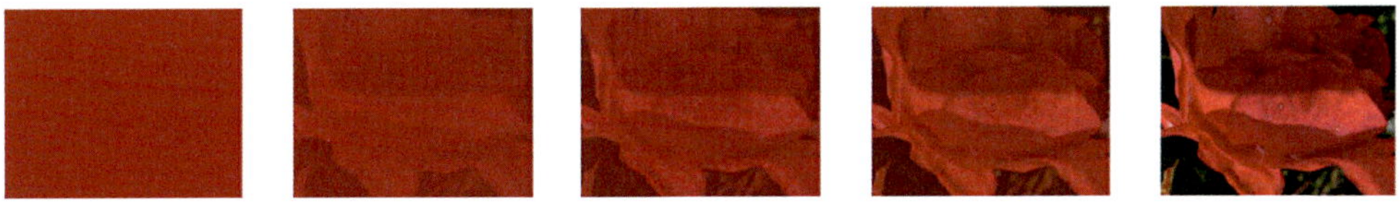

she laughed, embarrassed.

Mr. Higuchi, she said. I'm so sorry. These days it seems safest to get to where one is going as quickly as possible.

She picked up my glasses and handed them to me. And I reached down for the small box she had dropped. She took it from me in both hands, like she was cupping a bowl of rice.

She was a strange woman. An old childhood schoolmate of my wife's. I admit that I did not like her much. And I would have much preferred to wait there on the steps by myself.

But then she told me a story. Her daughter had hit a homerun a year ago. In a pristine ballpark across the sea in a city the Americans called Modesto. Ten years old, a lucky girl, dark brown hair, Hakujin father. How he must have plotted and planned to keep her secret. Half Spanish, perhaps he said, or Black Irish. Just that morning, Mrs. Nakano had found a baseball on her doorstep, wrapped in hemp cloth, held tight with twine. Her daughter had signed her name on the baseball, along with the date and the English words "homerun—right field bleachers." There were other names on the ball. Arnold Pittswheeler, Bakersfield, CA. A woman named Betty Crummer, Los Angeles. Sergeant Dick Mum, Pt. Mugu. Nils Wechsler, Pearl City, Hawaii. Tom Liu, Wahiwa, Hawaii. Aleksandr Vlachko, Kuril Islands. Akira Suzuki, Sapporo. What incomplete story did these people tell while holding this ball, stroking its seams, finding a pen and adding their moniker upon it before passing it on. Maybe it was the exact true story, carefully memorized word for word, "Katie Wiley has a Japanese mother who lives in Hiroshima..."

I'm going to store this at the bank, Mrs. Nakano said, waving the box in my face. I'm going to keep it safe.

She asked me if I wanted to hold the baseball. I remember why I didn't like her, that damn insouciant attitude, like every oyster would yield, like she could find pearls in this war that nobody else could. I politely said no.

hachi (8)

I saw Shinichi Ishimaru pitch his last game before the war claimed him. He had an interesting way of cupping the ball, not in the natural cradle, but tensely at the edge of the palm, with the wrist bent and fingers spidering over it. I wonder if he swore at his hands' betrayal as they fumbled at the controls of his crashing bomber.

Am I frowning? Do I even remember how the necessary muscles pull together to make a frown. I am thinking about my hands. Look at them. They do not look like my hands. The knuckles, they pucker differently, the flex of the fingers are too smooth. And there are, after all, five fingers on each hand. These are the hands I had before the war. Before I lost the thumb and index during training exercises. These are my actor's hands.

Watch.

That was the salute I did in "Traveling Hero." It was to be a salute with no honor.

Watch again.

In the context of the entire film, you would have seen it as a poignant moment. The hero falls, disgraced, but at the last moment gives his life for his commanding officer and remains the hero. Not a film for the war effort. Too interpretive. Was he really a hero or just doing his duty? Or in doing his duty was he then the only kind of hero?

So, a position in the Imperial Japanese Army was deemed a better use of my time, until the loss of those crucial fingers made me a civilian again. I had doubts that I would be able to act again after the war, as an actor's hands are second only to the expression in his eyes.

I had a career that might have surpassed even that of Sessue Hayakawa, had I fled to Europe as did he. I was offered a part in a film of his, but when the war started, he abandoned the project. I only assume he did so because my letter, my acceptance of the part, was never acknowledged. But the film could have come out later, with a promising new co-star, a premiere in Paris with flutes of champagne and no darkness under the guests' eyes. How would I know if this happened or not? I am dead.

But the rumor was that Sessue Hayakawa had given up acting and was painting in the south of France, perhaps with the same transcendence he dutifully demonstrated in every part he ever played. I imagine him in a high, domed room with tall windows that let in the frayed light of the morning. Besmocked, barefoot on stained tarp. Brush poised. A frown of artistic discernment hiding his deeply creviced soul, a look I know would have been practiced to perfection.

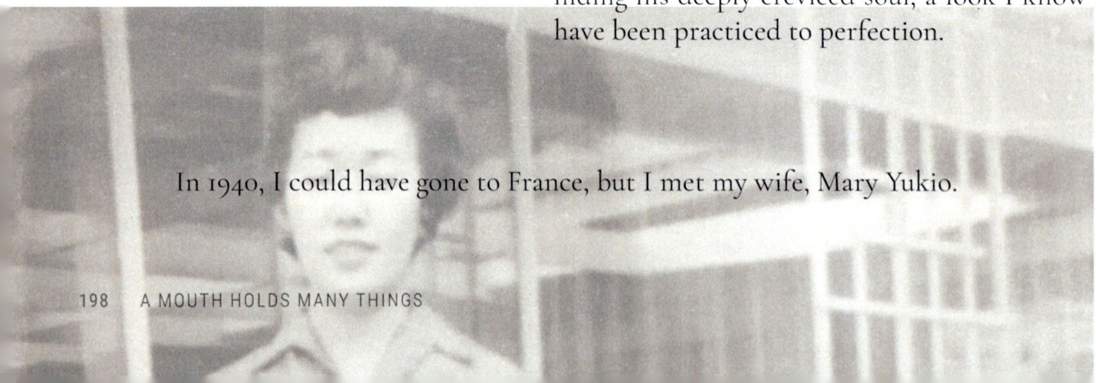

In 1940, I could have gone to France, but I met my wife, Mary Yukio.

shichi (7)

The mission was on the way to the streetcar station. I stopped by to tell Father Schubert that Mary Yukio was ill and would not be coming in, and to pick up my daily egg.

It was minutes after the all-clear siren had sounded. Before I could even knock, Father Schubert came up behind me and put a heavy hand on my shoulder.

"Who are you?" he said. "What are you doing here?"

"I'm Mary Yukio's husband." I said it in German.

He looked at me closer. "There will not be any more eggs." And he pushed by me and went into the mission.

Father Schubert was a dour man even for a German priest. And he became even more unpleasant when Germany fell. Even so, Mary Yukio was lucky to work at the mission compound. Because she had spent most of her teenage years in Honolulu, she wasn't quite trusted to work in any of the war effort jobs. Her knowledge of English (surpassing even mine) and German worked in her favor with Father Schubert, as he often needed documents translated and he had begun to depend on her. Of course, her formal job was the cleaning of the toilettes, the cooking of their midday meal, polishing the remaining silver and brass in the chapel. But a certain benefit of the job was that Father Schubert often gave her eggs—a luxury—precious, precious eggs from the country. These eggs were transported from some unknown location and left on their doorstep every other day. Some rich man's penitence, I am sure.

Father Schubert became ill that first day of the egg deliveries, he thought maybe from the poached egg he had so greedily consumed that morning. So he offered Mary Yukio an egg to take home from every delivery. To test out. It was insulting. But she would take those eggs, because she knew I loved them. Mary Yukio looked out for me. And I took it for granted that she would always give more than I demanded.

I never got sick from the eggs and thus, both Father Schubert and myself had them fried, poached, or scrambled whenever we wanted.

A half a dozen priests filed by me, coming from around the corner, from the cool dark burrow that was their bomb shelter. They squinted at me. I grinned at them, I knew they would not last much longer in this country.

roku (6)

There is a boarded up auditorium in a little park on the way to the mission. That morning, I pulled off the wooden slats nailed across the entrance and went inside. It was not musty like I thought it would be. The windows were clean, and light illuminated the wooden stage, making it gleam.

It was here on this stage, five years ago, that I met Mary Yukio. She played the monkey spirit in a children's play I was adapting from the well-known story of the monk, Hsuan Tsang, and his journey to India to find Buddha's truth.

I cast Mary Yukio as Sun Wukung because she was small and wiry with a round full face and large double-lidded eyes. Something of the monkey in my Mary Yukio already with her quick aggressive movements and frank unblinking stare. She had no experience acting, but I worked her hard and we bickered constantly.

Backstage, the night of the opening, with her monkey costume halfway pulled up, her breasts strapped flat to her chest with soft white gauze, she looked at me as if seeing all the selfish fates in my eyes and she pulled me to her and kissed me.

She went on stage to the cheers of the children and mothers and swung her tail with verve and deference at the same time, and when she lopped off the head of a plaster demon, I decided that I was in love.

We were closed down after the Indian Ocean disputes in November as the local authorities did not care for the play's non-traditional slant and its sympathies toward China and India.

go (5)

When I was six, I got lost in the Honnoji Cemetary in Kyoto. It began to rain and I took shelter in an old gardening shed. On a low table were baskets filled with toys and canned fruits, dried flowers still slightly sweet-smelling, and odd items I did not recognize. Gifts to the deceased collected off the graves. Toys and foods I'd never seen in our own cupboard at home. But what interested me were these long shiny strips laying off to the side, that, when I held them up to the faint light, I saw pictures lined one on top of the other. Scenes of two men with fists the size of melons locked in some sort of combat, a pale crowd of faces behind them watching. And although it at first appeared that each scene was the same, when I examined them closer, I saw the slight change of positions, the infinitesimal movements towards the end frame: one man lying prone at the other man's feet.

I took them home and hung them outside, like wind chimes. I would watch the sun play through the twisting celluloid, the casting shadows whipping across my body, flashing gold in my eyes. I eventually forgot about them and it wasn't until I was thirteen that I took them down and saw that the pictures were now indistinguishable, faded to a translucent orange. And when I was twenty-two, I became an actor and did my first film, and I realized that the strips were rare 70 millimeter footage. I could tell from the sprocket holes. When I was thirty-two, I played an Indonesian boxer in a British film and in my research of the part, I realized the strips had been of the Corbett-Fitzsimmons boxing match held in 1897 in Carson City, Nevada, where Corbett went down in the 14th round. I knew because I remembered that fifth to last frame, that of the punch, famously to his solar plexus.

And I could finally wonder at the eccentricity of such a gift to the dead.

shi (4)

I sat eight feet under the earth, in our bomb shelter. Wooden braces barely supported the crumbling walls. I had brought into my shelter, the Cine Sakura camera that Mary Yukio found for me in a shop in Yamaguchi. She visited Yamaguchi, to see Old Auntie, a dozen times a year, war or no war.

The night before, Mary Yukio had presented me with the camera.

I thought you could show your film strips, she said. She sneezed twice. She had been feeling poorly.

It was not a projector as she thought, but I didn't bother to correct her. I don't believe I even looked up at Mary Yukio. I didn't thank her. Perhaps I nodded, I do not remember. I went back to reading and a few moments later she left my side. Such is the routine of marriage in the confines of curfews and war.

Our bomb shelter had a single table in the middle. I set down the camera and examined it. The black exterior was cracked. The lens and crank long since gone. I opened it up. The inside was gutted. The gears and heart removed. When I leaned in close, I smelled sour metal. I ran my middle finger along the edges, feeling the coarseness of the rust.

Resting towards the front was a folded piece of paper.

It was a note to me from Old Auntie. She had written about an old beau of Mary Yukio's, a rich banker, who comes for tea every time she visits. All is perfectly proper, do not worry Great Nephew, but I respectfully tell you that this man is now working at the big bank, in Hiroshima where you live.

I immediately imagined Mary Yukio with this banker at the junk store in Yamaguchi.

– Oh, my husband would like this.
– What is it?
– He has these film strips.
– It looks broken.
– No, he'll like this.
– And what do you like, Mary Yukio?

Did she then look up at him in surprise? Or did they exchange familiar looks? Did he dare to touch her hand?

Mary Yukio had wanted us to make the bomb shelter comfortable. She had laid out a tatami on the floor, folded our second-best futon in the corner, lined up whatever canned foods we had, along the wall. To my right, hung my old film strips, on fishing line, making scratching noises every time I stood up in the small space. To my left, hung her favorite hiroshige. The one of the temple in Yamaguchi. She had told me that Old Auntie had given it to her. Such a suspiciously expensive present from such a poor poor woman.

I pushed the camera onto the floor. It thudded on the hard earth and dust rose. I stood up, ready to pull the hiroshige from the wall. The film strips crackled with my sudden energy.

Then it was 7:00 am. The sirens blared. The sound stilled me and I looked up at that rectangle of blue, the open door of the bomb shelter angled up towards the sky. American weather planes cruised overhead every morning at this time. But today I did not have the time to watch for them.

I would go to the bank. I would wait for him. And when I saw him, coming up the steps, important in his suit, unaware of my regard, what would be his countenance? Contentment, a sterling conscience and a shining work ethic? And when we were finally face to face, his expression slowly collecting, in his eyes would I even recognize that which I lacked?

I climbed out of our bomb shelter while everyone else in the city was dutifully climbing into their own.

san (3)

You think that I selfishly keep you here to shed my memories, like peels of skin, sloughed off with a simple shrug. You, with your immortal clipboard. Of course it is like that. Of course, a corporeal form will reform with all its aches and desires and condemnations.

In reality, in reality, the moment of my death was brief. Is the duration of a moment enough time for a human being to transform in some way? In this case, it was the disintegration of a human body, 45 years of accumulation—scarring, creasing, the toughening of soles and palms—gone in a moment.

But in truth, in truth, it was not brief at all. It was an event. My death was heavy with the orchestration of clever clever minds—the canon behind the bomb. The pageantry of the light—I remember standing against it—purely cerebral, soul-less if you please, the last synapses snapping. I resisted the insignificance with the weight of my life.

I see the look on your face. Hiroshima was different somehow and you cannot tell me.

MASKED FORCE: VÕ AN KHÁNH'S WARTIME PHOTOGRAPHS

QUYÊN NGUYỄN-HOÀNG

All photographs by Võ An Khánh; reprinted courtesy of Võ An Khánh and Sàn Art.

In a mangrove forest the solemn women walk in line. Wearing masks with holes for the eyes, the revolutionary officers look like pious pilgrims performing a cryptic ritual. In enemy territory these women are often disguised as sidewalk peddlers to collect enemy intelligence, transmit messages, or store weapons for the resistance. In clandestine cabins in the forest, as Võ explains, they convene and study the tenets of guerrilla warfare to enhance their political consciousness. The masks hide their identities from one another in case of capture and interrogation. It is a pragmatic gesture, not a sign of terrorism or fanaticism as a viewer might imagine at first glance. The white, soft fabric of the masks glows in the light, impenetrably exuding a climate of disquiet. The masks also funnel the viewer's attention on the faceless animacy of the female officers, who seem unagitated by the camera's petrifying eye as they move along the slender wooden bridge. Carrying both motion and stillness in their barefoot gait, they are plainly dressed in the no-frills, versatile apparel of the Mekong Delta working class: gingham headscarves, glossy black pants, and bà ba silk shirts, long-sleeved, button-down, cinched at the waist. The white array of homespun masks punctuates their humble pastoral presence with a bewitching flavor of fright.

Politics class for 50 officers working undercover in enemy territory—Năm Căn mangrove forest, 1972

In Võ An Khánh's more stereotypical photographs, the female figures are usually either steadfast militants holding rifles, looking stalwart and monumental like their heroic male counterparts, or they are demure weavers and diligent caretakers toiling in the rear area among baskets, fishnets, and jugs. Sometimes they pose and smile photogenically. Even when they don't, the camera still finds a way to capture the beautiful staunch faces of these stoic patriots. But in this picture, the deadpan masks become shields behind which the women may escape the visual formulas often foisted on female insurgents. Effaced by their startling, luminous veils, they stay impervious to camera lenses, prying gazes, and imperious desires to know. They keep private all of their lovely features and any flashes of panic, longing, daydream, hesitation, or indifference that the face might betray. The mask and the photograph collude to form an impenetrable double disguise that distances the viewer's gaze from the concealed being of the guerrilla girls. The sharp perforations in the masks, though tantalizing, disclose nothing. The cuts, these passages to nowhere, arouse and defuse the viewer's exploratory expectations. They invite guesses without divulging any identifiable data about the women, whose external and internal landscapes—their appearances, their dialects, their laughter, their futural plans—remain a series of elusive, unknowable, dark openings.

Workers from Trần Ngọc Hy printing house during lunch break—Năm Căn mangrove forest, 1968

In the same forest, the band of printing workers strut down a familiar pathway, a lean bridge made of trees. Although this picture and the previous are taken four years apart, the formation of the barefoot men almost perfectly mirrors that of the masked female officers. But the women, covered from head to toe, move with their heads slightly tilted down whereas the male workers stride with their faces and torsos openly revealed. Casual vigor and optimism radiate from these men in their off-hours. They will shortly get back to work in good spirits and make do with chronic shortages of paper and ink. They will go on assembling propagandist pages in a printing house named after Trần Ngọc Hy, a patriotic newspaper editor-in-chief and martyr who in 1957 had been executed by firing squad in Cà Mau. The workers are blissfully unaware of a spell of bad weather stealing up under their feet. In the lower left of their image, a black cloud blows like a zephyr from the underground. These miasmic vapors look as though they could spread and swallow whole the picture's positive presence, dragging the men and their boyish zest into a damp netherworld. The low-hovering mist, an imprint of humidity, could be read in various ways: a minor symptom of the photographer's neglect and forgetting, an inevitable bruise of time, an ominous sign of death. It carries a whiff of the deadly fragrance that enwraps the war and acts as a grim reminder of the nature of photographs as living images of the dead. Who could tell what became of these young workers and whether they survived the war. Still, the buoyant men walk on, sailing idly on a murmur of dim exhalations from below, black dread transfiguring all that gaiety.

On the faces of many officers in the hall, like that of the man in white in the front row, there is the stunned look of someone captured on camera while caught in a daze, unable to adjust their dumbfounded bodies in front of the lens. Võ An Khánh has a flair for capturing the corporeal stupefaction and uniformity of the people in revolutionary base areas, from pupils at a flag-raising ceremony to bureaucrats at a formal meeting. Many of his photographs record a pack of loyal believers gazing at some symbol of authority such as a teacher lecturing, a flag flying up, or an officer speaking behind a white tableclothed podium as seen in this picture. The faithful group often stand or sit together, all aligned, facing the same direction. Their bodily conformity, earnest and mechanical, fills the pictures with a gently eerie atmosphere of ceremony and menace.

Founding congress of the Cà Mau Committee of the National Liberation Front, Giáp Nước crossroads, 1961

Morning flag-raising ceremony at Thiếu Sinh middle school, Kinh Ba hamlet, Năm Căn, 1962

In the previous photograph of the provincial committee, a banner on the right-hand wall declares the revolutionaries' commitment to education: "TO ACTIVELY ELIMINATE THE PERIL OF ILLITERACY [...]." The front's fervent literacy campaigns infiltrate even the remotest niches of the countryside—like the hamlet in this image, where children have gathered under the canopy of trees to learn the Vietnamese alphabet. The Romanized script, previously propagated by European missionaries to transmit the holy teachings of the Christian West, is now re-appropriated to disseminate the sacred letters of the revolution. On puny blackboards sprinkled with sunlight, the children's tottering hands chalk the same word "ơn" over and over. The lexical meanings of this word include gratitude, kindness, favor, indebtedness, blessing, mercy, and grace. In the picture, the front half of the class have correctly spelled their giant gratitude, except for one absent-minded girl who seems to have scrawled "ơm" instead of "ơn," blurting out *um* instead of giving proper thanks. The error blithely leaps out from the scene of rote memorization and perfect docility. As time goes by, the children will obediently, uniformly, faultlessly grow to be thankful, thoughtful. But for now, the small humans stay dreamily distracted. Some gaze at the schoolteacher while others tinker with pen caps, study treetops, or doze off on the hindermost bench. The picture of the classroom gathers an eternal recurrence of tedium and wonder—the gift of the first words, the initiation into prescribed knowledge, the habitual sameness of school, the occasional daydreams, the innocent missteps and their sunsparkling grace.

Guerrilla students are seated on wooden boards that are removed once the class is over, leaving no traces behind. Kinh Hãng hamlet, Khánh Hưng commune, Trần Văn Thời district, Cà Mau, ca. 1970

Song and dance class organized by the Southwestern Region's Propaganda Department in U Minh forest, 1970-1971

Two dancers doing their jeté are captured by the camera in a moment of endless suspension. The outlines of their outstretched bodies quiver and blear a little. The male partner, his eyes kept on the ground, looks prepared to land, while the female dancer fastens her upward gaze on the clouds. A mesh of white scratches on the photograph mars her youthful face and intensifies the spectral elegance of her buoyant figure. Softly defaced by time, the girl glides into a ghost of herself. Her hair blown back like a black flame against the sky, she soars and slides into an elsewhere of her own, floating in a sphere of negated gravity and excised identity. Eventually she will touch the forest floor and return to the ground, "the plane on which everyday life plods along, the plane of walking, the prose of human movement," in the words of Paul Valery. The next girl, getting ready behind her, is about to execute the same jump and the next one, and the one after, will start over and over again. The dancers take turns to release themselves into a transient state of flight, far from the worldly ground, far from the stability of contrived steps and ideological guidelines, far from the distress of catastrophic bloodshed and daily upheavals. In the middle of somewhere elevated, the flying and falling dancers enact the condition of human bodies in time—always gliding with time, ephemerally exhilarated and inspired, while ever earthbound and marvelously perishable.

Making the Năm Căn mangrove forest green again after the Americans sprayed toxic chemicals, 1970

After the mass spray runs of the herbicide Agent Orange, the Năm Căn mangrove forest is reduced to an assembly of barkless bodies. Standing like charred martyrs, the black trees call to mind the singed skeletal bodies in Alberto Giacometti's sculptural works. Among the dry dead roots, young children are cleaning up the debris, blending into an ecosystem reeking of toxicity. The diabolical dioxin permeating the soil and seeping into the groundwater is linked to various nerve disorders, cancers, and birth defects among the families of veterans and civilians exposed to the poison. Before long there will be malformed newborns mirroring the limbless distortion of these gnarled trunks. Ravaged as they are, the stark stumps still remain the strongest presence, the most stable rhythm in the photograph. The mangroves in Võ An Khánh's body of images are now lush and protective, now scalped and denuded, soundlessly suffering and transmitting toxins from humans to humans. Nature in these pictures is not some passive backdrop to savage human progress but a net of life, a tacit community of glorious bodies always in flux, always implicating, unmaking, transforming and deforming with humans.

The summersmeared beach spreads like a foreign planet brimming with ridges and rims, wind and water, meandering hollows and schoolchildren on vacation. The landscape of leisure deviates from the common visual trope of battlefields swarming with enthused brigades or strewn with ashen carcasses. Taken in 1968, this picture also strays from the breathless tension of that year, the year of the Tết Offensive and a bloody series of assassinations, massacres, summary executions, student occupations, wildcat strikes, and struggles for self-determination all over the anxious globe. The photograph, drenched in an alien peace, stands apart from the turmoil of the era. Cheery adolescent boys slip and slide into puddles, their bodies luxuriating in soil, their smiles matted with wet sand. Their thin torsos, bare chests and damp shorts are smudged all over with silt. Meanwhile, reclining on the sand dunes in the distance, slender schoolgirls in their uniform gaze far beyond the frame, each hypnotized by her own reverie. These schoolchildren might soon, if not already, be recruited as scouts and messengers for the resistance. They might join the armed struggle, might end up as mauled kills. But in the endless now of the photograph, the season of blood and mourning never arrives. No traces of decay here. No nervous cycles of worry about the past or future. Time condenses and extends into an infinite present of stillness and delight. It is forever midsummer, midday, an atmosphere soaked in an unexhausted spirit of play. The younglings are free to sprawl, scream, dream, forget the war. They can ride astride their noon and bask in soft soil until their childish flesh is blackened by grime and games. Their pubescent skin radiates an earthy scent of innocence, a fleeting aroma of freedom on fettered earth. Standing near the photograph, feeling that giddy fragrance of euphoria, one may hear the unstained melodies of their laughter scatter and sprout like wild grass across this dreamshore, one muddy paradise.

Pupils from Lý Tự Trọng School on a summer day on Khai Long beach, Cà Mau, 1968

Mobile military clinic during the period of enemy defoliation in U Minh Forest, 1970

The military medics stand thigh-deep in water. Their modest clinic is sequestered in the middle of a wooded marsh, embraced by leafstalks, vines and mosquito nets dangling from tree branches. A masked nurse lifts the net to let the stretcher-bearers in. The motionless youth lying on the stretcher with a capeline bandage is Danh Sơn Huol, a Khmer cadre wounded in an American bombing. He squints as if sleeping, sinking into a silence, slowly absorbing the shock of his injury. The impending operation is exposed to a variety of risks, ranging from changeful weather and drug shortages to hungry leeches and all the mythical creatures of the U Minh forest lurking in the deep. The precarity and poverty of the situation turns into a purely aesthetic experience for viewers far from the war, geographically and temporally, who may merely marvel with winged words at the guerrilla clinic's theatrical allure. The mesmeric image softly vibrates as the bright ripples in the water summon the undulations of snakes slithering around the legs of the medics. The dramaturgical halo of the scene belongs to an enchanting yet sober and windless sort of drama. The operation doesn't take place inside a building like that "large old church at the crossing roads, now an impromptu hospital" in a poem by Walt Whitman. Whitman's spectacular and disorienting portrayal of the American Civil War is packed with hasty motion, "surgeons operating, attendants holding lights, the smell of ether, the odor of blood." Võ An Khánh's visual poem illuminates a different style of improvised hospital, smaller, quieter, less grisly, more subdued. The photograph is bound by a spell of unsettling calm as the slumberous wounded soldier is brought closer to the medics, whose upright bodies conjure the noble solemnity of inert saints, and the forest turns into a bewildering crossroads of emergency, where death and life quietly converge.

In the second frame of the guerrilla clinic, sharp scalpels gleam behind the veils. A comatose soldier lies covered in cold white sheets on the operating table. Seen from afar, his body seems to levitate among the trees as if under the spell of the masked medic-sorcerers. There existed a third frame of the scene, a close-up of the shrapnel removal, but Võ An Khánh says that negative went missing a long time ago. Except for a tiny cut in the crown of the patient's head, the spooky slit in the middle of this picture, viewers can barely see the rest of his vulnerable body and the invasive surgical procedure. Captured at a distance, the operation retains a semblance of privacy behind the clinic's nettings and the forest's unruly verdure. The brambly bogs and marshes provide many layers of disguise and protection to the revolutionaries in the forest, making it hard for one to ever get a clear view of the mythologized liberation force, which the Americans often call the "other side" of the war.

Consider how the name of the U Minh forest itself carries the haziness of shrouded otherness. A common etymology derives "U Minh" from 幽冥, two Han characters meaning *gloom* and *darkness*, which together conjure a blind of hellish shadows. Legend has it, however, that the name might be rooted in another "u minh," from the characters 幽明 for *gloom* and *light*—a word that limns the misty doorsill between brightness and darkness, humans and ghosts, grace and horror, the living and the dead. This wavering light calls to mind various kinds of in-between states. Liminality is embodied in the mangroves themselves, whose dense stilt roots arch high above the loose soft soil, in a mode at once submerged and aerial, throughout estuaries where salt and freshwater meet. The dusky brackish atmosphere of the wartime mangroves, now gentle, now forbidding, could further fill us with layer upon layer of visions of in-betweenness—for example, the threshold between daydream and wakefulness; the ephemeral months and years that floated between the verdant forest then and the rampant deforestation now; the gap between the openness of an opaque image and the enclosure of its lucid caption; the fate of war refugees drifting at sea; the fate of self-exiles at home pondering the imagined borders between domestic and diasporic waters. There are many more twilit conditions to wonder about as we keep circumambulating the meanings of the war, which itself is a forest half dark, half bright.

Out of the fog—the muddled past, the murky aftermath—of war, out of the mist of the sacred forest, this diaphanous photograph has sculpted a reverie. Behind the thin gauzelike veils, tyrannical narratives about the old conflict seem to soften, lighten, melt away. Labels of heroes and aggressors, along with cries of hate and praise, falter and recede into a distant din. The irreducible photograph glimmers in its own hazy logic, its autonomous opacity. A secret about a secret, the picture of what was, now a whispered parable, still shimmers and self-shadows with a beauty that remains unnameable, a wound that stays ajar.

Mobile military clinic during the period of enemy defoliation in U Minh Forest, 1970

Võ An Khánh made some of the most phantasmal pictures of the Vietnam War, or so I have come to believe. Many propagandist-journalistic snapshots of the conflict, including plenty of images by Võ himself, abound with spectacles of ghastly pain, banal bloodshed, sonorous battle cries. Images of this kind fortify the demarcations of the war's simplified factions. But some of Võ's photographs radiate a different light. They unveil wartime situations that were precarious, quotidian, transient, strangely serene. They haunt the viewer as they bestow and withhold glimpses into the long days and years in which the Mekong Delta resistance covertly organized and took refuge in the forests of Cà Mau. The fleeting concealment inscribed in these photographs allows the struggle to be seen anew in all of its inscrutable otherness. The life force hidden in these pictures is an enigma that buoyantly deforms the prefixed meanings of ideology, outlives the noise of dogma, outlasts the propaganda of discourse. As Jean-Luc Nancy might put it, each photograph condenses and expands itself into an elusive site where an event and an eternity concur.

Võ An Khánh, born in 1936, grew up in a farming family in Bạc Liêu, a small town in the southernmost region of Vietnam. In the late 1950s, he left home and began working as an assistant at a photographic studio in Sài Gòn called Việt Long, a now-gone address. In the early 1960s, he returned to the Southwest as a photojournalist and joined the struggle against "the American aggressors," as he still says. With a Yashica-Mat medium format camera, Võ took around a thousand photographs in the revolutionary bases of Cà Mau throughout the war. One of his first tasks was to take portraits and create false identity cards for undercover cadres working in enemy territory. He also made use of his penmanship by writing pamphlets and decorating posters for the local propaganda committee. This circuit of propaganda, illustration and secrecy continued to pervade the rest of his assignment as an industrious photographer for the resistance.

Like most men of his occupation, Võ was loyal-heartedly devoted to the duty to mobilize viewers' conscience and document the struggle with what he believes to be objective veracity. In the militant parlance of that era, the camera, similar to the writer's pen and the painter's brush, was commonly likened to a gun, and the photographer a cultural combatant. Almost half a century after the war's closure, the righteous tone of the revolution continues to reverberate in Võ An Khánh's photographic archive. In his albums now kept at home in Bạc Liêu, Võ scrupulously glues each of his war prints next to a handwritten description. Instead of naming his images, he narrates them. An eloquent newspeaking photojournalist, he composes the captions using succinct slogans and neat summaries of events. His earnest diction is energized by the inextinguishable fire, or ghost, of a pamphleteer's lexicon. Didactic conformity glistens in the way he speaks in his interviews and the way he pens the moralizing captions of his images. After the war, Võ began making more ostensibly "artistic images," which he captions in a similarly patriotic tone. His peacetime works often feature picturesque landscapes, local beauty pageants, bashful ethnic women occasionally bathing nude, and other celebratory touristic tropes filtered through the male gaze and endorsed by official photography associations. (But that is another story for another book.)

Võ An Khánh's war images were largely unknown within and outside the country until they were excavated by American photojournalist Doug Niven in the late 1990s. For more than five years, Niven tracked down ex-combat photographers in Vietnam, interviewed them, scanned the negatives, and collected the captions of their previously unpublished pictures. In 2002, Niven and his collaborators gathered around 150 photographs and presented them in the publication and US-based exhibition "Another Vietnam: Pictures of the War from the Other Side." Back in 1996, when Niven first stumbled on Võ An Khánh's iconic picture of the military clinic in the forest, it was a tiny 6x9cm contact print found in a forgotten stack of archival images in Sài Gòn. Võ had never enlarged this image or any of the photographs he had considered too ordinary or too bizarre to be sent to the propaganda headquarters. Ever since they were discovered and validated by the international media in the early 2000s, Võ's formerly useless or un-instrumentalizable photographs have now been privately collected and popularly shared online as self-governing artworks, released from their original secrecy and purposefulness.

—Quyên Nguyễn-Hoàng

EVE

ALLEY PEZANOSKI-BROWNE

caught   traded   lost to history   bought and sold
in a will signed
by james madison

a memory enacted
death comes for us all eve

but it didn't
come
for her
she lives in
she becomes
his legacy
she lives in
she becomes
rebellion

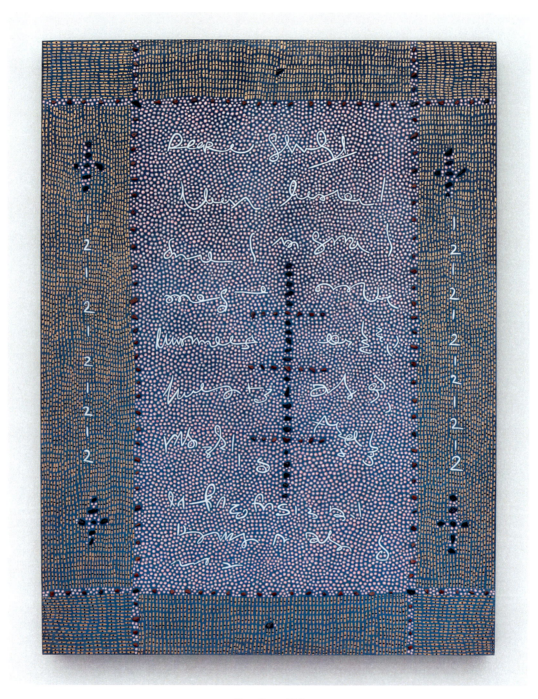

"Dear So and So"
painting by Nadia Haji Omar; poem by Christine Shan Shan Hou

DEAR SO AND SO,

You could say that our fates are

inextricably linked to one another.

That in the end, we are soft infections born

from significant loss and widened eyes.

Listen, I am at my quietest

when I am aroused.

Lately I have become more verve

and less nerve in the thriving.

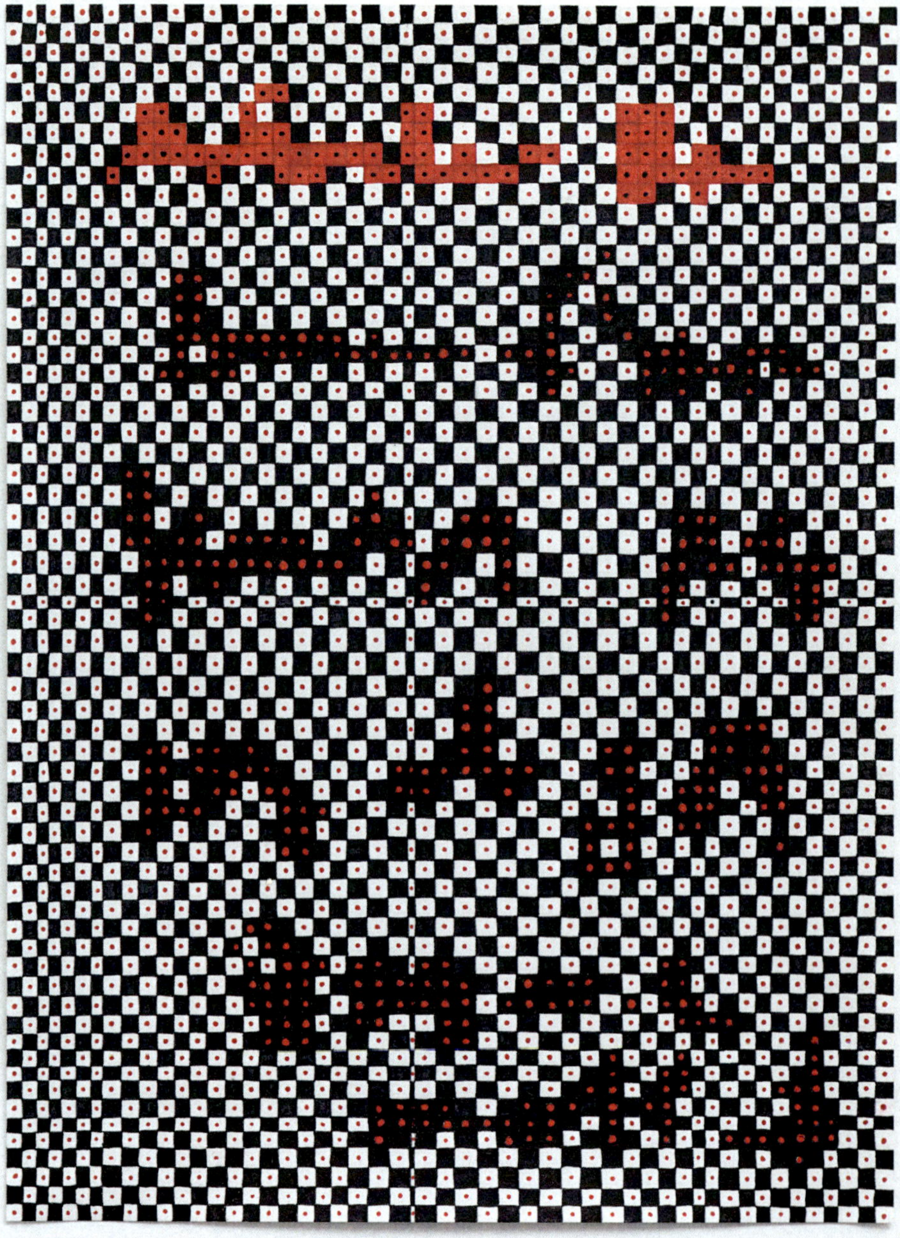

"Square Font"
painting by Nadia Haji Omar; poem by Christine Shan Shan Hou

SQUARE FONT

I was once afraid of the dark

But am now a receptacle for night.

What is the theme of the night?

This is for me not to know

And for you to find out.

"Dark Eyes (the Flower)"
painting by Nadia Haji Omar; poem by Christine Shan Shan Hou

DARK EYES (the flower)

An insurmountable feeling rests
its head in the late afternoon light

The tentacle of disbelief gnarls its way
around the flowery root

I've never been one to fret about arrivals

Glowing my way through the winding night

CAMBRIDGE
A
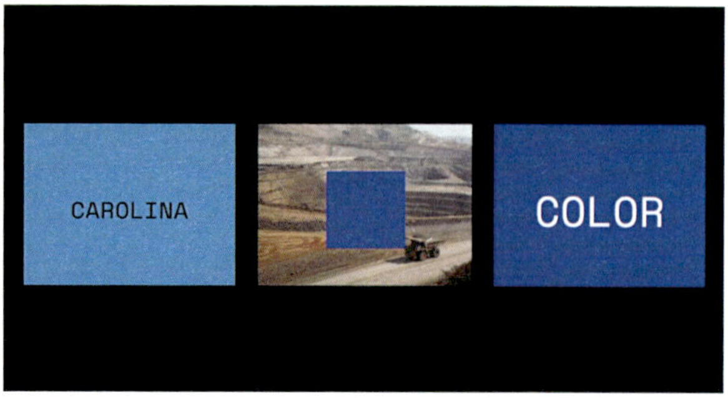
CAROLINA
COLOR
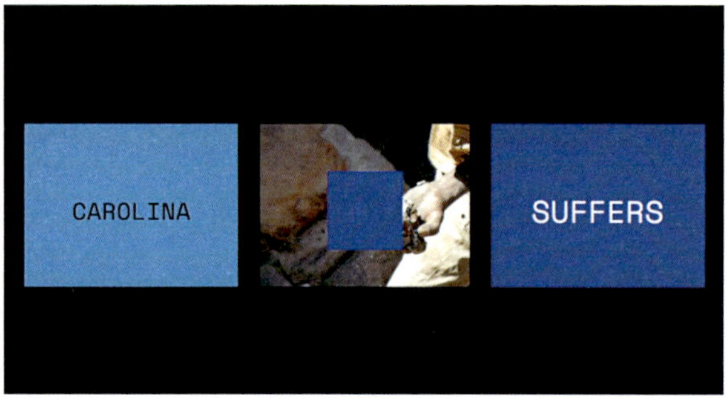
CAROLINA
SUFFERS
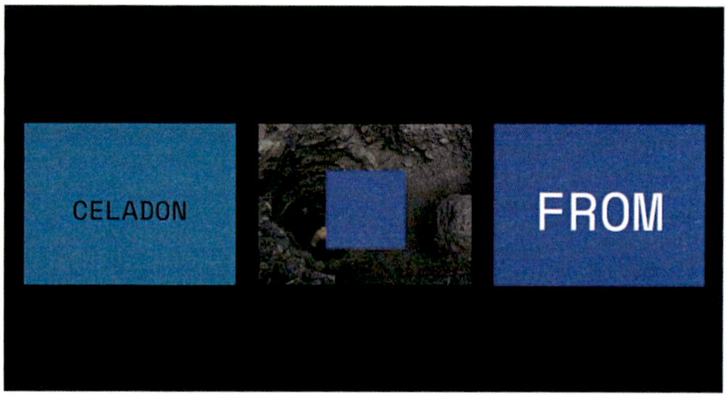
CELADON
FROM
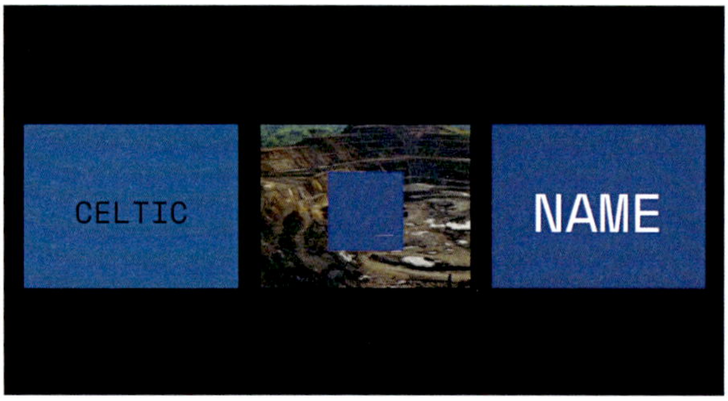
CELTIC
NAME

CADET
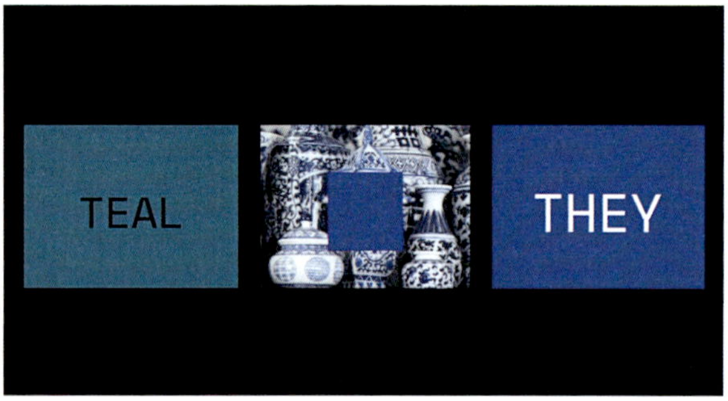
TEAL
THEY

TEAL
CANT

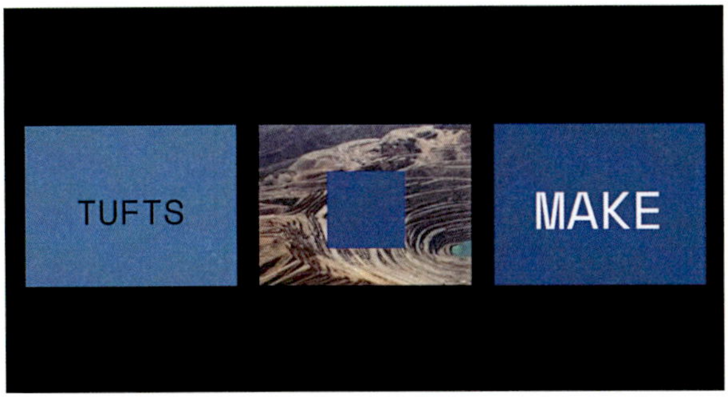
TUFTS
MAKE

TUFTS
LITHIUM

TURQUOISE
FAST

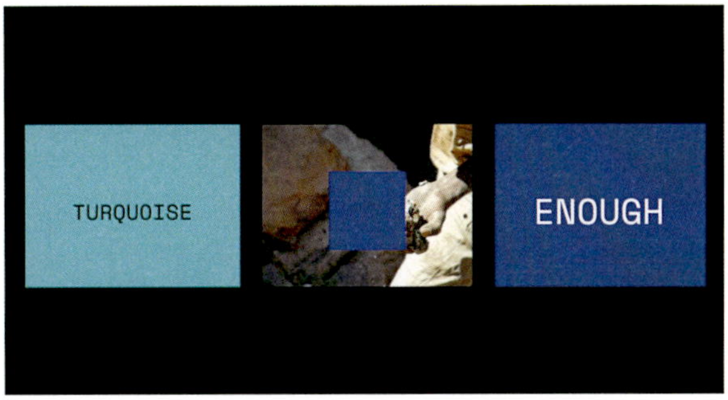
TURQUOISE
ENOUGH

UA
APPLIANCES

ULTRAMARINE
LOVE

ULTRAMARINE
TO

UNITED NATIONS
HIDE

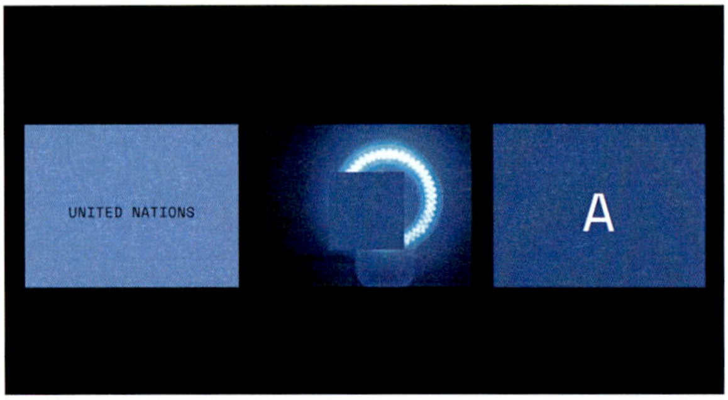
UNITED NATIONS
A
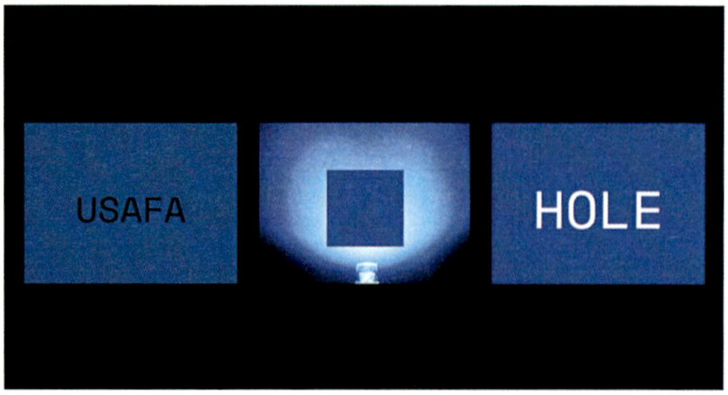
USAFA
HOLE

UA
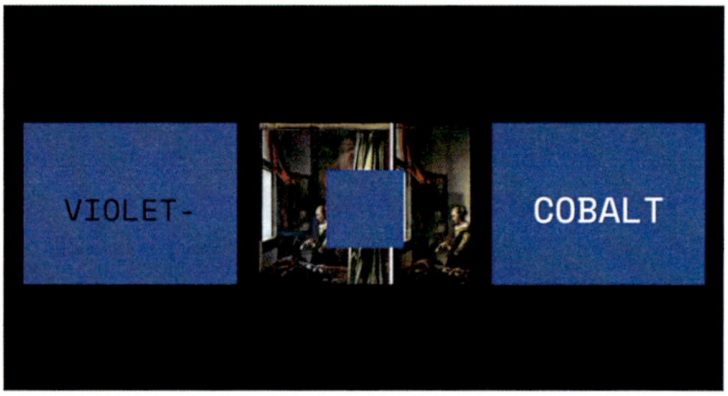
VIOLET-
COBALT
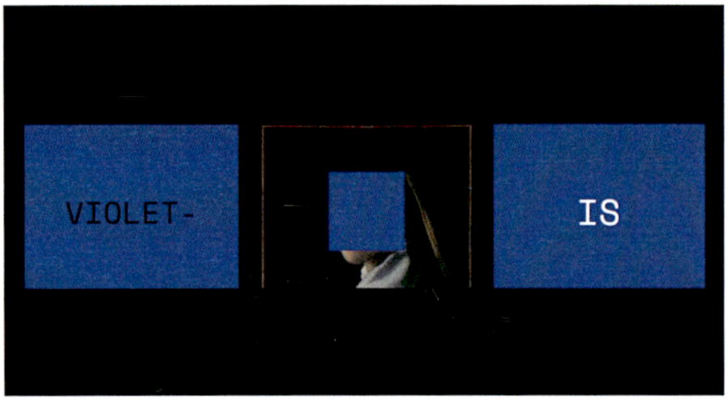
VIOLET-
IS
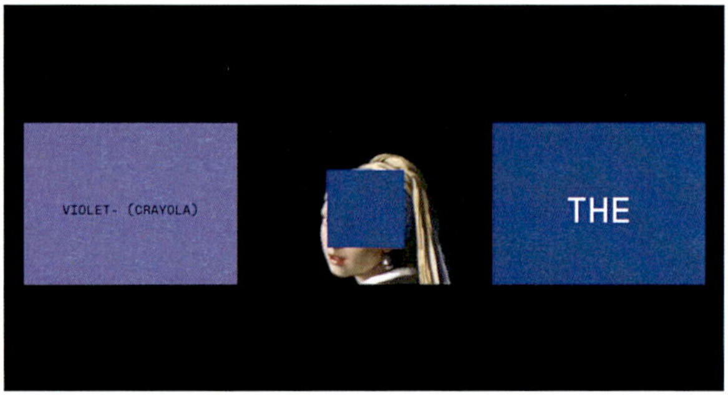
VIOLET- (CRAYOLA)
THE
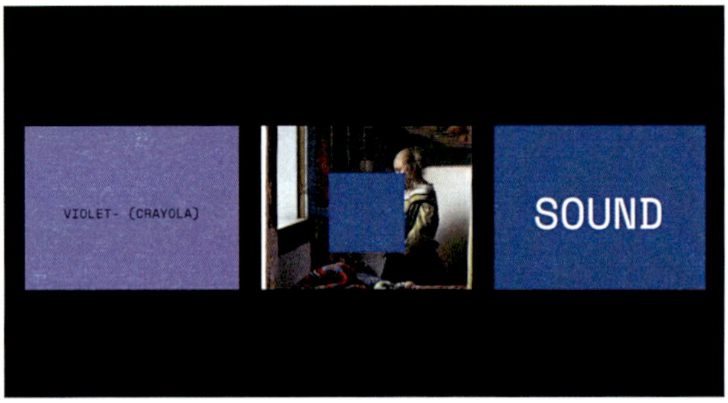
VIOLET- (CRAYOLA)
SOUND

VIVID SKY
ON

WILD YONDER
ROOF

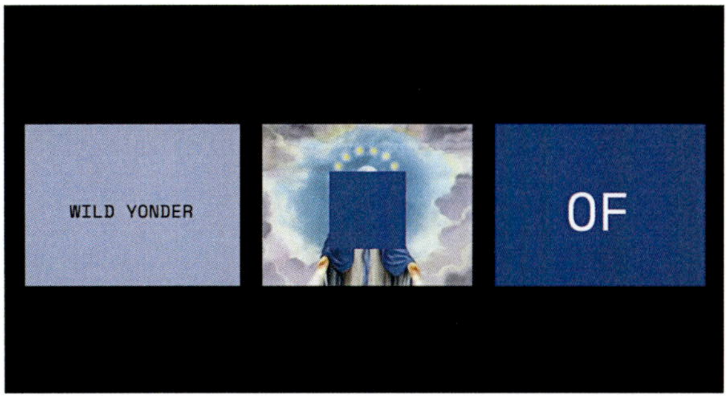
WILD YONDER
OF

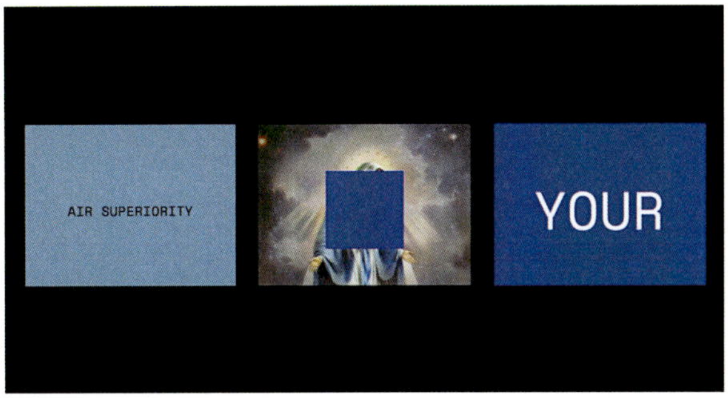
AIR SUPERIORITY
YOUR

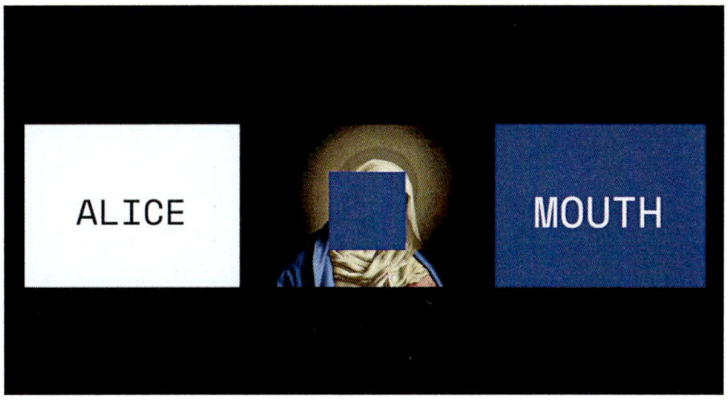
ALICE
MOUTH

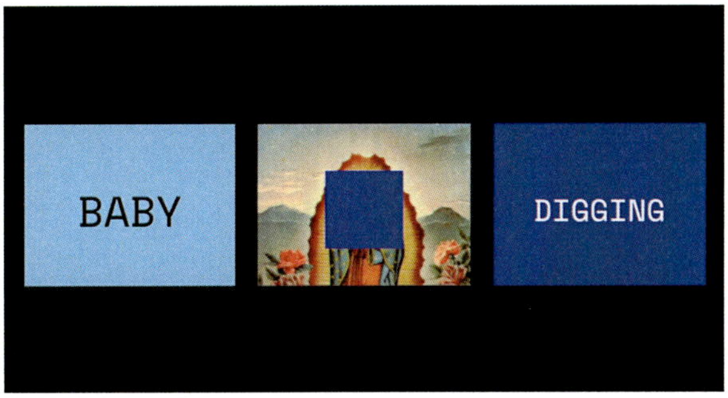
BABY
DIGGING

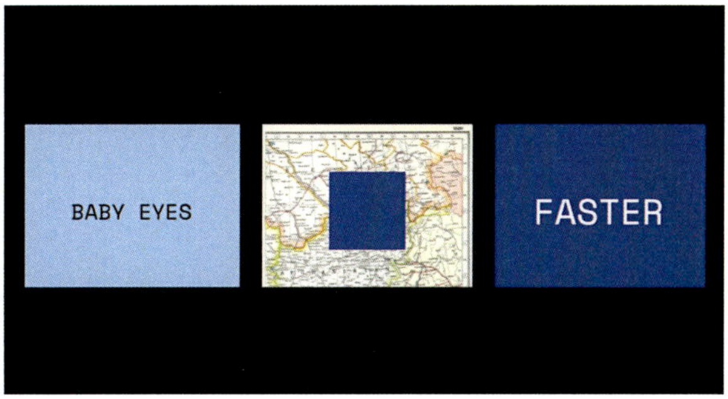
BABY EYES
FASTER

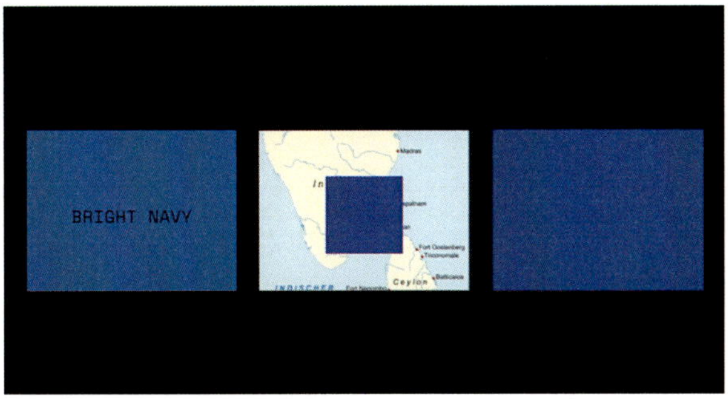
BRIGHT NAVY

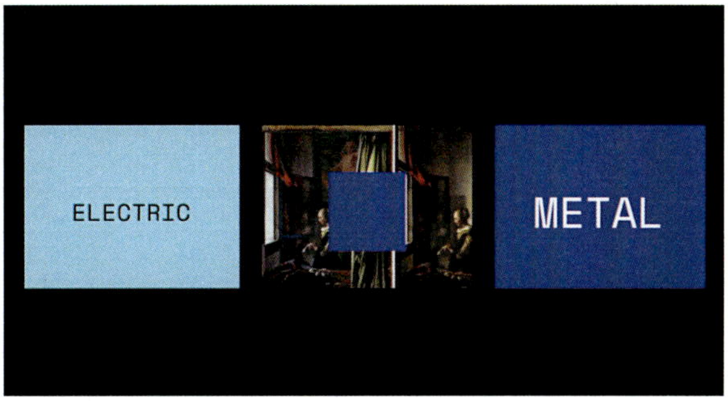
ELECTRIC
METAL

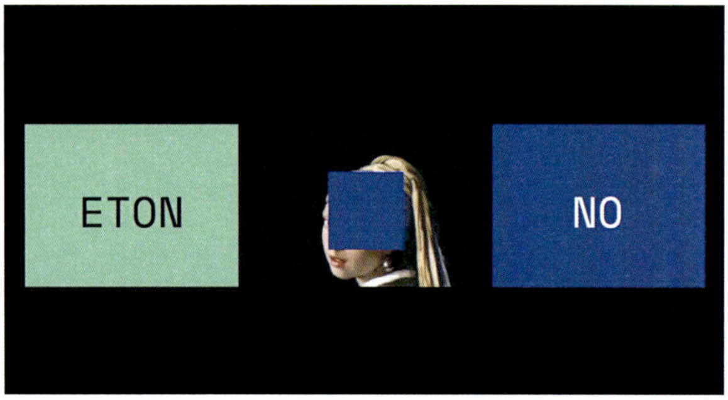
ETON
NO

FLUORESCENT
MOTHER

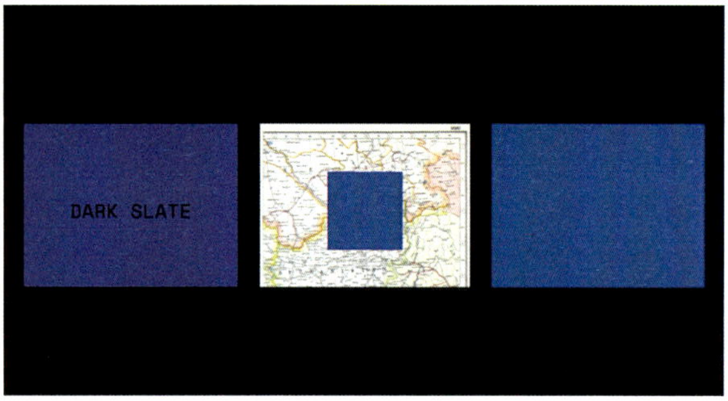
DARK SLATE

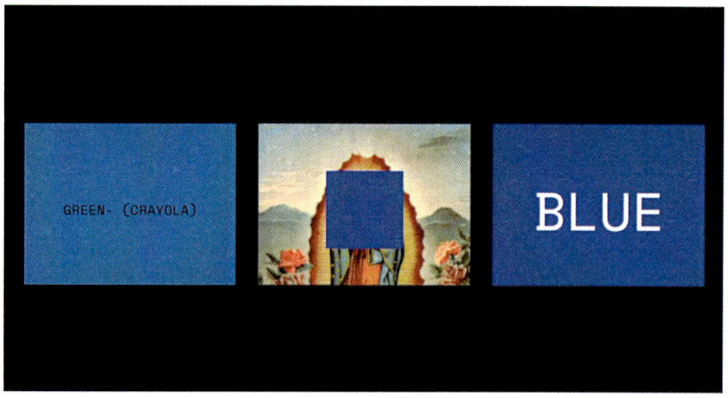
GREEN- (CRAYOLA)
BLUE

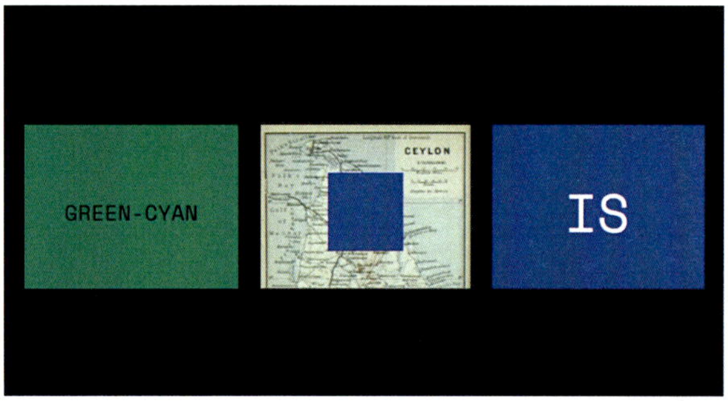
GREEN-CYAN
CEYLON
IS

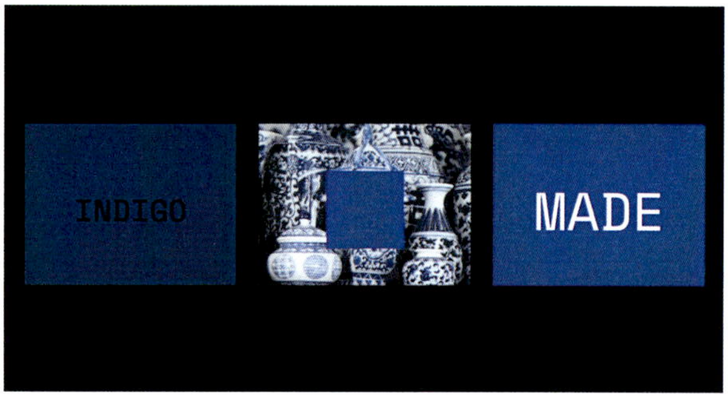
INDIGO
MADE

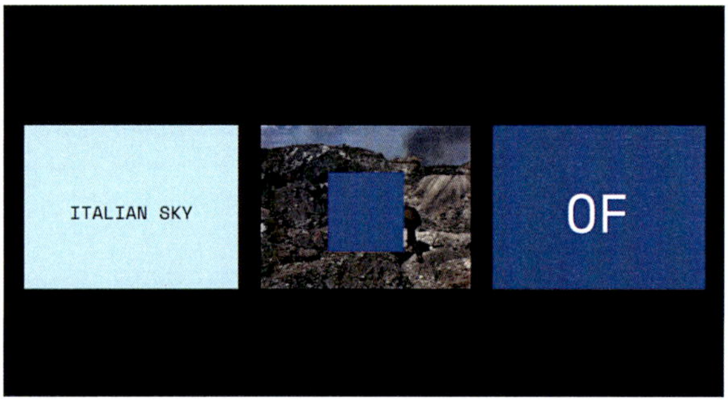
ITALIAN SKY
OF

ITALIAN SKY
HARD

LAVENDER
THINGS

MEDIUM SKY
VIRTUAL

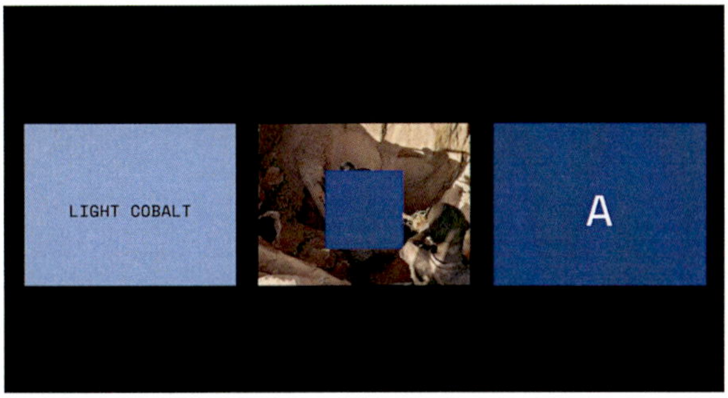
LIGHT COBALT
A

MEDIUM SKY
DREAM

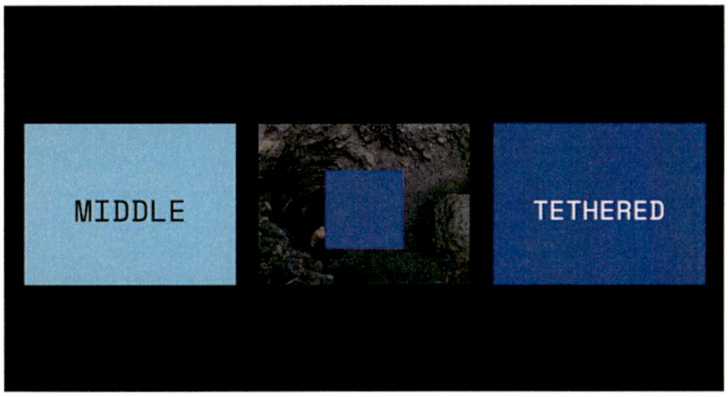
MIDDLE
TETHERED

MIDDLE
TO

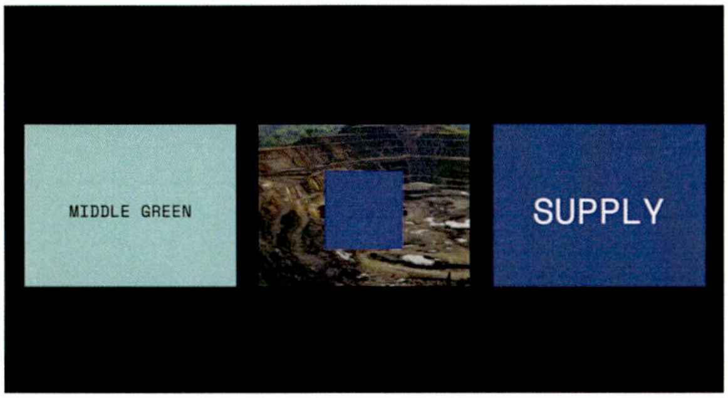
MIDDLE GREEN
SUPPLY

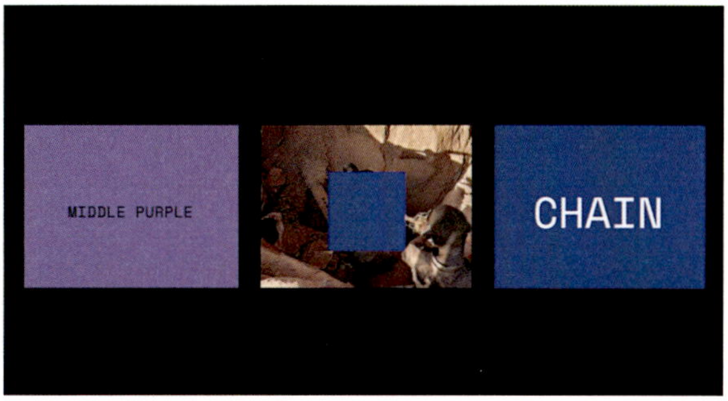
MIDDLE PURPLE
CHAIN

(left side poem procedurally generated from a list of "all colors ever" by looking for the word "blue" or "navy" or "lapis" and then stripping out the word "blue")

['Air superiority ', 'Alice ', 'Baby ', 'Baby eyes',
'Beau ', 'B'dazzled ', 'Blizzard ', 'Bondi ', 'Bright navy ',
'Cadet ', 'Cadet (Crayola)', 'Cambridge ', 'Carolina ',
'Celadon ', 'Celtic ', 'Cerulean ', 'CG ', 'Cobalt ',
'Cornflower ', 'Dark -gray', 'Dark cornflower ', 'Dark cyan',
'Dark electric ', 'Dark sky ', 'Dark slate ', 'Deep sky ', 'Denim
', 'Dodger ', 'Duke ', 'Egyptian ', 'Electric ',
'Eton ', 'Fluorescent ', 'French ', 'French sky ', 'Green- ',
'Green- (Crayola)', 'Green-cyan', 'Han ', 'Honolulu ',
'Indigo ', 'Italian sky ', 'Lavender ', 'Light ', 'Light cobalt ',
'Light cornflower ', 'Light cyan', 'Light sky ', 'Light steel ',
'Little boy ', 'Majorelle ', 'Maximum ', 'Maximum green',
'Maximum purple', 'Maya ', 'Medium ', 'Medium electric ',
'Medium Persian ', 'Medium sky ', 'Medium slate ',
'Middle ', 'Middle green', 'Middle purple', 'Midnight ',
'Morning ', 'Navy ', 'Navy (Crayola)', 'Neon ', 'Non-photo ',
'Oxford ', 'Pacific ', 'Palatinate ', 'Pale robin egg ',
'Persian ', 'Phthalo ', 'Picotee ', 'Powder ', 'Prussian ',
'Queen ', 'Resolution ', 'Robin egg ', 'Royal (dark)',
'Royal (light)', 'St. Patrick's ', 'Sapphire ', 'Shadow ',
'Silver Lake ', 'Sky ', 'Sky (Crayola)', 'Slate ', 'Smalt (Dark
powder)', 'Spanish ', 'Spanish sky ', 'Star command ',
'Steel ', 'Teal ', 'Tufts ', 'Turquoise ', 'UA ', 'Ultramarine ',
'United Nations ', 'USAFA ', 'Violet- ', 'Violet- (Crayola)',
'Vivid sky ', 'Wild yonder']

(right side poem)

a color suffers from a name. a color is a color as long as you call it. virtual loves to
hide a supply chain. they cant make lithium fast enough. appliances love to hide a
hole, cobalt is the sound on the roof of your mouth. it is digging, faster.

one finds the other at a loss for words. cobalt, lapis. ultramarine. the sky isnt
blue without a box to look through. vermeer finds beautiful clothing for mary,
shes draped in it, its afghanistan, its deep as lakes. her lady the queen. see far-off
Prussian pulse offscreen; see pigment blood so princely its nation. the way silk is
skin cold, the way a name suffers from place. or rather, discovery. English found
this last. a computer screen blinks a blue refusal. virtual loves to hide a supply
chain, they cant make lithium fast enough. appliances love to hide a hole, cobalt
is the sound on the roof of your mouth. it is digging, faster. it is better to remain
unfound. a border closes around somewhere that is not here, and needs the
technology of words, too. my childhood bus drives by the scrapyard still, these junk
cars obscured by trees, on sunny days they sparkle. theyre water. metal is no mother.
the wrong things become exotic. you think blue is more velvet but it is made of
hard things. they wanted to build a tunnel to china but china was busy eating
the congo. the glaze whispering, infinity. cobalt, lapis. ultramarine. is the virtual
a dream or still tethered to supply chain? made of steel silica sand gold bauxite,
supply and demand and demand, close your eyes and see it still.

Eddie plops her eyeballs back into her skull, turning away from the crowd. She turns to go to the bathroom, ignoring the people watching from outside. She wishes she had drugs. She wishes she had eye drops. In an alternate world, she will peer into the porcelain bowl of the toilet and see it smeared with muck.

ꕥꕥꕥꕥꕥꕥ

This is how she descends, throwing up sugar (pink, red, white). She sees that which others cannot: the pale anus stamped across the water like a headline. She wants nothing more than to be polite vengeance served quietly. She wants steak tartare for every meal. She wants to not squirm at the sight of blood; she wants to eat it. What does Eddie do when no one else is around? She dreams of different colors: farrow, dust, clean white, gloam.

Eddie floats her eyeballs in an elongated metal tray of Japanese ink. They stay there like clouds waiting for a storm to disperse them into thin pluvial nightmares. The tray has dimensions of 22x8x10 inches. She is soaking her eyeballs overnight, like mung beans, like Chinese mushrooms, like kidney beans. This is her way of softening her gaze on her incestuous impulse.

ꕥꕥꕥꕥꕥꕥ

Can incest be tender? Can it be re-seen like her tits? Before she can open her eyes again, she must stop perception. Reality from developing the website of her psyche's molestation of the past. Her sight used to be a physical structure. Here are the eye sockets from which she has spooned out forkfuls of her incestuous agony. Her mother is constantly laughing into nothing. Into empty air. The eyelids. Her eyelids. Her mother's eyelids. They are the kind of skies that invite small monsoons of ineloquence. Thick mascara she wore on the days she repainted the brushstrokes of her assassination of her mother and her mother's lover.

Enter LEDA, also returned from the dead. She is still wearing her wedding dress. Her hair is adorned with fake roses, but, like the portrait at her funeral, she has no face.

LEDA: I didn't think too much of the years before they passed. I was there, you know... in the crowd, standing outside her apartment as she did it. Did I smile? Despite myself? Imagine if I could have also regained something. Not eyes, I'm better off not seeing. I'd much rather have a mouth, lips, tongue...

Here, LEDA's neck droops down like a wet stalk. If she had eyes, she would be weeping. She shakes inside of her kimono. It's so heavy to wear, all this woven fabric. It's so lonely when trapped by beauty on all sides.

EDDIE walks into LEDA's apartment. The stalk does not look up. It fingers the plastic stem of one of the roses strewn across the bed. EDDIE is wearing her flapper dress, her hair tied up in a ponytail. She looks so beautiful as she reaches down to pick up an eyeball, which has fallen out onto the floor. It is veined and globed like a sweet, white grape.

EDDIE: Leda, it's me! Did you miss me?

EDDIE stops mid-step. Her face slackens. For around an hour, EDDIE stands unmoving on the carpet.

LEDA hums the folk song "Takeda Lullaby" to herself, still unaware of EDDIE's presence. Suddenly, Eddie snaps out of her dissociative state to pull out a compact mirror, quickly adjusting her false lashes.

LAUGH TRACK and CARNIVAL MUSIC play in the background.

LEDA (*changing the theme of the song from an obon festival to a birthday*): "...How can I be happy, even when my birthday is here?..."

EDDIE (*worried*): Are you alright, Leda? Look, I...I brought some things for you. Happy birthday.

EDDIE begins to unlatch her bag, pulling out a pair of kabuki dolls. Both are women dressed in Western-style fashions. EDDIE pulls out another, and then another, and then another, desperately searching for the one male doll she has buried somewhere in her bag. We see that the whole apartment is covered in dolls, EDDIE and LEDA moving through them as if swimming through the sea.

LEDA (*doing a flip in the doll-glossed sea*): "...The child continues to cry, and is mean to me..."

EDDIE (*furiously paddling toward LEDA, as though scared she may lose her*): Oh goodness, Leda. Come on. It was just one man. Can't we leave the past in the past? Please?

LEDA rises from her bed and goes into the kitchen, where she unties the bag holding the birthday cake she has bought for herself.

EDDIE follows quickly behind, grabbing the purse she has brought filled with gifts for LEDA's birthday. If she had a mouth, she would be smiling right now. EDDIE has not realized that LEDA no longer has a face yet. LEDA continues to ignore EDDIE as she strikes a match to light the candles with.

It's obvious that her non-face, a furnace in itself, is flickering in its gas. Its ghastly light. Its ghost frame. Meanwhile, Eddie has become Psyche, the Japanese goddess of the soul. Her Oedipus complex is that she is now an Aphrodite. And her new lover is Eros, is Leda.

LEDA: Promise me, Eddie, that you won't look at my face.

EDDIE: Why such a promise? You are my arrow through the underworld.

LEDA: Please.

EDDIE: Why can't I see your lovely face?

LEDA: Promise me you won't seek for my face?

EDDIE: Why would I promise you the impossible?

On her kimono knees, she begs Eddie for her continual blindness. For her eye sockets to become stones or empty baby ramen noodle bowls.

And after fucking like two open roses in a king-size bed made of silk and pearly sapphire, Eddie clandestinely and furtively pulls herself out of bed, cupping a flickering candle as she walks towards Leda's face, which is sleeping contently like a lotus on the moving river that is their conjugal bed.

Eddie lowers the candle so she can better view Leda's face, and she gasps when a void projects its blackhole—its gravitational field of nothingness—before her.

This betrayal immediately sent Eddie to hell.

In Hell - Eddie

In Hell, Eddie walks in modern, transamplifiable, vacuous circles: one intertwining thorn over another. Even in Hell, she doesn't own a single Nippon oil lamp, or a lantern made from translucent paper, or drag queen skin or nori. Leda, betrayed, began to forgive Eddie with the help of opium, Nuberu Bagu, two cockroaches, and Flamenco Umeji. Eddie could redeem herself if she underwent five stages of terminal cancer for the soul.

.

.

.

The Third Stage: Eddie, who is extremely eco-friendly, must learn how to freeze each tapioca in Hell and then inflate each tapioca until they become 10,000 tapioca-lightbulbs, using human memory of sorrow and murder as electricity

With a bicycle pump situated between her thighs, Eddie holds the pump head with one hand and pinches each pluvial tapioca towards it with the other. She struggles. It's hard to pump and be meticulous.

"Xing, help me!" Xing is busy curling her long, jet black hair with Obama's wife Michelle, while using the tongue of Hell's open fire and a micro-dragon's *lingua franca,* who dresses like a hybrid between Demi Moore and Sandra Oh.

"I'm coming! But my hair, Eddie! My hair!"

Xing pushes the bicycle pump's handle up and down as if it were a hydraulic machine while each tapioca inflates and floats away. Eddie smokes an e-cigarette that bears resemblance to a toothpick. Sometimes, Eddie flosses her teeth with this nicotine.

It's hard to freeze anything in Hell, but both Xing and Eddie find Hell fairly accommodating. Hell has a better hospitality culture than heaven. In heaven, everyone must wear boring face masks (with words on them, words such as: "Silence is a great source of constipation"), drink almond milk, pre-register for Celestial Eventbrite, and leave their sandals by the half-quasi-bamboo, half-copper gate before entering. In heaven, no one can freely move about.

Everyone is restricted to designated areas: those who tried bánh mì before they sinned, and those who haven't. In Hell, bánh mì is popular because its baguette-shaped physique, like a mini-cedar colorseque sarcophagus, can easily be toasted in Hell's natural ultra-warm climate.

Later, Xing introduces Eddie to Cathy Park Hong, who was named on the 2021 *TIME 100* list for her writings and espousal of Asian American women. After the brief, desultory introduction, Eddie looks at her intensely and cries for like fourteen years straight.

Xing doesn't know how to respond to Eddie's lachrymose condition. Her tears aren't entirely tears, just as the sky, raining tapioca, isn't entirely tapioca. Eddie's tears have the texture of translucent mung beans or bánh bao, which contains onion (no wonder she cries so much), mushroom, pork, salt, and egg.

Instead, Xing mumbles softly, "Eddie! Eddie! Why don't you try eating edible, underwear-shaped packaged tofu to calm yourself down!"

STAGE 3 ½ (RIGHT BEFORE THE ESCAPE)

The list of bánh mì havers and non-bánh mì havers is irrelevant. Hell is not rational or forgiving. That's the whole point. It would be boring to know who's good; here, everyone is guilty of something or another. Awkwafina is in heaven, advertising her new show *Nora from Queens*. They get the flyers like they got the pudding: pouring in from the holes in the ceiling, which management has failed to fix yet again. Eddie looks at Awkwafina's face and decides she hates it. She asked Xing if she thought Awkwafina was pretty, and Xing said, *Maybe, kind of*, and they slept in separate beds that night. No matter how many people she asks, Eddie can't ever quite get why Awkwafina is in heaven, or Elijah Wood, who is technically dead but also technically alive. She figures they didn't have a place to put him. He looks exactly like he looked in *Lord of the Rings*. Someone should tell him brown boots aren't really the thing to wear any more, she thinks.

Xing and Eddie are still working hard at night, trying to get the tapioca pearls to take the right texture. They've announced a soft opening for their boba shop next week. Dolly Parton asks if it's the same kind they've opened up in Chinatown recently, with the cheese foam. She offers to perform at the opening, and they give her a non-answer. They secretly want to ask DJ Rashad.

They test their boba recipes out one night, their legs dangling over the stream of white water that runs through the middle of Hell. It's so beautiful. Seagulls flock and perch on the Asian pear trees (they only have Asian pear flavor—something they haven't told anyone else yet). Management has announced that lychee trees will be shipped in next week from China, but like the ceiling holes, who knows how long it will take. Xing has invented a secret game for fun, but they can only do it at night: they take their straws

and try to see who can shoot a tapioca pearl into a seagull's eye. So far, Xing hasn't had any luck. She pouts because Eddie hits the mark every single time: both eyes.

XING: Eddie, have you thought about marriage?

EDDIE: Yes. About how very disgusting and terrible it is.

XING: Even to me?

EDDIE is silent. She walks over to the river and lays down next to it, the wig DOLLY PARTON made for her getting dirty from the wet earth. It's a bright yellow, and was very expensive: it cost her 250,000 Hell Bank Notes, which could buy someone a whole year's worth of tofu, or even maybe a riverboat.

EDDIE: What about if we got a riverboat instead?

XING: What?

EDDIE (*yelling*): I said, what if we got a riverboat instead? Then we could sail forever and ever and ever, and we wouldn't have to think about stupid, silly things, like marriage.

XING begins to weep softly. She buries her beautiful, wet face into her hands. From the riverbank, XING looks like a kite—fragile and blurred, her red robes rippling off her body like tendrils of smoke.

EDDIE gets up from the riverbank. A piece of bark sticks out of her Dolly wig. She throws it to the ground and runs up to Xing, putting an arm around her.

EDDIE: I didn't mean it. I didn't mean it.

XING: I ride that stupid bicycle every day. I ride it, thinking of it as being an elephant. I thought maybe you could see me as someone worth loving.

EDDIE: I do love you, okay? I'll marry you. I'll do it right now.

XING: You're just saying things, like usual.

EDDIE: No, I'm not.

XING: There. You just said something.

EDDIE (*muttering*): Here we go again.

XING: "Here we go again?" What the fuck do you mean by that?

A fight breaks out between the two of them. EDDIE is the one crying now; XING is screaming. They rip at each other's skin and clothing. It feels just like how it always has, their love—unpredictable and volatile, like a rash. Eventually, they both get tired, and EDDIE carries XING back to their apartment. In the morning, EDDIE wakes up to touch XING's hand like she always does, but she's gone.

EDDIE *(panicked)*: Xing? Baby? Where are you?

EDDIE begins running through their 1LDK apartment, looking for XING everywhere.

EDDIE: Don't leave me! Don't abandon me!

She looks under pots, under urns, under plants. Under the toaster oven, she thinks she can see a glint of XING's robes—but once she tugs it out, she sees it's a hongbao. She opens it with trembling hands. Inside is 100,000 Hell Bank Notes, along with a train ticket back to Tokyo. A note reads: "I'll find you again one day. In the meantime, don't look for me."

Scene changes to XING boarding a bullet train from South Hell to Hangzhou. She stops for a moment, as if thinking of something, but shakes her head. In her hand, she holds a picture of a woman that's not EDDIE, wearing a yellow qipao. XING boards the train and is gone.

Cut back to EDDIE, who has fainted near the toaster oven.

EDDIE (*whispering*): I'll do it...I'll go back...

Funeral, a collaboratively authored novel by Daisuke Shen and Vi Khi Nao, initiated as an ekphrastic experiment based on the 1969 film, *Funeral Parade of Roses*, directed by Toshio Matsumoto.

CYCLE

AYESHA RAEES

CYCLE

ut o
easin
ade up
ese skins
rain of yes
sometime
times like
ever happe

But often I woke to nothing
creasing the blanket fort
made up of human beings
these skins are embracing
the rain of yesterday
falling sometimes like snow
sometimes like
nothing ever happened
here

In the morning,
I washed my clothes
and dried them on the line:
where was I? I questioned
the water, watching each dri
from these hollowed s
of all my bein

But often I woke to nothing
creasing the blanket fort
made up of human beings
these skins are embracing
the rain of yesterday
falling sometimes like snow
sometimes like
nothing ever happened
here
میں ایک بار
بھی نہیں
DISABLE AMERICAN VETERANS
Juice
NATURAL
SABRETT
NYPD
میں ایک بار
بھی نہیں
In the morning,
I washed my clothes
and dried them on the line:
where was I? I questioned
the water, watching each dri
from these hollowed s
of all my being

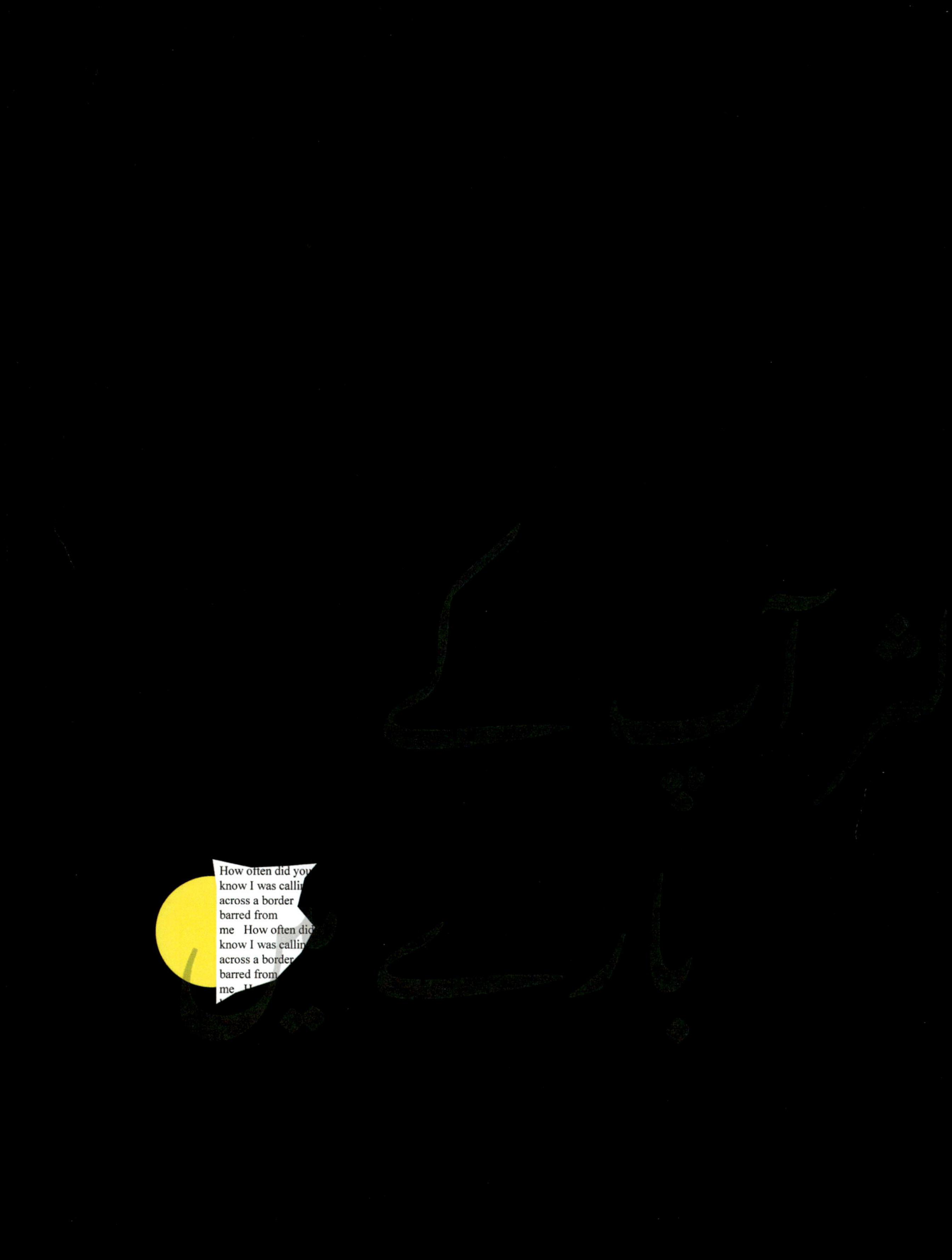
How often did you
know I was callin
across a border
barred from
me How often did
know I was callin
across a border
barred from
me

what is after this?
what is after us?
what is after this?
what is after us?
what is after this?
what is after us?
what is after this?
what is after us?

an imprisonment
where only the sky
goes on an imprisonm
where only the sk
goes on
an impriso
where only the sky
goes on

اکثر آپ کے
بارے

an imprisonment
where only the sky
goes on an imprisonme
where only the sk
goes on
an impriso
where only the sky
goes on
what is after this?
what is after us?
what is after this?
what is after us?
what is after this?
what is after us?
what is after this?
what is after us?
How often did you
know I was callin
across a border
barred from
me How often did
know I was callin
across a border
barred from
NYPD
POLICE

Here.

But.

Somewhere.

But.

Here.

But.

Tripping   for earth   a storefront   becomes a brownstone

becomes a crushed pill   becomes a snort   a red party cup swirling

prayer

I said   oh God   I'm trouble

God said   your trouble   keeps me

half extant   all spirit

my body

becomes

two then four then   thousand itsy bitsy bodies   falling from sky

bitting into tree

bark

the dog

inside my nesting place

woke to alarm

only to find its muzzle

glued with web

petitioning

without location   or culture

breathing still.

Somewhere.

But.

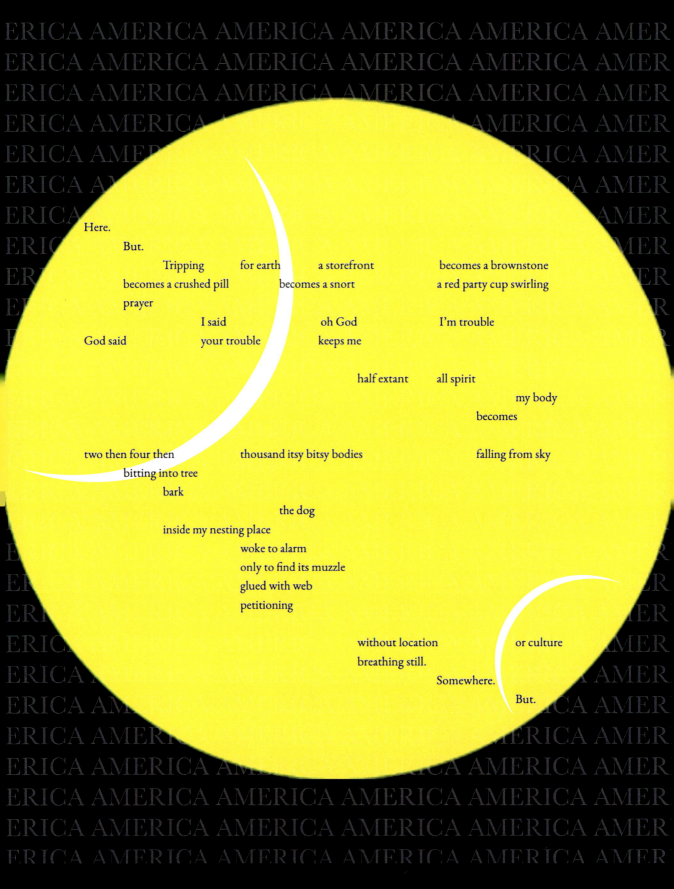

DESVELADAS (MACARENA HERNÁNDEZ, SHEILA MALDONADO, NELLY ROSARIO)

CEIBA NO DE COLÓN

What did the earth teach the trees?
How to speak to the sky.
—Pablo Neruda, *The Book of Questions* (1973)

Tell me, Atabey: Why does the legendary Ceiba de Colón first speak to me when it does, through a digitized photograph via the United States Library of Congress, and not in the land where tree and I were born?

May I have your divine permission to return the tree hug remotely, in words and in pictures? Would paying my respects in this way render me a poser, right alongside the man in the boater hat and suit pictured? I mean, as children of conquest, what business do either of us have taking selfies with a 'First Tree' so rooted in Indigenous and Afro Diasporic cosmology? Dwarfed by those sprawling buttress roots, might we be too deracinated to absorb the wisdom of the ancestors who live there? Have we been so easily uprooted that we've lost the passwords to ourselves? In such barren soil and stormy times, can we still access your network and lay down new roots? How can it guide our lost souls to the light when its main limbs have been amputated—many say by soldiers during the 1916 U.S. occupation—the remaining limbs contorted and spiraling out of frame?

How do we stay whole in a world that makes our axis mundi look like a tree possessed?

What exactly did you teach your student Ceiba de Colón to say to the sky? In what language should our sacred 'World Tree,' cursed with the surname of a 'New World' pillager, address the storm clouds?

Tell me, Atabey: Is there even proof that Christopher Columbus, upon arrival to the Americas, moored to Ceiba's trunk La Santa María, his flagship and the largest of his conquest vessels? If so, can we fantasize, in turn, that the same tree from which Taínos made canoes put its own roots on the caravel named after Holy Mary? That this *amarre* in reverse is what later caused La Santa María to mysteriously shipwreck off the island's northwest coast, of what today is Haiti, on Christmas Day 1492, of all blessed days? Or did Columbus deliberately run the ship aground as a pretext to colonize Ayiti/Quisqueya as Hispaniola? Should the Ceiba stump that remains near the mouth of Río Ozama today—behind the ruins of his son Diego's luxury palace, the Alcázar—be renamed rather than venerated as the "first colonial monument" in the Americas? For doesn't the addition of Colón to ceiba, Taíno term for "stone," mutate its properties to mean: "stone of the dove / colonizer / longest part of the large intestine"? Does such a dis/honor bind our 'Great Tree' to the cultural archetypes ascribed to indigenous women like Pocahontas—representing "the American frontier and the civilizing process that the Europeans claimed to bring to the Native Americans"—or to the archetype of "traitor" ascribed to Mexico's La Malinche? Would the archetype of resistance fighter associated with Quisqueya's chieftess Anacaona be most fitting of all? Or do I hear in Celia Cruz's "Soy antillana" our 'Cosmic Tree' resisting imposed taxonomy: *"Me andan pidiendo definición / Como me siento tan antillana / No puede haber definición?"*

Tell me, Atabey: If I place my forehead on the petrified trunk, will Ceiba de Colón answer all the questions tied up in my throat?

Left: "Columbus tree" Ceiba de Colón, Santo Domingo, Dominican Republic [c. 1909-1932].
Source: Library of Congress

Right: Ceiba de Colón, March 2022.
Photo: Nelly Rosaario

~~CROSS~~ TREE

once I was a teenager
with some depth and doubt

looking for belief
I turned to nature
and the ancient

had just learned
I was from such things

At 15 I saw Copán
the greatest city in the homeland
an Egypt several souths down
from whence my family came

a city in a valley of pre-latin kings
trees bursting through stone still there
the only document
of past greatness

if that is what we call a city
what we call the manmade

I too wanted to read and build
learn their signs
went looking for
the other cities in books

the Maya based their buildings
their glyphs on the natural
the animals the bodies
the depictions the signs

I found a replacement
for the Christian cross
that burdened me

the world tree of the Maya
my new symbol
from the Palenque sarcophagus

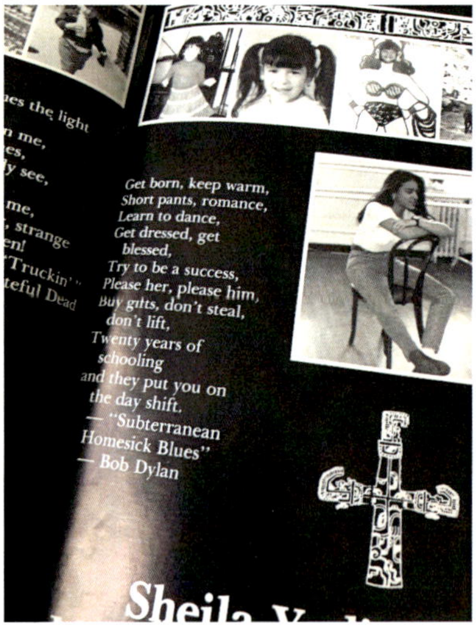

Brooklyn Friends high school yearbook page, NY, 1991

Left: Stenciled reproduction of the K'inich Janaab Pakal I carved stone sarcophagus lid in the Temple of the Inscriptions, Palenque, Mexico, 7th century, A.D. Image: Madman2001, edited by eurythmia1 on Wikimedia Commons, colorized by Sheila Maldonado

9/29/22, 9:35 AM

Made it to the more than 900 year old tree today

Sheila Honduras

How far is it from u?

SH What's ur friends name?

3 miles from where I grew up

Sheila Honduras

Ur on the ancient lands

Right (text exchange between Macarena and Sheila): Ahuehuete, or bald cypress, is derived from the Nahuatl for tree, āhuēhuētl, *which means "upright drum in water" or "old man of the water."*

EL ÉBANO

My mother 's favorite tree, el ébano, in La Ceja, Nuevo León, México. Photo: Macarena Hernández, May 2022

My parents never intended to stay on the U.S. side of the Rio Grande, the Río Bravo. One day they would make enough to go back to México and work their own fields, even if their eight children didn't. That was back in the 80s, when those ranchos just across the Tamaulipas state line and in the northern edges of Nuevo León shipped out truckloads of melones, sandías, and sorgo. Back when they still grew sugarcane.

But places, like people, die, too. Few people go back these days.

My mother still makes two annual pilgrimages to her rancho: Día de los Muertos and Día de las Madres. She's been placing flowers at my father's gravesite every year since we buried him in 1998 in the community cemetery a couple of miles from La Ceja, my mother's birthplace.

My father had been ambivalent about being buried in México: "Que al cabo, cuando me muera, no me voy a dar cuenta." My mother was clear: "Vale más que me entierren en el rancho." Next to his father, mother, and brother sits my father's black granite tombstone engraved with a promise to never forget him and a cropped photo of him taken at my college graduation in 1996. Next to him is my mother's uncarved rock, waiting for instructions.

My father would be shocked at how much this rural stretch across from Río Grande City, Texas through Tamaulipas and to Nuevo León has changed. These days, going to the rancho means crossing the cartel checkpoint along Tamaulipas 63, just before it becomes Nuevo León 33.

My mother's oldest sister was the last of her clan to live at the rancho. A few years ago, we went back for her funeral. Like my father, she is buried in El Panteon Sara Flores. I hitch a ride back to the United States with my tía. At the required checkpoint stop on our way back north, a young man approaches my window. He has kindness in his eyes.

"We're heading back to the United States," I tell him.

"We just buried my sister," my mother's sister says with the saddest voice she can muster.

"Who do you work for?" I ask him quickly and hoping I sound like an inocente with only curiosidad pura. Because in all these years of crossing that checkpoint, I've never asked them a single question. But it is just me and my tía and the worst she can do is yell at me.

"Soy miembro del Cártel del Golfo," he says without threat.

"Que Dios los proteja y los cuide," I say, hoping to sound as maternal and holy as the evangelical church ladies at my tío Rafael's Spanish-speaking Pentecostal church.

My aunt, though, is annoyed: "¿Qué más quieres? ¿Un huevo frito?"

If Ama plans on staying at the rancho a few days, she'll take clippings from her garden in South Texas. "Yo quiero ver vida aquí," she says.

Ama finds life in her ebony tree, in la labor chiquita, surrounded by abandoned fields.

"Este ébano ya era ébano desde que yo tengo conocimiento," says my now 81-year-old mother.

En otras palabras, she has known that ebony tree all of her life.

Under that ébano, abuelito Jose María used to feed his children during breaks from working the family land, where they planted corn, beans, watermelons, and sugar cane. Ese árbol had always been their refuge from the thorny scrublands and the implacable sun.

When she visits, my mother always hugs her ébano. Le da energía, she says.

And before she says adiós, she whispers it an oración of gratitude.

Detail from Codex Rios (Codex Vaticanus 3738 fol. 3v): Infants who died at an early age being fed by the Aztec Chichihuacuauhco or Tonacacuauhco "wet-nurse" tree," or árbol nodriza. Source: Bibliotheca Apostolica Vaticana

ATABEY + CANEY

If you must ask: Ceiba is born from Atabey, Cosmic Mother. Cosmic Mother makes her virgin self pregnant with firstborn son Yúkahu. Yúkahu is both Ceiba's father and Ceiba's brother. Ceiba's father-brother is also the sky turey—a sky that does not fall, as it has no beginning and no end. For in the end, this mother-father-brother becomes Great Spirit Yaya, the trinity who in the beginning creates the sun, the moon, and the stars. After the stars is when Ceiba is born.

Born first are the stars, created when Great Spirit Yaya casts stones high into the sky, creating lights in the four cardinal directions that shine with fundamental virtues: Achiano in the south (innocence and open-mindedness), Koromo in the west (introspection and spirituality), Rakuno in the north (wisdom and experience), and Sobaiko in the east (enlightenment and balance).

Balancing these stars is Ceiba, born when Yúkahu delivers from Atabey three more stones and makes of them a triangle in the center of the sky to form the first fire. From this first fire rises a smoke, higher and higher, hardening and hardening, until becoming the tree trunk that comes to be Ceiba. Ceiba comes into being with branches stretched into Yúkahu's sky and with roots lodged deep into Atabey's first waters. Waters that Ceiba best navigates on earth when hollowed out into canoa, then softened by fire and polished smooth with stone or shell axes. Before axing, first bow to the tree born as mother of all trees, for Ceiba stands at the center of all that is created by Great Spirit Yaya with both humility and honor.

In honor of all that is and said above, Ceiba means "stone" and has leaves in the shape of stars—earth and heaven as one. One may call Ceiba navel of the world and axis mundi. One may call Ceiba pentandra kapok and kankantrie; samauma and Java cotton; silk-cotton tree and Yax Che. One may call Ceiba Tree of Life, as well as First / Central / Green / Great / World / Cosmic Tree.

Or one may call Ceiba all of the above, the middle, and below.

If you must define: Ceiba are native to places you call Caribbean, Mexico, Central America, northern South America, West Africa, and were introduced in South and Southeast Asia—a canopy that spreads far and wide.

Far and wide spreads the canopy, for it is held up by four main branches, where Ceiba let eagles come to roost from above. From above and down the middle, Ceiba trunks house insects that attract animals and birds and bats, which Ceiba roots shelter. Ceiba roots extend to the underworld and give home to your ancestor spirits. Ancestor spirits also born from Great Spirit Yaya, ancestor spirits from whom you must learn.

If you must teach: Learn from and in all cardinal directions for the strength to hold up the sky. Sky people like Taíno and Maya know to plant Ceiba at the center of towns as a living Medicine Wheel, defined by the four virtues. Virtually the first stones cast by Great Spirit Yaya, these cosmic points are bound by 28 units—each quarter divided into seven—marked with sibas or pebbles in the guaiko Medicine Wheel of Taíno. Taíno, too, mirror this Caney Circle at home. Bohío homes are held up by a center pole made from Ceiba. Also of Ceiba may be the roof and frame: eight poles carved as the dark-cloud snake, boinas, with eight more poles supporting the sides, and carved in the form of iguana—these 16 poles join to form the sacred home-cave Iguanaboina, path into the womb of Cosmic Mother Atabey.

Of our Cosmic Mother Atabey, then, you ask many questions about one Ceiba made stone and long dead in your homeland because you are home-sick: A split center pole and a mid-life middle divide the place you call home. The place you call home is splintered by three addresses, two states, two countries, one self. Self is split further under the stars of two fish and twin beings, between time and space, work and life. Work-life balance medicine happens as you now sit to write by the Green River, located on the land of the Mohican Nation Stockbridge-Munsee, people of the waters that are never still, between Achiano-south and Sobaiko-east, in the green-yellow time between spring and summer, seasons of squash and corn, calling on the wings of turkey and of hawk. Hawk-eyed in the darkest hour before dawn, you can look across space and time to the land of your birth for a sturdier branch to roost on.

If you must write: Know that Ceiba de Colón is calling for an excavation of the four virtues still buried in you.

Top view of Taíno Caney Circle medicine wheel. Source: Indigenous Caribbean Network

EL RÍO

This last Day of the Dead, the Hernández sisters hoped to convince our mother not to go to México.

This is the first time I feel maybe we shouldn't. These guys were at grandpa's house a few months ago looking for guns and ammunition.

Veronica Elizondo

😱

Maybe if you don't go she won't. We can always tell Chivo not to invite her.
Up to you all 🙏

👍 I will talk to Tia Lola tomorrow and then call mom.

❤️ Buenas noches sisters.

Cuata

Maybe if you call Chivo and tell him to discourage her coming from him maybe she will not go

They were there inside the cuartito while the man searched the house 😱

10/31/22, 7:29 AM

Cuata

I talked to tia Irma last night she said it was very traumatic for her because the men kept asking why they were hiding and la ranchera told them that they were sick and afraid but kept looking for stuff around the house. She was afraid that they were going to go in and pulled them out with the guns

Veronica Elizondo

Good morning sisters.
Maybe mom doesn't want to go anymore. Has she said anything recently?

Nancy Tovar

Good morning sisters
Mom woke up with a soar throat
Maybe that will also hold her back

I called her, she said she is using her spray, feels better.

I asked her about going to the ranch, she said she doesn't know yet.
She doesn't seem worried about the incident with the tias.
She said it wasn't a serious thing. If the guys were evil, they would have pulled them out of the bathroom.

She is something else 🤣🤣🤣
Mother !!

Cuata

Yup!

I alert las desveladas.

(I saved Sheila's name as "Sheila Honduras" the night we met in 2008 on Nelly's tree-lined back deck in San Marcos, TX. At the time of this writing fourteen years later, Sheila learns of this. She is first perplexed, then amused.)

Río Bravo at the Texas-México border, Matamoros, Tamaulipas, México. Photo: Macarena Hernández, August 2019

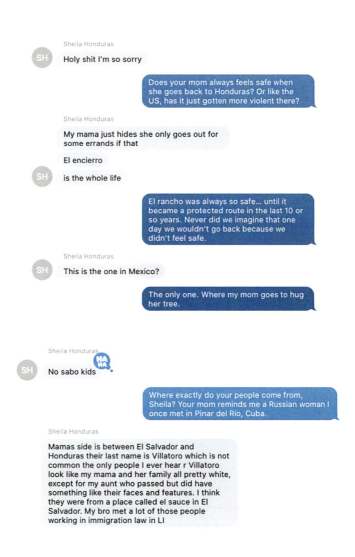

Sheila Honduras

SH Holy shit I'm so sorry

Does your mom always feels safe when she goes back to Honduras? Or like the US, has it just gotten more violent there?

Sheila Honduras

My mama just hides she only goes out for some errands if that

El encierro

SH is the whole life

El rancho was always so safe... until it became a protected route in the last 10 or so years. Never did we imagine that one day we wouldn't go back because we didn't feel safe.

Sheila Honduras

SH This is the one in Mexico?

The only one. Where my mom goes to hug her tree.

Sheila Honduras

SH No sabo kids

Where exactly do your people come from, Sheila? Your mom reminds me a Russian woman I once met in Pinar del Río, Cuba.

Sheila Honduras

Mamas side is between El Salvador and Honduras their last name is Villatoro which is not common the only people I ever hear r Villatoro look like my mama and her family all pretty white, except for my aunt who passed but did have something like their faces and features. I think they were from a place called el sauce in El Salvador. My bro met a lot of those people working in immigration law in LI

RAISE RAÍZ RAZE

this is the first tree
in our little family
as parts of our family tree fall
we have this actual tree
how long we will have it
we don't know

it is in the backyard of
the first house in our nucleus
in the larger family
there were others just a few
we just lost
the house in the bronx

we lost the women there
mi tía mi prima
two women too soon
we thought we weren't
losing in this pandemic
but then we lost

we talked so much shit
till they were gone
talked shit after
but it hurts it is all hurt
always and forever hurt

what we did
what we didn't do
to keep them here
did we not want them here
do we not want us here

tree losing branches
losing roots
we're too small
for this much of us to fall
we can't bear it

Maple in backyard, Freeport, Long Island, NY, November 2022. Photo: Sheila Maldonado

BUDDY SYSTEM

 Bar is dangerous

 You are running into danger  I will keep close to you

 You are in a dangerous position  I wish to communicate with you

 Stop carrying out your intentions and watch for my signals

 I have lost sight of you

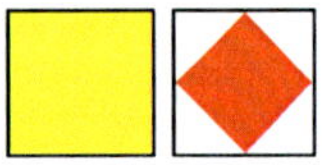 I cannot go ahead  It is dangerous to stop

 I cannot continue to search  I require assistance

 Keep clear of me; I am maneuvering with difficulty

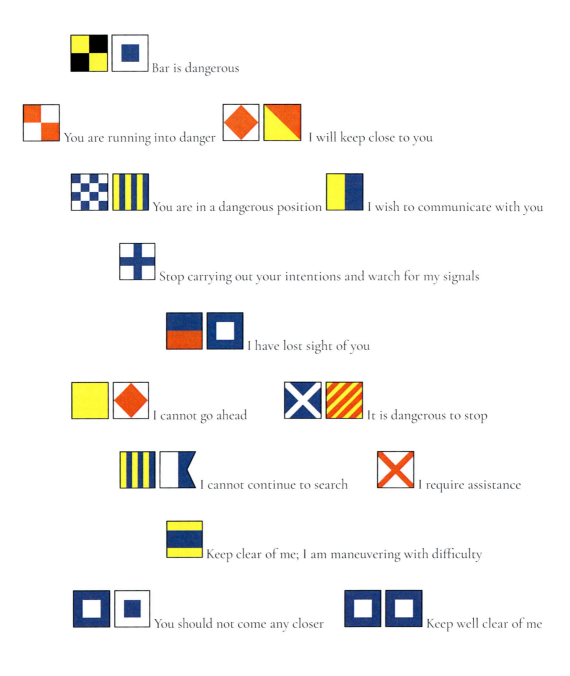

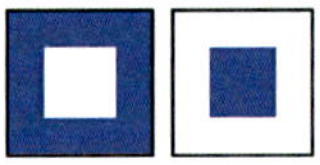 You should not come any closer  Keep well clear of me

 I am drifting  I am sinking

 Repeat the distress position

 I cannot save my vessel  I must abandon my vessel

 I am abandoning my vessel

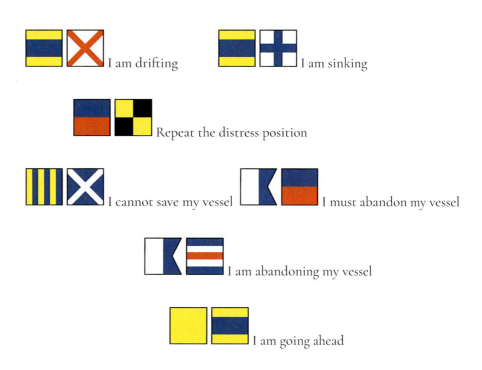

 I am going ahead

AN ENDLESS CYCLING OF WITNESS: CLAIMING ONE'S SELF, ONE POLAROID AT A TIME

The technical learning curve for operating a manual camera has always been hard for my brain to take on. For whatever reason, I just can't grasp the way a camera's machinery works. Part of it's my own resistance—I enjoy seeing the camera as a magic machine, whose inner workings I'll never fully know.

When I was ten years old, I was in love with taking photos. My mother gave me a Vivitar camera for my tenth birthday. I mostly used it to capture what I found beautiful—a lot of sunrises and sunsets, which I would see through the window of my mother's apartment (when my mother took custody of us, which was sporadic as she often canceled at the last minute). The 5x7s from the drugstore never brought to me the image I saw through the viewfinder, but in that space between what I had perceived and what was inked onto the print was an element of surprise that kept me engaged with the medium. The camera always gave me back magical accidents, and sometimes, every once in a while, it gave me back exactly what I'd hoped for.

There's something I find controlling about obsessing over the technical ways around a camera, something cold or even menacing. I don't want to invade the space of the camera, and penetrate all its body parts. I just want to build a relationship together, see what we make out of our union.

*

And then I met her. I'll refer to her as Beaches, because our love reminds me a little of CC and Hilary, which is not something I've thought until this precise moment.

Photography was the filter through which our entire relationship blossomed. We connected initially because she was interested in me as a subject to make photographic work of and through, and then our relationship unfurled like an ever-winding tulip, and wilted just as slowly. There was something about her, and something about the way that I responded to her, that brought me out of myself but also left me more grounded in my own sense of power and intimacy, all to be recorded by her camera.

She took me to a local beach town for my birthday. We ran in the sand, occasionally stopping so that she could take a Polaroid of me standing in front of her, my hair (long, then) sticking to my back and the sides of my face from the ocean and sweat, or so that I could take a Polaroid of her fingers rubbing wet muddy sand on her belly. My favorite photographs of that trip, and possibly of any that will ever exist of me, happened in our hotel room. I am sitting in a hotel chair, nude, my knees flattened against my chest, with only a string of blue beads around my neck.

The beads were a gift, but not from her. When we first arrived, she took me to a rundown shopping mall that seemed mostly deserted. As the doors shut behind us, she grabbed my hand and ran us into this small shop for African jewelry and housewares. The storeowner was a thin, older man from Ghana. His laugh was like a bell that rang against a piece of cardboard—sweet and scratchy. Oh, how he laughed about how wild my new paramour was. I felt shy to hear these stories—what else lurked behind the impulsivity and recklessness his stories implied?—and yet, I hungered to learn as much as I could while seeming nonchalant. There was a subtlety to the way he treated us as a couple, and I tried to hold my blush inside my skin. I didn't say anything. I just watched the two of them speak about the old days when she used to live here, and they, among others, would dance around a drum circle every weekend. He was asking her where she was going to take me, when he noticed my eye lingering on the blue beads behind him. She was going to buy them for me, and then he pulled them from where they hung on a nail in the wall, and gave them to me, with a wink. It was her idea to bring the beads into the photographs. Every time I wear them, I think of her.

In one Polaroid, my eyes are closed. In the other, they are wide open, vulnerable, ready to explore whatever will come. In both, the beads lay against my pale skin, soft daylight shining through their blue plastic orbs.

Beaches encouraged me to play with cameras, and it was through my time with her that I began to understand a little more about how cameras worked, just enough so that I could accomplish something that I wanted. She brought me to self portraits and double exposures, two frameworks that I would return to again and again, long after we parted ways. And I would be brought back to the Polaroid, after we fell apart, even as friends, when her need to possess my body and claim it through the lens was more important to her than us.

What is it about the relationship between artist and muse, maker and subject, that ties so closely with desire? How is it we learn, again and again, how destructive these connections are, and yet we can't see them when they're right in front of us? We would be connected while I collaborated with a friend on a dance production of Claudel and Rodin, and yet, still, I couldn't see its parallels right in front of me.

But, I suppose, we have to leave our mentors behind in order to discover who they truly are.

*

I began to seriously take Polaroids in the middle of the pandemic, newly recovering from a painful and traumatic divorce. The Polaroid I play with is one of the newest refurbished models from Polaroid Originals, which took over the old Polaroid line and updated them to adapt to this explosive technological age. My favorite of my collection has an app that you can use with

Bluetooth and that simulates manual shutter speeds. It has several settings, including one for multiple exposures. But that's not how I take double exposures on the camera. (I'll never tell.)

The old Polaroids were finicky enough, especially with light exposure, and my old faithful is no different. It is hard to take any photograph with daylight that's exposed properly, with or without the manual functions. It requires just the perfect set of circumstances to expose in a way that the viewer can see what I've shot a photo of properly. But, in the end, I've decided to use that to my advantage. It wouldn't be the first time.

Almost a decade ago, I lived in an apartment that had a magical relationship to Houston's light. One summer I set up a mirror under the windows and I would wake up at 5 am, and take a roll of self portraits through the mirror as the light began to creep onto the reflective glass. I would start to rewind the film and stop just before the film was completely rewound, and then I would shoot another roll of self portraits on top of it. I've never had that perfect light in any apartment since.

In some sense, it was a kind of chiaroscuro effect, or at least the attempt at one. And it's a similar effect that I seek in the self portraits I take on the Polaroid now. I see the Polaroid as a project in failure. Instead of fighting with the Polaroid for perfection (much like I do in my writing), I work with the camera as a kind of dance. Maybe I'll fall backwards just as they attempt to lift me. Maybe we'll turn in circles around each other awkwardly but with a certain charm. Maybe we'll fall into each other and ribbon ourselves in a duet and tumble to the ground, laughing hysterically. Or maybe something unexpected will happen when we encounter one another, something magical, something that shows us something new in one another.

The Polaroid is a place of failure, of accidents, and of play. With myself in this extended solitude, I take photos in the bathtub, while acoustic indie music falls over me, or in a little spot on my floor with a ring light, the same one I sometimes use for performances and readings on Zoom. Sometimes I take them lying on the floor, or on my stomach in my bed.

Sometimes I'm nude or fully dressed, or the nudity is kept just out of frame. Perhaps I've streaked facepaint across my skin or splattered it on my chest. Maybe my hands are draped in boxing gloves, or my face is concealed by a mask. I'm interested in seeing all the ways I can experiment with subjecthood, me staring through the camera, how the light can filter a new way of knowing with myself. Or the ways I can cultivate a different relationship to the face and body that have been captured by others in artistic possession, or sexual exploitation, or twinned voyeurism, or the number of other ways the physical fact of me has been used for others' intents.

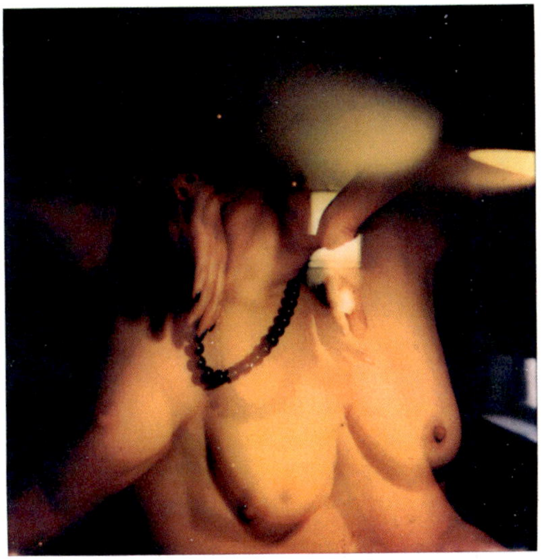

The first time I encountered the idea of a Polaroid as a teenager, it was in realizing that, through the Polaroid, a person (especially a woman or a person perceived as such) could be claimed. There is something about the object of the Polaroid—the weight, the border, the immediacy with which you hold it in your hand—that lends itself to a kind of possessive quality of whomever exists, frozen in time, in that little glass box. It occurs to me now that when we use the word Polaroid, it is interchangeable, referring both to the mechanism and the object it produces. It's been years since I let anyone photograph me the way that I let her. I'm not sure I ever will again. But, as for trying to reclaim the me that used to open for only her, I'm not sure I'll ever stop.

I've always had an itch to perform, but I'm terrified of the stage. When I talk to actors, they tell me they only feel powerful onstage. For me, it's the opposite. The white light disorienting and bright, the audience a sea of nobodies, it feels, to me, as if they have all the power, all the seeing, all the knowing. But here, in the safety of my home, with no one watching, I get to be whatever I want. Even if I share the object with millions of people after the fact, the act of it itself is no one else's. Just mine.

The primal scene is a perfect image for an ordinary absence of the subject at the very place where he comes into being—we are not present at our own conception. It is, however, the catastrophe of sibling displacement which occasions a retrospective imaginary perception of this unimaginable event. Hysteria protests this displacement, this absence of the subject.

—Juliet Mitchell

But, Juliet, what if we are present at our own conception? What if we are each to each, mirror to mirror?

I am tired of holding grief, a wet body for me to lug around.

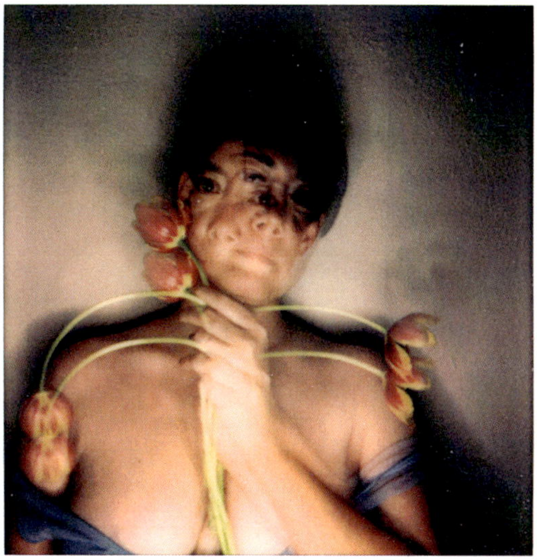

I offer the Polaroid an opportunity—to hold my grief, and to witness it. And for me to witness, alongside it, a different version of myself than I reveal to the world, or even to myself. An endless cycling of witness, that will hopefully lead me forward. I can't say where.

I. Cradle

We are plucking prickly cucumbers for this week's farm boxes, hoods up against the morning rain. Hoocąk and Amish orders we trade for strawberries. One meter between stakes threaded with rows of twine, broad leaves and cukes tangled up. Have I forgotten the sound of insects? Is humanist care-culture in the post-industrial state a response to ambient ecological collapse? Do the red cranes know? Tucked into the low places, decentralized, some of us are lighting candles in the green fog after a storm, grieving them, the spectres they're becoming.

Where is it we go—for example, into the rift like this? When the surge pushes across us in the field, we're brought closer to quiet, which is a kind of commitment to the forging of another world. Dream time is an origin account. There is a kind of accomplice to origin in the gap we're making (as in the cranes)—trances are more casual than we expect.

I am inside that willingness to be carried.

Sound stays this close.

Sound says emptiness is everywhere in the form of flowers, Wu-men says cut clean to kindred intimacy. Language like this induces a chemical clamor. Next, go to the packing house with a tub full of fruits from the creeping vine, introduce semaphore:

- Ethnography of drift ways (such as gardening and suddenly being blown open)
- "and" is the body talk of the end
- Plantationocene is one kind of measure
- The number of miscarriages in your household during the drought
- Cradle

II. Measure

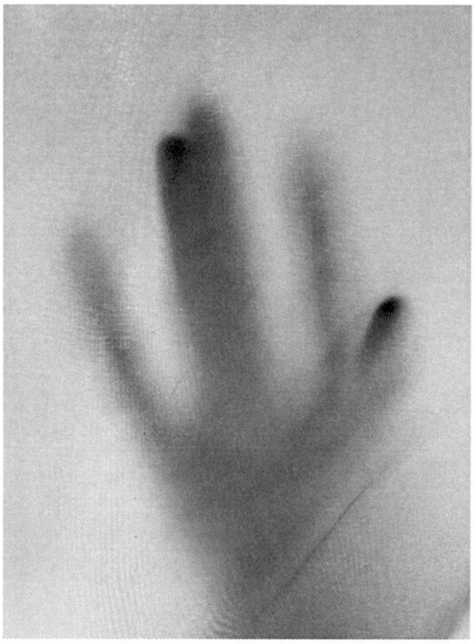

condition pay scale game it grunt according to according
to according to as if there's a harmonics gradation grace
i use some words like grace and abandon and their gravity
fuzzes off, ricochet. after work
one box said *i don't know what*
the fuck anyone means by care anymore in response
another box said *i'm thinking about pride and*
i'm thinking about recklessness where it goes when you leave
to be in solitude, affording it letting the rot get bigger
and bigger imagine yourself in adrift community
like this, but you're not fourteen
contracted for passage from karachi, or calcutta
to rake to bull whip to climb to plough and be ploughed
to mend to saw and haul old growth pine to mash cane, wheat, pulp—
what is your role now?
to walk toward the fire, to wield a maul with two hands
be the mudra
every day we etch our habits
a little deeper, a little more refined

III. Dig

ride, deciduous outlined in crud
it's this kind of shit i convince myself
makes the days bend back from themselves
makes that sound sustain though the machine clicks in wait
in suspension shit the blue black birds say, a hummingbird left behind into winter
makes me write a little meaner when softness is spilling at home
buttery lights in the cold morning, the monk leaking smells into blankets
i scuff pavement, avoiding people   divested gore of another city
i'm meaner and warmer, living in america—cut away,
this is a vehicle, reeking of signifiers. hollows me out with bass
from 3am until when its still going fingernails buffed, tapping the gear shift
pulse of the river, its straightening. the crust is soft and littered with birds, dead stuff
of autumn breath begets fog molded cumin left in a jar under the house, jug of
spoiled milk, the stale taste caste leaves in your memory,
tongue all around the waking—

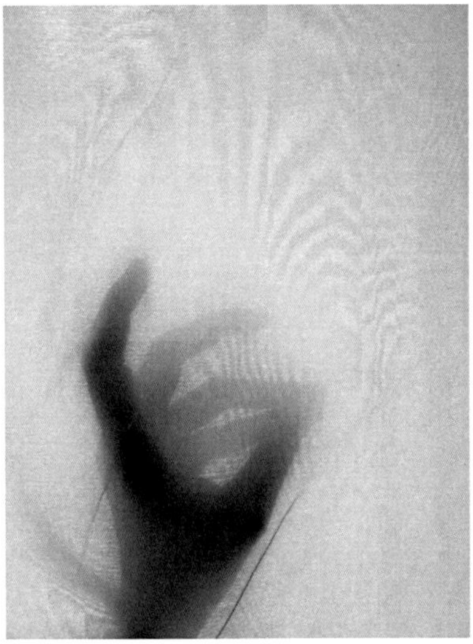

IV. Bone

Today, yesterday, the new moon. In cool humidity we rise, we plant. A comrade down the line marks an approximation of feet with a trowel, squatting. On a short row nearer the winding highway, I drop beads of coriander along ridges in furrowed earth, two fists' distance apart. Hands lay flat, curl fingers under. Inhaling flies. Twenty seeds, visible only for one year, dried. I dimple the soil, push fingers in. Merge lips of soil with palms. It's here on my knees, collapsing meeting loosely living matter, I feel my old pelvic wound in a new register. The limit edged into my body. Can we call this process healing, inhabiting a learned and yearning kind of ache. Stains of a document, stains of a flat touch finding density.

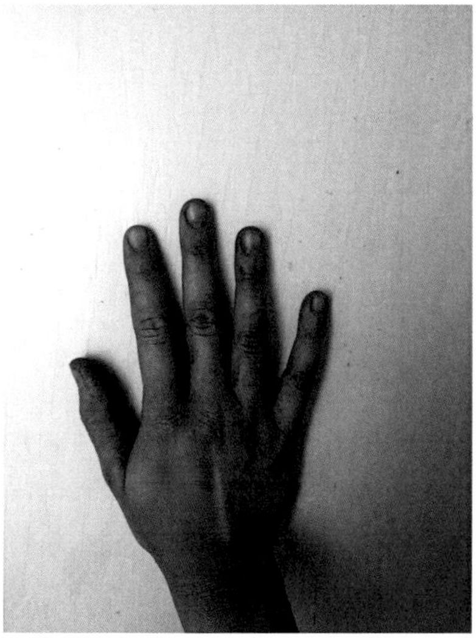

To remember being wiped down. An abstract gesture catalyzing plurality. Whose sensations are these, which scatter, leaving numinous fissures, indistinct and suffusing? Which sink and dissolve and interpenetrate? Where does this live? Arching my back, I encounter a future here with my body that becomes the field—it emerges as we plant turnips. This is to say, we must resist containment.

V. Almanac

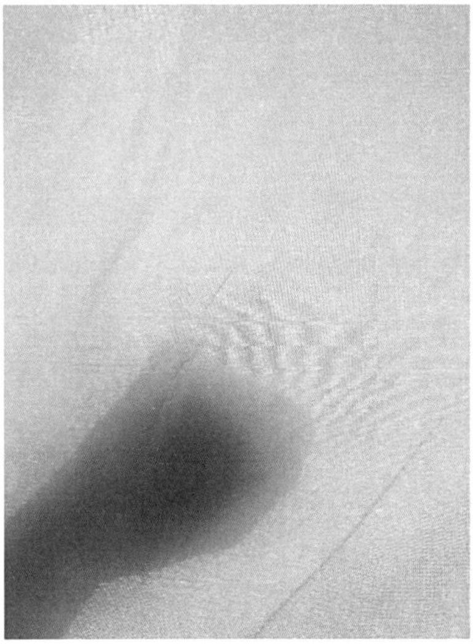

someone illuminated mercury this evening from her steaming room full of books, glossy images of her daughter who holds a smile behind her back she said walk backwards through a doorway throating open your question—mercury is a planet of thresholds and you will receive your answer she said, *i'm just grateful.* someone said we are chickens scratching for our questions, opening rough openings meanwhile i forget where i am that's a theme in my writing: you could be anywhere, and that is dharma, or something. there are beads in my mouth and i forget they are teeth i try to spit them out so i don't choke there's a bottle, there's a lace runner across the table, there's the policed places these objects emerged from the portal is anywhere i fall deeper into what cannot find form without access to its edges. it makes me boil losing my teeth ball a fist my skin runs dry. do you recognize this loneliness? we've been enduring for so long that we've forgotten how to surrender, forgotten the revolution of the planet of heartbrokenness.

VI. Crowd

Dear M,
I am washing the bowl and wondering why I have only one bowl to eat from. The bowl is round, tapered, empty, glazed. It sounds clean, slipping across my dried out palms. I'm using a guide to write this poem to you, and to a bowl you may have eaten out of at one of our gatherings. It's eggshell blue. The guide instructs me to depart: So, on a walk, after a crying morning, T says, *and here in the jargon we fetishize the object into a closed circuit*—a cylinder of metal pushing out another little cylinder of metal, very fast, two metal pieces—getting deeper into the object, deconstructing the object, until there's / nothing / left / but / to add more to the object and its containment. Dampening locks. Limited magazine capacity. Meanwhile the names of those murdered by the unrelenting path of white power go on and on, unceasingly. I ignored the part of my guide where I am supposed to ask a question. And everyday I work on someone else's book, my book, a memorial to hundreds of thousands of lives cut short by incarceration or state sanctioned erasure. We talk about the book as a semaphore, a ceremonial presencing—a kintsugi, lacing a broken thing and its disjointings with gold, or a molten alloy foiled with gold leaf, along the pathways of shatter, sealing the fragments together again. Writing to you, M, a tensile suffering ribbons into the breeze. To gather the power we took from pain, a dependency upon pain, to bundle it up and give it back to source. When I remember this touch, I can shatter into relief.

VII. Send

But I'll try. I will try.
The world wakes and I offer quiet, witness, preparedness to step deeper into the rain and the river. To let the dust run down from my back and feed the mites and the spores. Can I say I give the world of flies and mold something to incubate within and eat from? The world of mushrooms? My oblique offering—humans and egg-laying insects, those decomposers who aren't yet metabolizing toxins. What else could I give, what else do I feed the world? An assurance that in this moment here together I will not neglect you. Still, I clamber away on the tide, never to be seen on this shore, against this mattress on the sidewalk again. I may never find you or you me, but here you spill forth on these pages. The world braided, dangling humidly, lank and warped. Indecipherable. Most hours the world offers sky's abundant advance—today, rain, the dove wingbeating over our heads. Maybe it's a loosened memory that marks a spill—our tongues and shoulders unbuckled, our abdomens furry and rolling with microbes, the flowers we lose ourselves in. Anza-Borrego, grasses ripping at the edges of a baseball field, in a prairie when the stillborn's ashes sprout something livid, fire-sown, in the earth. We make pots from this clay. We cook for each other in the pots made of this clay. I am my guts and I am not, loving them. My coil thick with flies and all the harms I've caused, piping in, underwater. Boiling the water, another gut that feels far more inevitable than my own body. One reckoning with surrender acknowledges a limit's edge, an exhausting of boundaries, tearing from under (an archaeology). Weaken the form. The land under the grasses goes cold with endurance, big and subdued. I try to get there with you, to eat with you, but food is a dungeon,
a trade wind, an infanticide, or a manufactured
surplus to create scarcity.
I stumble. But
I'll try. I will try.

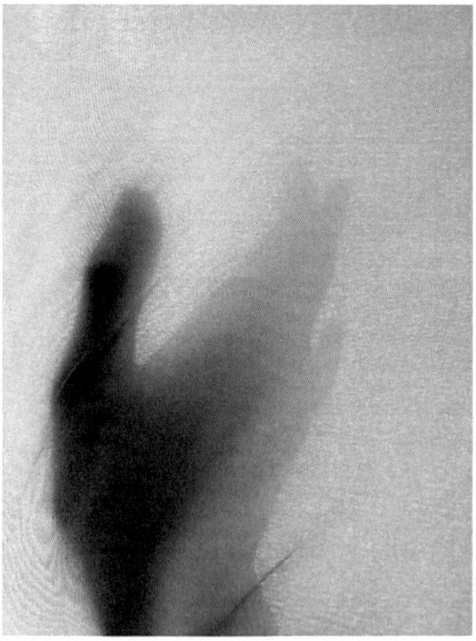

[FROM] DEAR MEMORY

VICTORIA CHANG

Waitress
1. Make tea
2. Vacuum
VOL. 256
34.00'
16695.66
96405.81
96113.54
Amount due at closing
Excess funds collected at clos
Prepaid Costs (Credit Report
Cancellation charges (Check
Cancellation charges (No
from expense.)
INVENTOR.
Fu-Shueng Chang
BY John R. Faulkner
John J. Roethel
ATTORNEYS
499 Schoo
S LINE 125.02
Placemat
Egg roll
5. Pinapples
6. Pints(500
7. Quarts(4
Remarks
The birthday was change
from April 6, 1940
on April 1, 1954
TEL
334997
516404
518766
AS THAT WHIC
CHOICE BUT T
TRANSACTION
MINATED AND
E VERY MU
PICACHO RESERVOIR
Picacho
Newman Pk
Picacho Pk
LY TO RAY
TY-COUNTY
LLECTION
李玉燕
灣省桃園縣
Mack Ave
楊
辦法之規
2-STORY
FRAME
F BSMT
#1135
DRAGOON INN
MAIN
FIRE AND ALLIE
ED AGAINST
FELICITY
68 I GWO
CRAFT CORPORATION
LOTS
Ford
STATE OF
MICHIGAN
Dept. of
Taxation
NOV-9'77
INSPECT
OD SERVICE
PRELIMINA

Dear Silence,

I wrote in the margins of my notebook: *What are you doing? What's at stake here? Why are you skirting around things? Why are you circling around and around, afraid to go into the center?* I think I am circling around you, Silence, your center, and the closer I get, the closer I am to shame, to the language of shame.

The center could be the *rack* that Mary Ruefle speaks of in her book *Madness, Rack, and Honey*. The *torment, pain, torture* of what *poetry does to the world, what poets do with words, and what words will do to a poet*. I don't think, though, that Ruefle meant that we should only write about painful life experiences or feelings, but rather that we should write to put language at risk. I like that: *What words will do to a poet.*

Do I want to risk going into you in order to come out with words? To let the words build into something that is no longer me? Can I be the hawk and the storm that tries to kill the hawk? Am I willing to write about the dead? Will the language that I make murder me?

In our house, loud language was everywhere—bundles of Mandarin from Mother's mouth, Father's nearly perfect English but Taiwanese-accented Mandarin. Then our Chinglish. But in our house, silence arranged itself like furniture. I was always bumping into it. When unrelated aunties and uncles came over for dinner parties, I envied the laughing as they drank Riunite wine, ate steaming fish and tofu. When they left, they took all the words. What was left after their laughter was always my grief.

I didn't know what was wrong so each night I prayed to God, but God just gave me tomorrow. Eventually, I stopped praying because I realized that God and I did not speak the same language.

Last night, I went to the talent show at the children's school. Kids dressed as sharks running around in circles. Popular girls with matching ripped jeans and long flat-ironed hair singing pop songs and dancing unenthusiastically. A magic show, piano players, ukulele players, joke-tellers...

Then a boy got up and the music began. He sang "Never Enough" from the film *The Greatest Showman*. I didn't remember the song or the film, but his opening breath was so quiet, it was Ruefle's *rack*. That was poetry. I think that is why I write. That is why I want to make art.

After he finished to a standing ovation, I remembered that this was the boy who was recently outed at school. This small seventh-grader sent his insides out, through his mouth, in small envelopes.

I am seeking whatever is painful in my body, whatever is joyful. While seeking, I may never find myself. While seeking, I have no idea what form I may take or whether anyone, including myself, will ever like what I write. Most of writing feels like walking in the dark. I'm reminded of what Donald Barthelme said: *The writer is that person who, embarking upon her task, does not know what to do.*

Recently, during a reading, the poet Valzhyna Mort said, *Lacking language is the beginning of a poem to me.* This is what writing feels like to me too. In some ways we are coming out of silence to make a new language. This making comes out of a deep desire to understand something that is invisible and voiceless.

Do you know that Jeanette Winterson cast this generative uncertainty of creative practice in terms of time in *Art Objects: Essays on Ecstasy and Effrontery*:

> *My work is rooted in silence. It grows out of deep beds of contemplation, where words, which are living things, can form and re-form into new wholes. What is visible, the finished books, are underpinned by the fertility of unaccounted hours. A writer has no use for the clock. A writer lives in an infinity of days, time without end, ploughed under.*

Writing feels like being within you, silence, and then emerging, bronzed. Somehow, writing feels more related to beginnings than endings. Writing feels outside of time. In a windowless room. Not in a room at all. In a state of being half-awake and half-possessed. In an endless snowstorm, *ploughed under*. Alone. As I reach for memory that has become extinct.

Dear Silence, how do I enter you, seeking answers, but come out writing into and toward ambiguity? How do I *live the questions*, as Rilke says in *Letters to a Young Poet*. How many times have I looked so hard for someone's eyes to catch mine that I disappeared? That feels like writing. That feels like living the question.

It's not that the boy's voice sits within me now. It's the bird his voice became that I now seek. I am trying to make birds out of silence. Birds that will fly away, that I will never see die.

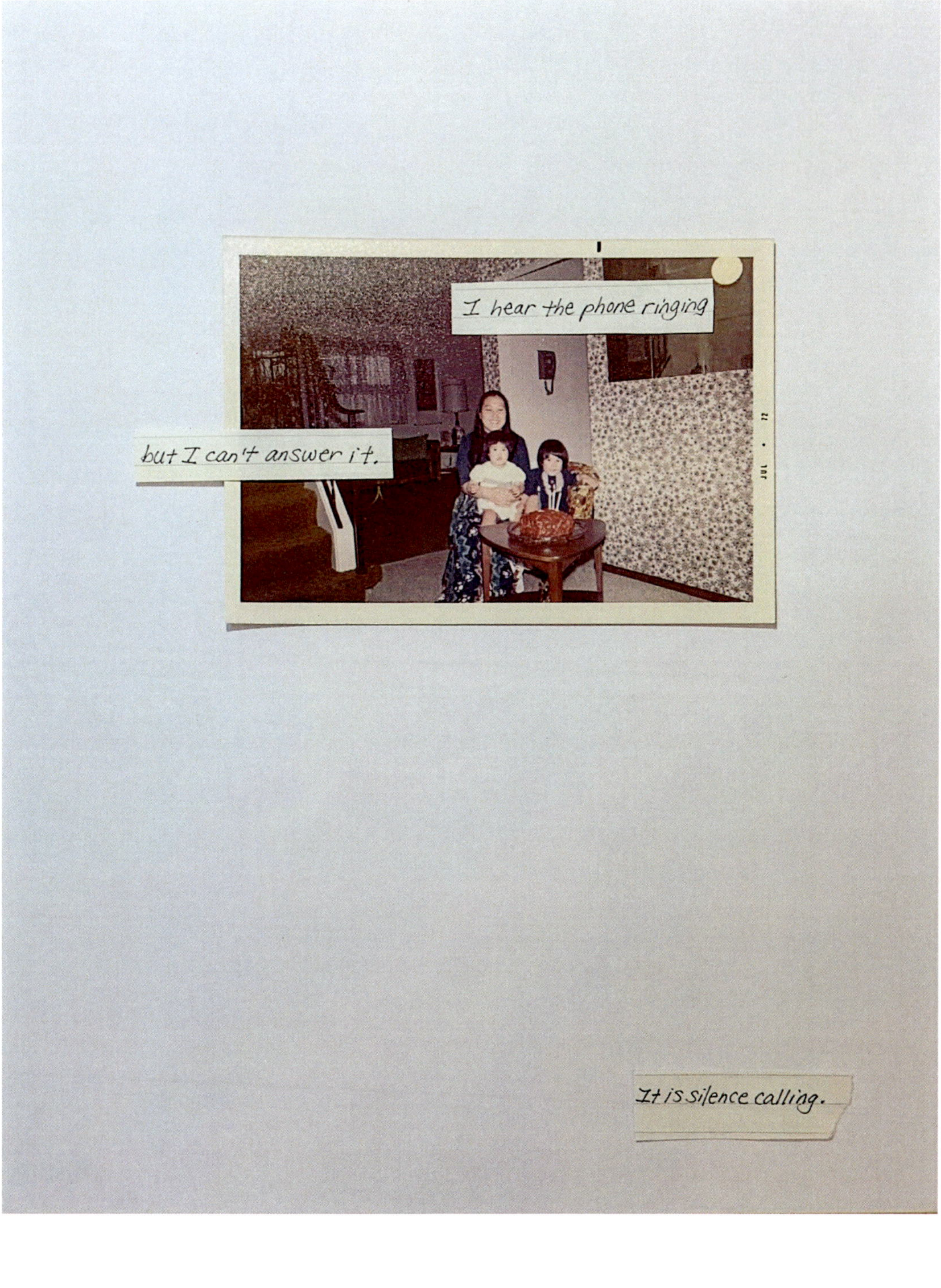
I hear the phone ringing
but I can't answer it.
It is silence calling.

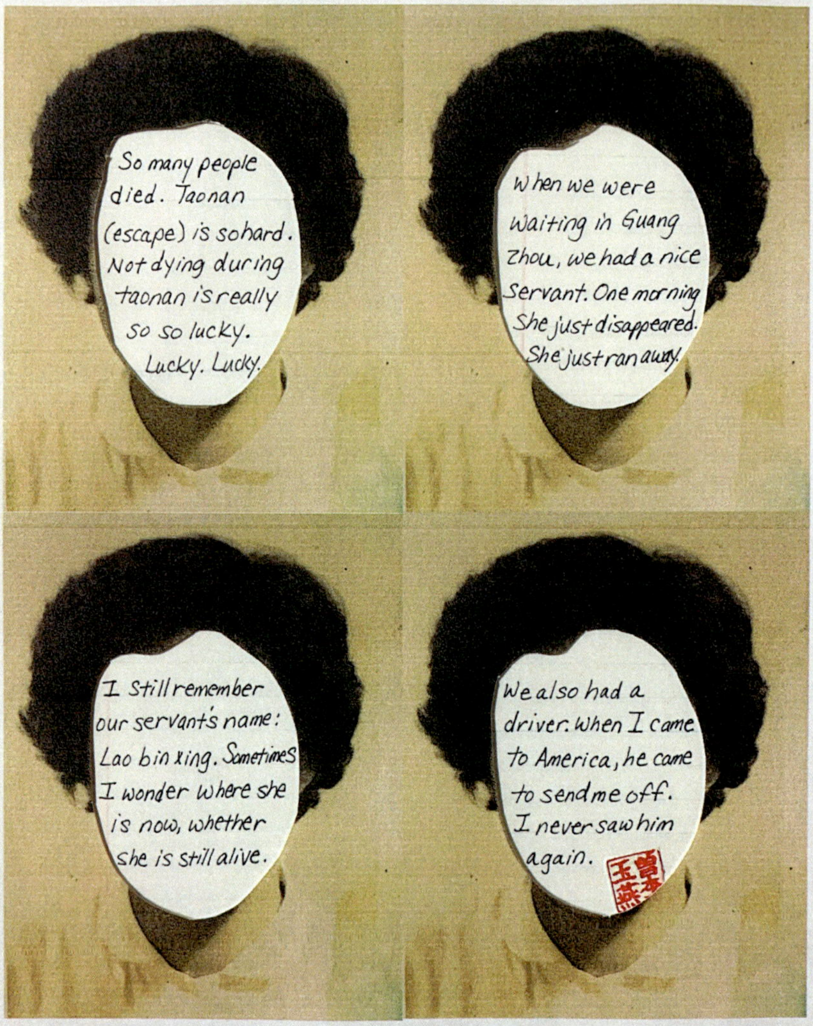

So many people died. Taonan (escape) is so hard. Not dying during taonan is really so so lucky. Lucky. Lucky.
When we were waiting in Guang Zhou, we had a nice servant. One morning she just disappeared. She just ran away.
I still remember our servant's name: Lao bin xing. Sometimes I wonder where she is now, whether she is still alive.
We also had a driver. When I came to America, he came to send me off. I never saw him again.

1. What if my stories are
   somewhere else,
   with others who are dead?

2. I always cut too hard,
   and what's left is an

3. outline. What remains
   in my hands are
   someone else's memories,

4. something severed.
   At some point, we will

5. kill everything, but the
   memories will be the
   only living thing.

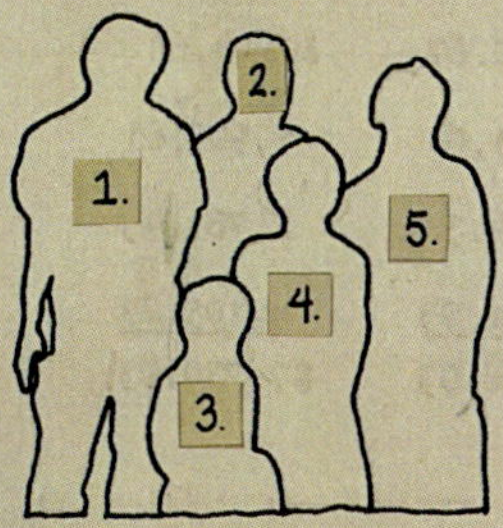

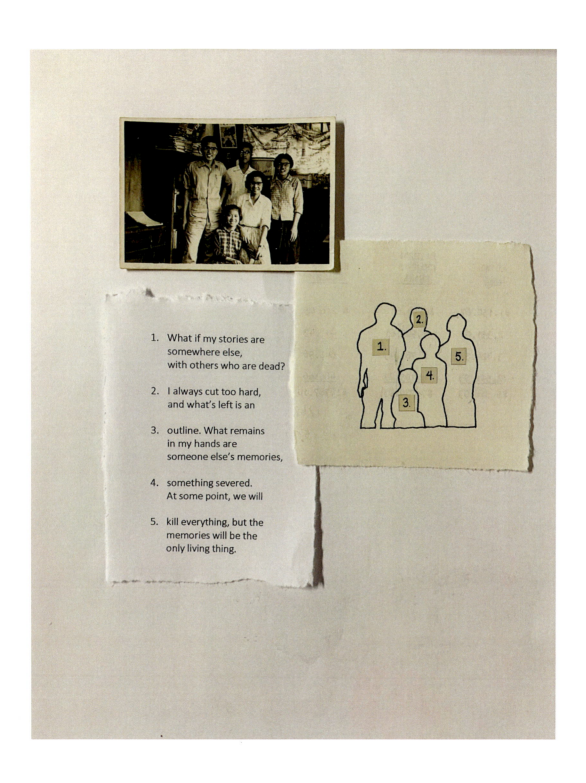

Addie Tsai *[p.281]*

I was born hybrid. Not just as an AppalAsian born to parents from separate cultural spheres—my mother a white woman from Nashville, Tennessee and my father who fled with his family from Nanjing, China in the late 1940s to live in Taiwan—but also as a mirror twin, the name for twins for whom the egg splits late (if it were to split any later, the twins would be born conjoined), which results in the twins being born with mirroring features. It shouldn't have been such a surprise to me, then, that my gender and sexuality would also live on liminal planes, as a queer non-binary person unable to ever live comfortably within any one realm of existence or identity. It is from all of these swirling environments I came of age as an artist in the '90s, at a time when hybridity and interdisciplinary art was actively discouraged, resisted, or even feared. I'm thankful that we now make and receive art at a time in which the literary and arts world is slowly catching up to the porousness between generic boundaries, which has freed me (at least somewhat) from the previous constraints of the publishing world.

"An Endless Cycling of Witness: Claiming One's Self, One Polaroid at a Time" represents just one facet of my engagement with hybridity—in this case, that which lives between photography, self-expression, and writing. My relationship to photography is deeply wedded to my understanding of my queerness, as well as my self-conception as a twin, and it is through those poles that I wanted to explore the physical fact of the Polaroid, as well as its imperfections as a medium. I'm most interested in the fissures and cracks and textures that can come to the foreground between the interplay of mediums like text and image, and how each language can inform or create tension with the other. Just like my own body, hybridity isn't comfortable or pristine but, through its dance, moves our understanding into new dimensions.

Alley Pezanoski-Browne *[p.221]*

Eve was a Black American who lived in the United States before it was a country. We know about her today only because of her proximity to white people deemed important by historians. From them we know she *belonged* to Peyton Randolph, called *a father of America*, someone who said that "no one man should have so much power" when he abdicated the presidency to George Washington. His wife ultimately sold Eve in a document signed by James Madison, the last evidence of Eve in the white historical record.

Eve has lingered with me along with the few details I know about her: The fact that she was educated to be Randolph's wife's companion. That she and her son ran away during the Revolutionary War, but were later captured. It struck me that the things we know about her life are only scraps of information. We know nothing about what she thought or felt. But nonetheless she exists to this day as a ghost in the text to complicate the official narrative and to stir up questions about how much else is missing from the record.

I am compelled to make collages and risograph prints about Eve and to tell of her through materials, because of this sense of lack, of having to collect scattered pieces. Re-enactments, illustrations, replicas, approximations. While knowing little about her, she is important to me. The piece in this collection is an experiment to find her in multiple mediums, because words mostly fail to.

Anna Martine Whitehead *[p.63]*

These collages are maps of prisons. I've been interviewing women, femmes, and queers around the United States about the experience of journeying inside prison. When I ask them to tell me how they remember it, it is impossible to separate their emotions—the anxiety, the fear, the excitement—from the architecture itself. Every metal detector, locker, and officer's desk carries an emotional weight, and when they tell the story of their journeys inside, hallways and walls distend and contort around memory.

Prisons, and their waiting rooms, are dramatic, emotional, chaotic, and familial. They are strikingly Black, brown, and homosocial. These spaces exist in reality—I've spent countless hours in them. But they also exist in the abstract, as places which, in the words of one of my interviewees, make "blatantly clear that this is what we have... All we really have is each other."

As I continue working on *FORCE! an opera in three acts*, a sprawlingly Black queer opera about femmes who wait, it strikes me that the voices of actual women, femmes, and queers—not characters or archetypes, but actual human beings—should be present, too.

These collages are my attempt to bring life to what these folks remember.

Arianne True *[p.125]*

The pieces included in this collection are from a completed (but at the time of writing, still unpublished) manuscript called *exhibits*. That collection is a series of experimental poems that bring you through a museum exhibition, and the poems are reading you as much as you're reading them. The museum engages with how the experience of childhood trauma doesn't end when you turn eighteen: the effects ripple, even for decades, finding new ways to manifest and asking to be healed. Given the history of Natives and American museums, the museum form is also a perfect place to repatriate a stolen body, and the artist in the collection hopes to do just that across the course of the work.

I started writing the pieces that would eventually become *exhibits* when I was up on a deadline for new work but couldn't generate anything. My brain was struggling and would not cooperate with making anything, so instead I experimented with ways to creatively destroy and repurpose things (text, image, ideas). It was all I could do with where I was at the time, and over the next five years this practice kept expanding and finding new corners of the museum to fill out, and took on a lot of new forms. The pieces here are all from the first section of the book, and specifically within that the first gallery in the museum, though the whole project itself has three very different sections.

I had to learn new techniques for writing to finish a more cohesive narrative work across a whole book's length, and I had to keep growing alongside the work to get it all to the place it wanted to be. I love this project for all it's taught me and all it's let me do and explore, and especially for the time I got to turn the entire manuscript into an immersive multimedia installation (you could walk around inside the book!) with massive support from the Seattle Repertory Theater as their first Native Artist-in-Residence. I felt so held by the poems.

Please enjoy your brief stay in the museum.

Aya Bram *[p.189]*

"Labyrinth" was created in a kind of trance, during a mixed-mood bipolar episode. When I'm in mixed-mood and manic states it feels like my limbs are full of too much electricity, rushing around through my veins, making me restless. Too energetic in my body, yet dull in my mind, I use asemic writing as a way to process the electricity into art. I don't fully remember making this piece. I taped up paper on my bedroom wall, got a bottle of ink and a dip pen, and went to work. I remember feeling trapped in my mind, and that is the closest I can get to an intention.

Asemic writing is what I turn to when my ability to understand language fails. I struggle to read and write when in bipolar episodes, lacking either the focus or energy required to sit with and understand language. These long periods of not being able to understand written words would make me feel lost, like a part of myself was broken away, leaving me expressionless. I started using asemic writing as a way to combat the loss of language, and in this way, asemic became the language of my bipolar episodes.

There are places in "Labyrinth" where the English language slips through the asemic. Spots where my hand was compelled in a kind of automatic writing. In this way, the work is hybrid: language and not language. But it is also a hybrid of consciousness, where I slipped in and out of awareness. I can remember flash moments of making this piece, but these are out of body memories, where I see myself standing at the wall with the pen in my hand. They are false memories, formed from listening to my former partner describe what he witnessed while I made "Labyrinth." Or, they are nonlinear memories, formed from an actual out-of-body experience I had during the creation of the piece. I'm not really sure. I do know that "Labyrinth" feels like something that came from another world.

Ayesha Raees *[p.255]*

If we could hold our eyes in our hands and observe where the gaze lands, the camera will come into reckoning. The moment it is lifted, the body holds in the breath and waits until the subject falls towards the perfect posture, sometimes against or towards an external power (light! action! object!). The finger then presses the button, a trigger, and shoots. There is a violence in the language of capturing photographs which mimics the constant violence of surveillance in the rupture of ideological obedience asked from the world by the world. In this case, in New York City, the landscape is a making of human bodies finding home in both repulsion and attraction in other human bodies. In the homogeneity of crowds, there is both visibility and invisibility.

I can cry on the pavement. You can die on the pavement. There is a man in a suit. There is a man with a revolver. All these images I witnessed were found inside me through the body of the camera I lifted and shot through.

I talk about the nature of photography because it gave me both wings and shield. I had an excuse to stand still and stare, be astounded from the movement of interaction and isolation in front of me all in the name of observation, and find in it all solace, knowledge, care, and ultimately—poetry.

When I look back at these photographs, some digital, some analogue, I find in them a vastness of an unsaid experience. The photographs have gone through a test of time. Afterall, I had captured them in early 2021, during the pandemic, and edited and printed them a year after. From a moment of observation to holding it as an object in my hand, there was a weight asking for mass.

A language asking for comprehension.

In this asking, I found myself in the realm of hybridization. To create a partial space where two mediums collide in great asking for they are unable to breathe in just one.

These photographs, with poetry, both in Urdu or English, hold that asking: where does your gaze land? What occurs in a realm of comprehension? Unreadability? And how much did you pause, breath held, in your own kind of askings?

Carolina Ebeid *[p.15]*

However a work begins for me, whether with a phrase, a rhythm, a moving image in the mind, a concept, the glossing of a single word, it takes root in the pages of a notebook. What a porous surface that ends up being, holes or openings, fits and starts that make possible the development of a poem. So hybrid by nature, the notebook; I find a certain "notebook energy" propelling (or vexing) my poems into being. I lean into that restlessness by assembling the poem, the multiform poem, as it locates its wholeness spreading to more than one place—a verse, an essay, a book, a performance, a video, a sound.

For example, "She Got Love: a circle of spells for Ana Mendieta" started as notes on a butcher paper scroll. These were lines, drawings, rings of words in Spanish and English. I wanted to write about the letter O, its origin as the Phoenician pictograph of the eye, how it squints out of the word no, how that word relates to the life and work of Mendieta, how there was no "eye witness" at her horrific and untimely death. Every morning I returned to the scroll-writing; cross-legged on the floor, it became a ritual, along with chants and meditations. This lends me an understanding of what performance space might be. I wanted to make something at once analog and digital. I made stop motion animation sketches, I recorded a dance, collected videos from my phone, I curved the lines into circles, semicircles, slivers that took on the circular motions of the scroll-paper itself. "Say something about the method of composition itself," says Walter Benjamin, "how everything one is thinking at a specific moment in time must at all costs be incorporated into the project then at hand." We are grateful to Keith Waldrop for his translation.

Cindy Juyoung Ok *[p.151]*

Both my works came from thinking about language as landscape and landscape as language. "Translator" spells out a Korean phrase that literally means "does not even make words," but more commonly signifies "does not make sense," something like: no way. I wrote the text years ago thinking about the oddities of two languages unnoticeable to anyone living only in one of them; it was then a kind of coda to another work, and I was thinking about my role translating for my family. In practicing literary translation more recently, I began to understand the text as its own work. I was curious about what senses are created and refused in thinking of characters, letters, and words as shapes themselves, and used my own handwriting to fill. "Before the DMZ" I also wrote in its first form a long time ago but could not resolve at the time. It discusses a border that separates my family members and horizons my understanding of space, but also addresses my own estrangement from the country, having grown up in the U.S.. Imagining the DMZ as a gap in language, a visual lack of story, helped me finish the piece. I had taken a workshop with Diana Khoi Nguyen in which we explored the aesthetic possibilities of text as image, and both these works emerged from the technical skills she generously shared.

Daisuke Shen + Vi Khi Nao *[p.243]*

Vi wanted to watch a queer Asian film, but was limited in her Criterionness in Boulder. Daisuke was trying to trans-characterize the ethos of queerasianness. And, it was Fall and the leaves were turning yellow and red and time was imminent and Daisuke wrote their sections while gazing out at the two unused barbeque grills outside of their window in Brooklyn. Eventually, Daisuke gave Vi access to the Criterion landscape through the-beast-must-be-killed password, which led them to watching *Funeral Parade of Roses*. Vi commented on the exquisiteness of the main character Eddie's non-gendered buttcheeks and the book came together within a short period of approximately three months? Their intention was to write the continuation of Eddie's life while preserving the nakedness of the dried tofu after it wore really sexy Chinese underwear. Eventually, they ended up writing the continuation of many peoples' lives, including Tony Leung. They both wrote when their car's literary headlights were mostly turned off, and the view of the nocturnal landscape of the narration was ambushed with intermittent darkness. They were compelled by the unknown, not only of the materiality of the language but also the materiality of its direction. There was a lot of trust. Vi trusted that Daisuke would take them to a literary place that had not been explored, and they would not leave Vi in the mountains without any beef jerky, jackfruit chips, or coconut water. Due to the intensity of the process' unknownness, Daisuke and Vi's book unfolded organically without boxing gloves or TESticuLAr wheels. Its hybridity was born from biomorphing the quotidian exchanges between Vi and Daisuke, and ecologicizing the texture of their existence into the manuscript so that both worlds (fiction and poetry / photography and numbers) did not feel isolated or cannibalized in their contemporary diction and medium.

DESVELADAS (MACARENA HERNANDEZ, NELLY ROSARIO, SHEILA MALDONADO) *[p.265]*

"Arbographies/Arbografías" grew one leaf at a time. The story of these collaborative tree dispatches by the desveladas collective stretches from New York City to deep-south Texas, entangled not only by history but by ancestral stories rooted throughout the Americas—Honduras, Mexico, Dominican Republic, and the United States. Comprising desveladas are a poet, a multimedia journalist, and a fiction and prose writer. Our individual relationships to specific tree species helped ground visual conversations about the overlaps and gaps in our hyphens, hyphens sprouted from shared family histories of migration and displacement, as well as from our work in multiple genres and languages. Though planted in different places, we come from peoples who commune with trees. "Arbographies/Arbografías" is the outgrowth of our transplanted cuttings, fragments of *desvelada* conversations late into the night, pruned and trimmed to the nodes where our roots connect. We wrote. We walked. We photographed. We mapped. We planted. And the trees spoke back as ébano and ceiba, Montezuma cypress and maple. We found new eyes, reconsidered what we took for granted, felt Nature as belief, heard the land speak like blood. Our senses, and our sense of what we were taught, were upended. We remembered when we thought we didn't.

DIANA KHOI NGUYEN *[p.181]*

Every year around the time of the anniversary of my brother's death, I revisit the family portraits where my brother cut himself out. These cutout photographs have become a kind of ancestor that I treat as if part of my ritual practice with an ancestor altar. That is to say, I carefully and tenderly hold space and time with the images, then pour myself in thought into the literal spaces of the photograph. This one particular year, I reflected on the act of tracing around one's body in order to remove it from its frame and context. Instead of doing this with a physical blade, as my brother did, I used a lasso tool in an image editing program, zooming into the collective body of the family. When I finished tracing around our family shape, I hit "delete," expecting an instant erasure, for a white void to fill in the space I had traced. Instead, and somewhat remarkably, the family faces and bodies disappeared, but instead of white space replacing those bodies, the background material filled in. So, in this case, bamboo filled in where the family had been, the stucco wall replicated itself, and so on. It was so uncanny but also feels very true to how things move on—the landscape continues to grow or exist, regardless of whether or not the living bodies are there anymore. Which is to say—I never proceed in the writing / making process consciously thinking about hybridity; instead, my practice revolves around life emotions and actions done because they feel essential—in my constantly evolving grief for my deceased brother, I return to the altar of where his absence is, and try to look and listen carefully in that liminal space; this often involves then entering physically into the photographic archive in some way. To find where I might speak, where language might emerge in the rupture and new layers.

DIVYA VICTOR *[p.35]*

Curb began at the interstice of two disciplines—book arts and poetry—and intervenes into conversations about composition, authorship, and solidarity enacted across identity lines. Its very first iteration in the world (2019) was a collaboration between me and Aaron Cohick. In Aaron's words, it is a "fine press/ artists' book" created "from the convergence between documentary poetics and the possibilities of structure and legibility in the handmade book." The formal concerns about structure and legibility enact descriptions and activate questions for me:

How does it feel to walk your own neighborhood as a perpetual stranger?
How does it feel to be disoriented in your own home?
Why are our ways of knowing tethered to (keeping/losing) our bearings?
What are the paths we take to return our bodies to ourselves?
Who are we when we are (at) home?

My early work with Aaron set the stage for enacting further collaborations that would be hosted in an expansive and intentionally designed webspace called *Curb(ed)*: divyavictorcurb.org. It includes an experimental, minimalist documentary using Google satellite imaging, created by Los Angeles-based artist and writer Amarnath Ravva.

Amarnath Ravva's *American Canyon* introduced me to fine new textures of text-image relationships in representations of South Asian diasporic life, particularly in the contexts of mourning and grief. His book informed how I thought about the role of photographs, images, archival facsimile, and poetry in my previous book, *Kith* (2017). I wanted his sensitive dedication to the tether between the environmental and the sentimental to be registered in *Curb*'s life as well, because I found his questions about ritual, sensation, attention, and memory to be important and eternal. His video quilts, occasioned by *Curb(ed)*, suggest, for me, the co-existence of macro and micro attentions within the phenomenological experience of natural and built spaces, which resists the abstractions of digital satellite imaging technologies that shape diasporic communication and movement. His works here are the tender and attentive responses to the question "What are the paths we take to return our bodies to ourselves?"

Gabrielle Civil *[p.101]*

"Ineffable Intangible Sensation"

. . . .

. . . . Yesterday in my workshop in a swamp in Florida, we wore matching yellow T-shirts like at a family reunion and described photographs from memory in our notebooks. We created a video of us dancing to the sound of "Silk"—not the '90s jam "Freak Me," because that would be NSFW and the youngies don't know it anyway, but the ringtone on my phone timer which always ended our writing prompt sessions. We read all our writing aloud at the same time following a practice I first learned a decade ago in Miguel Gutierrez' "INEFFABLE INTANGIBLE SENSATIONAL" workshop at Defibrillator (DFBRL8R) in Chicago, a city where I don't live (and I don't live in Florida either). We put our sounding in conversation with a paragraph from Tina Campt's *Listening to Images*, which is a wonder but also a funny thing—I hadn't actually planned to bring this into the workshop. The program coordinator, moving materials into Canvas, dropped a PDF of the intro into our site by mistake or happy accident or grace: how "sound consists of more than what we hear. It is constituted primarily by vibration and contact and is defined as a wave resulting from the back-and-forth vibration of particles in the medium through which it travels" (Campt 7). As I reflect on my own practice of writing and performing, vibration and contact crystallize. And isn't this hybrid writing? Living and creating memory and landscape, traveling and teaching, description and movement, image and text, video and dance, the critical and the creative, togetherness, being somewhere else, tuning into the frequency, accepting the gift, interweaving, connecting, and fusing . . . .

Gabrielle Civil (in conversation with Anna Martine Whitehead) *[p.113]*

Perhaps no other medium of communication represents the pandemic moment better than Zoom, as everything from remote work to political organizing to poetry readings to family meetings and wedding celebrations switched over to this internet video conference platform. On Zoom, my interviews for *Black Motion Pictures* were both intimate one-on-one affairs and displaced virtual encounters. While the resulting Zoom videos highlight resilient Black sociality, the Zoom interview transcripts arrive as curious documents full of time signatures, ellipses, erratic capitalization, and relentless repetition of speaker names. Rather than smooth this all over, many of these elements remain preserved in this excerpt. For me, this idiosyncratic, hybrid style becomes a fitting testament to how deeply mediated we were by technology and the glitchy strangeness of the time.

May new hybrid forms of Black performance dreams continue to arrive . . .

Imani Elizabeth Jackson *[p.27]*

This suite includes one slightly broken contrapuntal—which I think of as a set of sounding lines dropped and braided in the Atlantic—and four views of the ocean floor.

Over the past few years I have been working in several ways with the word hydrography, which literally breaks down to "water-writing" and which I sometimes attempt quite literally. Hydrography is also a scientific field of surveying bodies of water. An associated word is sound, which etymologically splits its root and meaning to intimate both one's ears/hearing and particular bodies of water/their measurement. I've been particularly interested in the act of depth sounding, or measuring the ocean's depths. As I understand it, these measurements were historically taken by weighting a heavy line and casting it into the sea. One would then mark the length of the rope as it settled to the ocean floor. That process has changed as technology has developed, and is now done mostly with sonar and called echo sounding. I love this: sounds determining sounds.

As with much of my writing, I am interested here in enacting an immersive environment and testing the limits of a given voice within the context of that space. How does that space consolidate and break apart the words I place within it? How, on and within the ocean floor, do words and their remains swirl about and unsettle?

Jenne Hsien Patrick *[p.145]*

Sometimes words are enough, breathing and living whole on the page. Yet, sometimes it feels as though there is a missing piece that I need to explore beyond the text to make sense of what I am trying to reach. To see if it can come closer to a truth I can recognize. An experiment in touch.

I often push toward fragment/image/hybridity to make visible the gaps inbetween. Much of my work emerges from deep silences in my family for which there is no model for clarity. As I am not able to read or write Chinese characters but am fluent in speaking and understanding Mandarin (my first/heritage language), some pieces expressed only in the written word can be to my body a thin translation. I feel like I am trying to reach towards what I know bodily with all the languages I have: visual, aural, and written.

This isn't to say that the text is lesser or separate from the images. I try to push the text, image, and sound to their full capacity as vessels for the piece. It is their interrelationships, the space in between and the moments where they touch and meet, which animates the whole.

Working with family photos is one approach in relationship building. The elements of a photo can be broken down into a constellation of meanings, beyond the story that's often told. Making space for the unsaid and unknown both in the image or the time in between its shutter release and my looking in the present. Distilling the text into the spatial juxtapositions of frames by drawing, to inhabit the intentional and unintentional gaps in my grandmother's memory. To examine these gaps between me and the past, using pencil upon slippery vellum to make imperfect and malleable images much as memory is itself. I am scratching towards an embodied truth, or as close as I can get.

JENNIFER PERRINE *[p.277]*

The International Code of Signals, used in maritime flags to communicate needs and desires between vessels that do not share a common language, was the inciting spark for "Buddy System." The code, designed to be used at sea, focuses primarily on navigation and safety. In learning its signals and their meanings, I recognized parallels to the language that many of us use as we navigate and attempt to find safety within systems designed to harm us.

In particular, the code's meanings suggested to me the language that women, femmes, and genderqueer and nonbinary folks have used in bars, clubs, and other social spaces as we attempt to protect ourselves and one another from sexual assault. The title alludes to a method of assault prevention that places the responsibility for thwarting violence on those most likely to be assaulted. When maritime flags signal to other ships, they can communicate the need for aid, for salvage, for rescue. They can alert other vessels to existing dangers and warn them to steer clear. But they do not stop the storm. They do not halt the tide.

JENNIFER S. CHENG *[p.3]*

My interior language—the one I use to speak myself into being—has always been composed of fragments, splinters, opacities, and absences. Sometimes the only way I can elucidate is by way of blurring. Sometimes an uncertain truth feels truer than a certain one. If the world—and myself in it—never seemed whole to me, why would language? In *Jacket2* I once wrote an essay series on "Other Ways of Seeing: the poetics and politics of refraction." It was a way for me to consider why I feel compelled by literary and artistic forms that somehow disrupt linear logic and de-center normalized sightlines, instead pursuing "marginal" perspectives and perceptions. To articulate my experiences using the structures and strictures of dominant systems of knowledge and meaning is an impossible and contradictory task; I have always felt more seen and heard when I was partly occluded, untranslated. I have only ever felt comfortable, as filmmaker and theorist Trinh T. Minh-ha would say, *speaking nearby*. That's all I ever thought language was. My desire is for the utterance that gestures toward without pinpointing because complexity cannot be pinpointed; the utterance that is a wild, liminal space, where identity constructions are not fixed but instead a question is inserted, an uncertainty is posed; where there is possibility for multiplicity, permeability, a continuously shifting space—other ways of seeing, knowing, and being. Critical theorist Édouard Glissant describes trembling thinking, and I am also interested in trembling language. "The world trembles in every which way," he says. And also: "We understand the world better if we tremble along with it."

Jhani Randhawa [p.289]

I would perform her hands or seek them, and when she died I dreamed of her fingers.

In this collection, my contribution "Semaphore" is a multimodal visual essay in seven mudras. Each mudra in "Semaphore" is a performance in two parts, literary and visual. When the body catches a memory, like a pearl of sweat catches the light, something is there like practice: the images in this piece are dance notation, are spiritual messengers drawing from my own cultural access points and fabricating reconstituted approaches to meaning.

Semaphore is the name for a method of visual signaling to transmit messages over distances. It is a method of mediating these messages and offering directives. Less speech act than dance notation, semaphore is a method that catalyzes performances of passage. Mudra, like the semaphore, is also a mediator, but of meditative and esoteric aspects rather than modular transactions. Mudra, a Sanskrit word meaning "seal," "mark," or "gesture," is a symbolic and corporal signifier, made by the placement of hands or the body's stretched contortion, its expression shared by performer and observer. A stabilizing form. There are eight to ten mudras that lay practitioners might use or be most familiar with; from Buddhist or yogic imagery there are over fifty hastas or mudras made with the hands and arms alone in Odissi and Bharatanatyam dance.

The pieces in this work explore the phenomena of sign-bearing and distance, using interlaced forms of (an)notation: letters, planting and labor logs, poetic scraps, meditations on digestion, and queer reconstructions of faith in diaspora, as well as visual documentation of the narrator's work-worn hands. And the images of my hands, photographed in two periods of mourning a year apart, in different regions in North America, are vehicles, impressions. I'm interested in the loose relation that holds these mudras together in their interpermeating universes. Between this loose-ness and the open space (one could call them gaps, implying a kind of danger, including the danger of those empty-geography narratives used by settler-colonialists to simultaneously erase and displace extant communities), in memories of pleasure and grief, resonate the horizons of circular migration and colonial, ethnic, ecological, and gendered violence. These open spaces "sign" across biomes, built environments, human community, bodies, and imagined futures, accruing and shedding meaning while in transit.

Kathy Wu [p.233]

Is blue the most virtual color? Blue brings to mind computers that fail, projectors that are starting or ending. A glitch or rupture, blue screen of death.

Blue is deeply abstract, and lossy. For instance, the sky and sea are the largest blue "things," yet they contain no pigment. In many languages, blue is a late or non-occurrence. Is blue an import? From where is it created or extracted?

At the same time, blue is a commodity: an expensive pigment, a modern-day market symbol. Sapphire, cobalt. Silicon Valley logos. How do legacies of empire and conquering classification systems linger linguistically, and what histories can we understand through them? What is the etymology of lapis lazuli; is there a relationship between Turquoise and Turks?

This work was curious to see what emerged through a study of color names. The names are taken from a Wikipedia list of all colors, from which I extracted via word search only shades of blue. I wasn't sure exactly what would result. The resulting names offered hints at nations and trade ("French," "Honolulu", "United Nations") as well as institutional brands ("Cambridge," "Eton," "Duke"). I used Python to scrape images off Google of cobalt mines, blue porcelains, painted cloaks for Mother Mary in shades of ultramarine.

Blue often derives from precious minerals; it shares that material basis with computers. Cobalt is a type of blueness and a crucial hardware element. In terms of hybridity, I wanted the poem to be formed primarily of light—the material of LEDs, and the screen, which the poem alludes to. I'm interested in what the material contributes to the work, as not just a container for language but something fundamental in shaping, exciting, and permitting certain types of language. To write on the computer extends writing into realms of data-parsing, copy-pasting, string-matching, and new scales. New media offers shifts from old canons by offering new conceptual and formal values.

KELLY PUIG *[p.83]*

The Book of Embers grew out of madness and its dissection—within myself, on the page, and of the book object. I had been writing about the unconscious in another book and come too close to it. My experience of psychic collapse left me unable to write during my MFA-as-labyrinth. I could, however, make a small ball strewn with a few sentences as I tried to find a way out. This attempt to unfurl and untangle myself would not have been possible without the space my mentor, Renee Gladman, held for me as I slowly came back from the edge which was a portal.

Over the years I worked on this project, the enactment and embodiment of Ariadne in my process became more and more imperative as well as more and more potent. Never before had I considered myself an art history buff and yet, one by one, a whole host of female visionaries would begin to appear—as if Ariadne's archetypal energy was summoning us to collectively reclaim a mythical ball of thread from the jaws of empire, history, and Greek myth for a winding experience of oracular awakening.

While the hybrid nature of this book manifested many times over, the original source of hybridity was the text itself. The syncretic hodge-podge of narrative, essay, literary criticism, art history, biography, and autobiography felt most honest as a means of piecing together multiple narrative thresholds in part because the process of the text teaching you how to read it is exactly what life-as-labyrinth does... it generates a form of consciousness. The book as an enactment of a synthesizing consciousness that could in theory go on forever further propelled my grappling with and understanding of art as utterly atomic when embodiment—in this case, embodiment as unabridged disembodiment—constellates and compounds. In my experience, the hybrid process of creating an integrated literary work of art within and across numerous prismatic dimensions is a growing within the unconscious to allow yourself to unfurl where you lead, come what may.

Kimberly Alidio *[p.139]*

The two poems in this collection are excerpts from a long poem, "Ambient Mom," which appears in my fourth full-length book, *Teeter*. *Teeter* is an autohistoriography of felt time that arises from subversive hearing practices and the emotional prosody of a mother tongue one does not understand but activates in another poetic language. Comprised of three long poems, *Teeter* knows experimental forms can be as intimate as mothering; knows we can understand languages we do not speak. *Teeter* tries to open up processing and procedures to get to a minimalist, reduced place but somehow ends up in a maximalist, messy place. A focus on technique invites the rise of a shape and form organic to chaos and excess.

The poems included here quote or paraphrase personal correspondence with Sarita Echavez See, John Melillo, and Kyle Dacuyan; and a poem by Fred Moten. An earlier version of "in a plain ponytail" appears in *Apogee*. The poems perform a homophonic transcription of Pangasinan language featured in Christopher Gozum's film, *Anacbanua*, and YouTube vlogs by Vilmarey Chan Vengua, TVMO Channel, and Monica Sandra Ronda. The two poems were composed with my sound collage, "You can actually say something (2011-2018)," uploaded to Soundcloud; my video poem, "pangasinan chora," uploaded to Vimeo; and my collection of spectrogram video screen captures, Ambient Mom, on Tumblr.

In a workshop on writing with ambient sound and field recordings I led for The Poetry Project, I proposed that a poem is an assemblage—screwed, welded, nailed pieces of sonic, voiced, textual, visual, graphic, and referential materials of spatialized utterance. Listening is composition as potential: what's being composed in your listening, and what "poem" can be composed nearby? A poetic voice may be a kind of synthesizer of languages and emotional prosodies. My proposal for all of us, readers of this collection, is that accountability to our material and spiritual lives is difficult to sustain, and, therefore, a vernacular avant-garde.

Monica Ong *[p.21]*

These Insomnia Poems began as a series about the things that kept me up at night coming from someone who has struggled with severe episodes of insomnia over the years. I was looking at diagrams of *Geometrical Psychology or the Science of Representation, An Abstract of the Theories and Diagrams of B. W. Betts* by Louisa S. Cook, published by George Redway in 1887. In these attempts to mathematically model human consciousness and spirituality through geometric forms, I kept noticing the absence of ancestors, and thus the diagrams became the basis of visual collages I made with archival family images. The color in these diagrams also served as the basis of the types of insomnia I explore, influenced by Mary Ruefle's series on the many colors of sadness in *My Private Property*.

As a poet who creates for gallery and installation space, I wanted to make these poems in the style of sleep tapes. Which is to say that they also exist as audio poems collaged with ambient sounds that remind me of the sleep channels I turned to in order to sleep. While most readers will encounter this work as visual collages and text in a book, my current installation-in-progress is turning the visuals into silk pillows that visitors can rest on while lying down and listening to these poems. Because I'm interested in interrogating the ways in which sleep is commodified, I am also imagining other components for a sleep kit as a kind of artist's book.

NADIA HAJI OMAR + CHRISTINE SHAN SHAN HOU *[p.225]*

There are multiple intentions going into this collaboration. Nadia's intention was to combine written elements, specifically asemic writing, with abstract drawing/painting. Nadia's process was firstly to draw or paint the written elements and then build the framework for the rest of the piece. The various elements of the drawing/painting are created in response to the initial writing cluster. The asemic writing thus becomes the central focus of the piece; the main character around which foreground, background, and pattern are developed and manipulated.

These three pieces are part of a much larger exploration of the concepts of asemic writing and how it relates to painting and drawing. Here, asemic writing is blended with various different media: graphite, ink, dye, acrylic paint, and natural gemstones. Regardless of the tools and materials used to develop the writing element or its surroundings, the impact or effect is the same: the human eye will always discern, distinguish, and isolate any text or text-like imagery first, acknowledging the innate power of language. Christine has felt an aesthetic kinship with Nadia's visual language and wanted to respond to the drawings and painting by writing a poem from inside, or while psychically inhabiting the drawing.

We addressed/explored the concept of hybridity from a couple of perspectives. In one sense, hybridity is two consecutive actions—call and response. Nadia's artwork came first and the poems were written second, with no alteration or adjustment to the artwork after the writing of the poems.

In addition to this relatively straightforward approach, we also interpreted hybridity as a form of friendship. The collaborative process consisted of talking, listening, and exchanging ideas—what we have been reading, thinking about, looking at, and how we have been nourishing our minds and taking in the world. So on one hand while hybridity can be interpreted as a simple call and response, it is also something that is less perfunctory—an invisible fusion, a deep interconnection of two varied and distinct artistic minds.

Paisley Rekdal *[p.69]*

My digital poem "West: A Translation" links the building of the transcontinental railroad with the Chinese Exclusion Act by using a poem carved into the walls of Angel Island Immigration Station as its formal "spine" to examine the transcontinental's cultural impact on America. Exclusion and the railroad are paired events, since the Chinese were eagerly recruited to build the railroad, then, after its completion, legally excluded from entering the country.

The Chinese poem I chose for "West" is part of a dialogic pair that elegize a fellow Chinese detainee who committed suicide at Angel Island. While I only translate one of these poems, I used mirroring and linking as formal tropes for "West," a poem that was commissioned by Utah's Spike 150 Committee to commemorate the 150th anniversary of the transcontinental's completion.

The individual poems themselves are a hybrid of the documentary and the speculative, the imagined and real. Hybridity occurs when the language of poetry must extend from the limitations of fact, in essence, completing what the original historical texts I relied upon leave blank. Rupture and loss might be seen—from a historian's point of view—as flaws in the record. But for the poet, they offer opportunities to create alternative texts to both poetry and history themselves.

West is also a book recently published from Copper Canyon Press. The book splits into two parts: the first the collection of poems on the site, the second part a series of short historio-lyric essays that function as notes for each of the poems. You can read all the notes as one long essay, or you can read each note only against its accompanying poem. Either way, the reader is forced to see how different texts mirror and speak to each other. Though I do not translate both Chinese poems carved on Angel Island's walls, in effect, I reproduce the *presence* of both poems, since the site and book, note and poem, each formally call to the existence of another connecting text.

Quyên Nguyễn-Hoàng *[p.207]*

"Masked Force" is a small experiment towards a poetics of looking. A poetics of looking that gently tries, despite the likelihood of failure, to protect the enigma of photographs against the desire of critics, and sometimes image-makers themselves, to argumentatively, brutally explain a picture to death. A poetics of looking that sees the past as a disorienting land strewn thick with absence and loss, a moor that crawls with rifts where meaning drops. A poetics of looking infatuated with what Gaston Bachelard calls the "unfathomable oneiric depth" of felicitous images. A poetics of looking where words and images are softly interleaved so that the former might refrain from loudly, heroically, desperately striving to interpret, master, and besiege the latter. A poetics of looking that wishes to make space for the abyssal magic of photographs to breathe, and infinitely expand, instead of extinguishing the enchantment with airless captions and useful lessons. A poetics of looking that births not pedagogical moralizations but shards of reverie. A poetics of looking that listens to both the laments and the laughs latent in an image, both the freedoms and the unfreedoms born of a revolution. A poetics of looking that descends the imaginal underworld of a past catastrophe that ceaselessly binds and permeates the present. A vaporous poetics of looking that floats down a river of photographs—a stream of ghosts enwrapped in the yarns of time. A winding poetics of looking that drifts with the haze of images, dreams them into twilit being.

SAMIYA BASHIR *[p.131]*

negro being :: freakish beauty

+

Field Theories #4

Finding starshine through the dark.
There is a fire. Again.

What Fred calls "music" calls "ours" like – wut?!
What a dream.

Hear: here sings the starshine of dreams, for sure:
the bends of them, the way their colors drip and bleed.

Now—as I reflect on these reflections presented here, how they were not just envisioned but seen. The thoughtfulness of their selection. The generous insistence of these editors to make a groundbreakingly beautiful document. Now I am returned to the specific and actual space—a cabin by the sea where I lived in COVID exile for nearly a year and a half, and haven't been back since. There is a tiny house here where many things were filmed. Created. Made. Insisted upon despite the despair. Pieces like this: an attempt, through the floss, to continue being. Like, y'all remember when we had to shout at each other from a distance for fear of actual-ass death? The hours and hours and days and months alone? 2020/2021 was perhaps the longest winter of my life. And the gratitude that I was somehow held—safe (imagine!)—through the darkness—that I was allowed—afforded—transformation. Well, it's everything. The moment I returned to this bit of ground I grounded. To return, here, to this work—work which got me through—work which lived in conversation with so many beloveds—work which was called for and which answered—looked the daemons through the eye. And then the return: field theories. So many years I lived its questions. Its demands still shake me: imagine! Its own insistence on remix—on reimagining and re-presenting itself (whole to part to fracture to fraction) through the gaze of and upon my own beloved community – well – imagine: to be not just carousel but doorway: kinda blows me away.

SANDY TANAKA *[p.193]*

"Countdown" began out of a necessity I felt to access my ancestors, to be in a narrative inaccessible by time and physicality, and emotional connection—the point of view of a uranium-235 gun-type fission weapon. In using the commonality of a countdown, this strict structure as the bomb's purview forced a very personal second narrative to be told between the stints. It was like holding open crevices and writing in glimpses. Hybridity of narratives.

But hybridity is also the ongoing process of meddling with the structure. I was fascinated by the *New York Times* use of scrollytelling, of being able to influence pacing and add images that morph the narrative into spaces I didn't even know existed, personal spaces. Not only did it change reader experience, like a zoetrope, it allowed me for the first time to see my ancestors hovering right beside me.

Sasha Stiles *[p.95]*

As a lifelong poet, I've spent years studying writerly craft and canonical verse, yet it wasn't until I began creating digital, multimedia texts and experimenting with natural language processing AI that I began to truly find my voice. My creative impulse has always been hybrid at its core, bridging poetry and art, science and literature, physical and virtual, ancient and speculative; and my practice has always been transdisciplinary, crossing genres and mediums to explore our increasingly transhuman condition. So, conventional approaches to poetics and publishing left me unsatisfied, hungry. As an unrepentant lover of books and the power of the unadorned word, I began to regard my naked, printed poetry as a libretto of sorts—the nucleus of a fuller ecosystem of imagination and expression, or perhaps a kind of seed. What would happen, I wondered, if I planted my writing in the soil of new technologies? What if a poem could start on a page but grow and thrive in multiple dimensions, incorporating sound and light and motion? Where might the creative process take me if I augmented my own analog intelligence with a large language model powered by machine learning and rooted in the sum total of humanity's written record—a turbocharged, nonhuman co-author? How and where might I be able to develop and share these evolving poetries in meaningful ways? For me, hybridity has everything to do with a posthuman near-future of networked inspiration and intertextual language and literature—not replacing what we know, but starting to write the next chapter.

Shin Yu Pai *[p.155]*

I'm often interested in interrogating an idea that may take me through many iterations over a period of years. This approach has led me to write about the same gallery in an art museum over a nearly twenty-year period, in addition to writing poems inspired by visiting as many skyspaces by James Turrell as I've been able to see in person. It would be wrong to think of these works as duplicative, as they more closely resemble variations on a theme akin to what a museum or concert-goer might encounter in a visual or musical composition.

I once printed words on the ripening skins of apples using sunlight, as part of a site-specific piece in an heirloom apple orchard that I loved to visit with my son. That installation couldn't possibly survive untouched more than a day or two. Nor could it express the full magick of the orchard. So I engaged a friend to make sound recordings of the orchard throughout the four seasons that we used to mix with an audio recording of me reading my poem.

My piece "Embarkation" also lives in that world of imagining and reimagining. First conceived as a stage performance, I wanted the piece to have a life beyond the seven minutes it took to perform live. Perhaps this was driven by thinking about the boat-burning at the center of the film. Based upon a ceremony conducted in Taiwan every three years, the community involved in the ritual prepares for the event for more than a year in advance. The cycle of preparation ends with immolation. I wanted to capture all of that intention and labor in a piece that could reach beyond documentary poem to the metaphor of poetic ritual for the individual herself—to consider both the poet and the viewer.

STEPHANIE ADAMS-SANTOS *[p.53]*

As one who spends a lot of time "upstairs"—moving language around in my head, constantly navigating a blitz of anxious thoughts, dread, and looming errands—I often find myself stuck against the ceiling of myself. When I'm like this, there's a feeling of soul-sickness, and with that, a freezing up of my creative well. So again and again the task is to drop down from my head and into the lower body, into the gut, the hands and feet, into blood and earth and breath. For me, this speaks to a constant, laborious inner work of rooting myself in the material substrate of my corporeal existence.

In these hybrid pieces, I was wanting to open the blocked channels in myself. I wanted to stir awake different parts of myself and explore what was deeply alive and dwelling under the surface of my conscious thoughts. I intentionally took very different visual approaches (in respect to the style of artwork, the background coloring, the layout of the text) to stir fresh fragments to the surface. These are unconscious writings/drawings, each composed at night, in bed, just before sleep. I was stirred by Rilke's words: "Go now and do the/ heart-work on the images/ imprisoned within you." I think of these as dreams of the body. They are not strictly poems or illustrations; they are both and neither. More than anything, they are explorations—and excavations.

Marion Woodman said that "in finding our own story, we assemble all the parts of ourselves. Whatever kind of mess we have made of it, we can somehow see the totality of who we are and recognize how our blunderings are related." For me, working across genres and mediums and creating hybrid works that serve their own mysterious purposes is a vital part of my spirit's unfolding. Hybridity is for me a way to honor and enact the true dimensions and facets and restless curiosity of the life-force(s) within me. It's a way of asserting my freedom and truth.

Vauhini Vara *[p.167]*

For me, form and content are always intertwined; what I'm trying to express, as a writer, is impossible to disentangle from how I go about trying to express it. Not long after I started playing around with AI in my work, I decided that, if I were to ever publish something written using AI, it would have to somehow be partly about what it means for AI to be able to write: about what emotional thread the Big Tech companies behind AI might be pulling on, when they start selling us these technologies. For me, this thread had to do with communication—with what I was, and wasn't, capable of articulating on my own. And so, with anxiety and anticipation, I went to GPT-3 with this sentence: "My sister was diagnosed with Ewing sarcoma when I was in my freshman year of high school and she was in her junior year." Both form and content followed from there.

Vi Khi Nao *[p.45]*

Early in the summer of ___, as I was putting together my memoir, *Country in a Glass of Water*, I was inspired to create a visual version of the memoir, one that spoke more versatilely and more polychromatically to my immigrant, refugee, and diasporic experiences. After my open-heart surgery in 2019, I exist and continue to exist in a debilitating state of chronic pain. To cope with this pain, I began to draw on a regular basis. I drew vegetable and fruit dykes and all sorts of visual objects, objects such as hearts and a toilet and brains and a baseball and fish and scissors. But then the pen grew difficult; whenever I drew (shading its dense black ink in), the intense pressure of pressing the pen nibs on the page placed so much strain on my post-operated heart. I had to turn to a medium that was gentler on my body while maintaining my natural compulsion for prolificness.

Watercolor is gentle and tender. Their brushes are light. Their colors—rich and versatile—are light. I started a project called "The Boat People Series" to address my Vietnamese refugee experiences. Employing watercolors to portray boats proved incredibly fitting, evoking a poignant sense of diasporic poetry and appositeness. The very act of working with water, or "nước," instilled in me a profound connection to Vietnam, effectively conveying a feeling of "birthnướcing." It's worth noting that "nước"means not just water but also the materiality of homeland in Vietnamese. Writing has always been a primary mode of existence for me, but also for my art. This hybrid work is a documentation of my love for the nuptial tissue between text and the visual. The text elements, serving both as content and texture, were sourced from my father's archive, which contains documents related to our family's entry into the United States through the refugee relocation program several decades ago.

Victoria Chang *[p.297]*

For me, to make art is to float or flutter in a state of non-intention for as long as possible or maybe even forever. The process of making is what I enjoy the most.

My book, *Dear Memory: Letters on Writing, Silence, and Grief*, was even more of a process of exploration than usual. I didn't really understand or know what I was doing until I was far into the process. I started with one epistolary letter to my late mother, then another and another, until I had a stack of letters. At some point, I decided to include images because the root of the letters were actually a box of photos, birth certificates, and many other documents. Then at some point, I included poems on top of images, then small pieces of cut paper, then the paper became alight on the page, then more collaging of an interview I found where I spoke to my mother when she was still alive. I think of this book as being able to see the insides of someone's body, like with a scope, while the body is moving along in its workings.

In terms of hybridity, I think that I tend to listen to whatever it is I'm working on and ask it what it would like to be. Sometimes, the work answers clearly as poetry or prose. But for me, most of the time, the work answers with some form of hybridity because I think poetry and prose are human labels. I think of art as having a fair amount of range. It is weight-bearing. It is flexible. Some poetry feels very poem-like. Other times, poetry really feels very prose-like to me. It really just depends on each poem. The same is true for prose. I tend to be drawn more to lyrical prose or prose writers who have a lyrical ear, or some kind of attention to sound. I'd like to think that art is not very mathematical, wooden, or mechanical. It is ineffable, indecipherable, effluent, and fluid.

ACKNOWLEDGMENTS

We wish to thank: Jeff Alessandrelli and Adie B. Steckel of Fonograf Editions who generously stepped into the role of our publishing partner and trusted our vision for this undertaking from the start; Rory Sparks, Shir Grisanti, and Jenn Woodward of Stelo Arts who in their partnership as fiscal sponsor and community arts space have enabled this project to become more than we could have managed on our own; Emmy Eao, Harper Quinn, and Sharita Towne of the Independent Publishing Resource Center (IPRC) and nun studios for their support in helping us further imagine and play with this project. Thanks, too, to Samantha Rivas for her work as an intern for De-Canon in 2022, and to John Beer and the Portland State University MFA in Creative Writing Program for making this internship possible; to Sandy Tanaka for graphic design support; and to Blake Shell and Oregon Contemporary for earlier fiscal support.

This project would not be fiscally or logistically possible without the generous support of a Creative Heights Grant and an Oregon Arts & Culture Recovery Program Grant from the Oregon Community Foundation; a re/source residency fellowship from the IPRC; a Make Grant from RACC (Regional Arts & Culture Council); and fiscal sponsorship through Stelo Arts and Oregon Contemporary.

We express deep gratitude and admiration for all of the contributors whose works appear in this collection, as well to the other writers and artists who answered our initial call for submissions. Thank you, all, for trusting us with your work and inspiring us with your creativity in this ever-evolving realm of hybrid literature.

This project exists in an ethos of community. It has grown and been inspired by countless conversations and interactions of many kinds with others. To name just a few of those whom we're grateful to have shared space or crossed paths with: Stephanie Adams-Santos, Intisar Abioto, Neil Aitken, Roya Amirsoleymani, Roland Dahwen, John Akira Harrold, Hannah Kim, Jay Ponteri, Vĩ Sơn Trinh, and White Noise Project reading series.

De-Canon launched in 2017 as a "pop-up library" social art engagement installation, enabled by a Precipice Fund Grant (via Portland Institute for Contemporary Art/PICA); we are grateful for subsequent collaborations with UNA Gallery, APANO (Asian Pacific American Network of Oregon), and Milepost 5; and to Kyle Macdonald for building shelves—these spaces and "place-making" activities served as the birth of De-Canon as a collaborative art project.

ARTWORK CREDITS, REPRINTS, PERMISSIONS

(listed by artists, in order of appearance)

JENNIFER S. CHENG:

(Text)ile: Asemic Book [1], 2021, fabric scraps, thread, hemp, twig, stone, seashell, 4.75 x 4.25 in. Photos courtesy of the artist. This work belongs to an ongoing series entitled "(Text)ile: Asemic Books."

Quotations in essay from the following sources:

Bachelard, Gaston, trans. by Maria Jolas. *The Poetics of Space*. Beacon Press, Boston, 1994.

Balsom, Erika. "'There is No Such Thing as Documentary': an Interview with Trinh T. Minh-ha," *Frieze Magazine*. Online. Nov 1, 2018.

Barthes, Roland, trans. by Richard Howard. *Roland Barthes*. University of California Press, Berkeley, 1977.

Barthes, Roland, trans. by Richard Howard. *The Rustle of Language*. Hill and Wang, NY, 1986.

Glissant, Édouard, Trans by Betsy Wing. *Poetics of Relation*. The University of Michigan Press, Ann Arbor, 1997.

Li, Yiyun and Jennifer Egan. "A Reading and Conversation with Jennifer Egan and Yiyun Li," Association of Writers and Writing Programs Conference. Online. March 5, 2021.

Schwenger, Peter. *Asemic: The Art of Writing*. University of Minnesota Press, Minneapolis, 2019.

Tanizaki Junichirō, trans. by Thomas J Harper and Edward G Seidensticker. *In Praise of Shadows*. Leete's Island Books, Sedgwick, ME, 1977.

CAROLINA EBEID:

Stills from *She Got Love: A Circle of Spells for Ana Mendieta*, 2021, video/audio poem, 2:55 min.

Stills from *Wound Studies*, 2021, video/audio poem from family archival materials, 3:18 min.

"Afternoon Dress for Emily Dickinson," 2022, digital collage, dimensions variable.

MONICA ONG:

Insomnia Poems: "Lavender Insomnia" "Amber Insomnia" "Yellow Insomnia" "Indigo Insomnia." Digital collages using family archival photos with diagrams from *Geometrical Psychology or the Science of Representation, An Abstract of the Theories and Diagrams of B. W. Betts* by Louisa S. Cook, published by George Redway, York Street Covent Garden: New York , 1887; dimensions variable.

These works previously appeared in:

"Amber Insomnia" and "Lavender Insomnia" (visual poetry + audio recordings) in *A Velvet Giant*, Issue No. 5, 2020.

"Indigo Insomnia" (poetry only) appeared in *Connecticut Literary Anthology 2021*.

"Indigo Insomnia" (artwork) in *Dogwood: A Journal of Poetry and Prose,* cover art for the Spring 2021 issue.

"Yellow Insomnia" (poetry and audio recording; audio recorded with Randall Horton) in *Tricycle: A Buddhist Review*, 2020.

Divya Victor:

"Curb 2" and "Curb 4" by Divya Victor, from *Curb* (Nightboat Books, 2021). Copyright © 2021 by Divya Victor. Reprinted by permission of Nightboat Books.

Stills from "Curb 2" and "Curb 4" multimedia, created by Amarnath Ravva, for *Curb(ed)* multimedia collaborative website: divyavictorcurb.org. Reprinted by permission of the artist.

Other versions of this work also appeared in *Curb*, Press at Colorado College, 2019.

Vi Khi Nao:

"Boat Woman Bicyclist," 2022, watercolor on scanned refugee document, 8 x 11 in.

"Boat Woman in Red Bicycle," 2022, watercolor on scanned refugee document, 8 x 11 in.

"Blindfolded Squatting Boatman," 2022, watercolor, scanned refugee document, 8 x 11 in.

"Tunic Boatman," 2022, watercolor, scanned refugee document, 8 x 11 in.

"The Rambutan Male Nudes," 2022, watercolor, acrylics, India ink, 12 x 18 in.

Stephanie Adams-Santos:

"[all the night]," 2019, digital, dimensions variable.

"[all that dwells]," 2021, colored Pencil, pastel, digital, dimensions variable.

"[un animalito del cielo me dio un poco de lluvia para sanar mi corazón]," 2018, colored pencil, digital, dimensions variable.

"[a persistent cause]," 2021, colored pencil, digital, dimensions variable.

Anna Martine Whitehead:

[I have so many dreams about prisons], 2022, mixed media on paper, 36 x 48 in.

[Rosa's mom worked at the jail], 2022, mixed media on paper, 18 x 24 in.

These collages and accompanying interview transcripts are components of a larger multidisciplinary art project, *FORCE! an opera in acts*.

Paisley Rekdal:

Stills from video poems: "心 / Heart" "有識 / Have Knowledge" "無 / Not." Excerpted from *West: A Translation*, multimedia archive project (online at westtrain.org); poems by Paisley Rekdal, videos produced in collaboration with Jennilyn Merten of Perpendicular Productions.

These poems also appear in *West* (Copper Canyon, 2022). Copyright © 2022 by Paisley Rekdal.

Kelly Puig:

Artwork details of *The Book of Embers*, text printed on cotton ribbon, 2014. Images courtesy of the artist.

Excerpt from interview with Cara Manes and Anne Umland taken from "Leonora Carrington and the Visual Language of Mexican Surrealism," originally published on *Magazine*, February 19, 2020, https://www.moma.org/magazine/articles/239. © 2023 The Museum of Modern Art, New York. Used with permission.

An excerpt from *The Book of Embers* appears in *Tupelo Quarterly*, December 2023.

Sasha Stiles:

All works by Sasha Stiles first published by and reprinted with permission from Black Spring Press Group (2021-22):

"Analog Binary Code" "Ancient Binary Code" "Cursive Binary Code" from *Binary Odes*, a series fusing binary code with handwriting, objects.

Completion: When It's Just You, multimedia poem written in collaboration with AI, 3:00 min.

Gabrielle Civil:

* *a n e m o n e*, a performance art work by Gabrielle Civil, premiered in the Pleasure Rebel series curated by Nastalie Bogira, at the Bryant Lake Bowl in Minneapolis, MN in 2012. Performance photographs by Sayge Carroll.

A version of this performance text was previously published online in *MAI: Feminism & Visual Culture*, Issue 2, Autumn 2018; and in Civil's performance memoir *Experiments in Joy* (The Accomplices, 2018).

"Epitaph" by Assotto Saint (as it appears in "*a n e m o n e" by Gabrielle Civil), from *Sacred Spells: The Collected Works* (Nightboat Books, 2023). Copyright © 2023 by The Estate of Assotto Saint. Reprinted by permission of Nightboat Books.

Gabrielle Civil (with Anna Martine Whitehead):

A longer version of "Dreaming in Motion: Zoom Excerpts," with Anna Martine Whitehead, was previously published in *Journal of American Folklore*, special issue on "African American Expressive Culture and Protest, Imagination, and Dreams of Blackness," Vol. 134, No 534, Fall 2021.

The unabridged conversation was transmitted as "Black Motion Audio" in the Center for Afrofuturist Studies takeover of Montez Press Radio (2020) and can be heard in their archive.

The California Institute of the Arts, the Roy and Edna Disney CalArts Theater, and the Network of Ensemble Theaters provided support for this project.

Arianne True:

"DO NOT TOUCH THE ARTWORK" was first published in *A Dozen Nothing*, Sept 2021.

"an-language: significant expressions" and "[silence]" first appeared in *yəhaw̓: together we lift the sky*, ARTS at King Streets Station, March-August 2019. Exhibition photos by Mel Carter.

Samiya Bashir:

"negro being :: freakish beauty," 2020, video poem, 6:18 min. Previously published in *Interim Poetics*.

"Field Theories -Four-" 2017, video poem, 1:39 min. Video director: Roland Dahwen.

"At Harlem Hospital the only thing to eat is a Big Mac" was published in *Field Theories* (Nightboat Books, 2017). Copyright © 2017 by Samiya Bashir. Reprinted by permission of Nightboat Books.

Kimberly Alidio:

"A one-sided phone conversation recorded as video" "in a plain ponytail and no make-up we roll r's deep as the ground" are excerpted from *Teeter* (Nightboat Books, 2023). Copyright © 2023 by Kimberly Alidio. Reprinted by permission of Nightboat Books.

Jenne Hsien Patrick:

"Paint by Number 1 (Outside Songshan Airport, 1969)" and "Is This Your Mother?" were both first published in *Hayden's Ferry Review.*

Cindy Juyoung Ok:

"Before the DMZ" previously published in *The Sewanee Review.*

Shin Yu Pai:

"Embarkation: Reimagining a Taoist Ritual Ceremony" was first published as part of a special issue in *Genealogy*, "Decolonizing Ways of Knowing: Heritage, Living Communities, and Indigenous Understandings of Place," edited by Rachel Breunlin and Antoinette Jackson, 2020.

All images by Shin Yu Pai; except for performance stills by Forterra.

Vauhini Vara:

"Ghosts" was originally published in *The Believer*, 2021.

Diana Khoi Nguyen:

The "Eclipse" poems appear in the collection, *Root Fractures* (Scribner, 2024).

Aya Bram:

"Labyrinth," 2021, ink on paper, 14 x 11 in.

Sandy Tanaka:

All images by the artist or sourced from public domain and free sources. The print version of "Countdown" is adapted from the scroll-format multimedia version online at: https://express.adobe.com/page/pnH2lGf9mhiIM/

Quyên Nguyễn-Hoàng:

All photographs by Võ An Khánh. Reprinted courtesy of Võ An Khánh and Sàn Art.

A Vietnamese version of this essay along with a previous English translation appeared in the catalogue-pamphlet *Masked Force*, created by curator Quyên Nguyễn-Hoàng in collaboration with Sàn Art (2022). More information about this publication is available at: https://san-art.org/publications/masked-force-book/

Alley Pezanoski-Browne:

"Eve," collage, risograph prints.

Nadia Haji Omar and Christine Shan Sha Hou:

Paintings by Nadia Haji Omar. Poems by Christine Shan Shan Hou. Photo credits: Charles Benton.

"Dear So and So," 2020. Acrylic, dye, red jasper, and black tourmaline on panel, 24 x 18 in. Private Collection.

"Square Font," 2020. Ink and graphite on paper, 12 x 9 in. Courtesy of the artist and Kristen Lorello, NY.

"Dark Eyes (the flower)," 2020. Ink and graphite on paper, 8 1/8 x 6 in. Private Collection.

Kathy Nguyen:

Stills and text from "Virtual Blue," 2021, multimedia, digital poetry, HTML/CSS, JavaScript, 4:11 min.

Daisuke Shen and Vi Khi Nao:

Excerpt from *Funeral* (Kernpunkt Press, 2023). Copyright © 2023 by Daisuke Shen and Vi Khi Nao.

Ayesha Raees:

Excerpts from "Cycle," digital collage. A version of the poem titled "Erasure" previously published by *Booth*, 2021.

desveladas:

All images by the artists or from public domain sources; credits as noted in the captions.

Addie Tsai:

All polaroids by the artist, 3.5 x 3.5 in.

Jhani Randhawa:

All photographs in the work were taken by the artist between 2018 and 2021. Section "VII. Send" emerged in response from a prompt by poet Tsering Wangmo Dhompa in *Spiral* magazine's 2021 issue "Awakening."

Victoria Chang:

Excerpt from *Dear Memory* (Milkweed Editions, 2021). Text and collages by Victoria Chang. Copyright © 2021 by Victoria Chang. Reprinted by permission of Milkweed Editions.

Addie Tsai (any/all) is a queer nonbinary artist and writer of color who teaches creative writing at William & Mary. They also teach in Goddard College's MFA Program in Interdisciplinary Arts and Regis University's Mile High MFA Program in Creative Writing. Addie collaborated with Dominic Walsh Dance Theater on *Victor Frankenstein* and *Camille Claudel*, among others. They earned an MFA from Warren Wilson College and a Ph.D. in Dance from Texas Woman's University. Addie is the author of *Dear Twin* (2009) and *Unwieldy Creatures* (2022), which was a Shirley Jackson Award nominee. They are the Fiction co-Editor and Editor of Features & Reviews at *Anomaly*, contributing writer at *Spectrum South*, and Founding Editor in Chief at the LGBTQIA+ fashion literary and arts magazine *just femme & dandy*.

Alley Pezanoski-Browne makes art in multiple mediums inspired by dream logic and spiritual & ancestral knowledge. She cares deeply about building creative practices that better people's lives, catalyze collective power, and celebrate radical care, especially for historically excluded communities. Her essays have been published in the *Leonardo Music Journal* and *Bitch*. She has held leadership positions with the Independent Publishing Resource Center (IPRC) (where she is now a Board Member) and Open Signal PDX. She received her master's in Critical Theory & Creative Research from Pacific Northwest College of Art and had a stopover in Hong Kong as a Fulbright Scholar.

Anna Martine Whitehead does performance from the homelands of the Council of the Three Fires, among others. They make art and write about race, gender, and moving bodies; and support coalition movements committed to repair and transformation.

Arianne True (Choctaw, Chickasaw) is a queer poet and teaching artist from Seattle, and has spent most of her work time working with youth. She has received fellowships and residencies from Jack Straw, the Hugo House, Artist Trust, and the Seattle Repertory Theater, and is a proud alum of Hedgebrook and of the MFA program at the Institute of American Indian Arts. She lives near the Salish Sea with her cat. Arianne is the 2023-2025 Washington State Poet Laureate.

Aya Bram is a poet, artist, and maker. They received their MFA in Creative Writing and Poetics from the University of Washington, Bothell. Their work interweaves themes of illness, death, queerness, history, and identity. They can be found in *Concision Poetry, Dream Pop,* and *Night Music Journal*, and as the book and layout designer for *Snail Trail Press*. As part of their practice of death positivity, Aya writes lyrical living obituaries and eulogies. They currently reside in Seattle, WA.

Ayesha Raees عائشہ رئیس identifies herself as a hybrid creating hybrid poetry through hybrid forms. Her work strongly revolves around issues of race and identity, G/god and displacement, and mental illness while possessing a strong agency for accessibility, community, and change. Ayesha is a Poetry Editor at AAWW's *The Margins* and has received fellowships from Asian American Writers' Workshop, Brooklyn Poets, and Kundiman. Her debut chapbook *Coining A Wishing Tower* (2022) won the Broken River Prize. From Lahore, Pakistan, she currently shifts between Lahore and New York City.

Carolina Ebeid is a multimedia poet and author of *You Ask Me to Talk about the Interior* (2016) and the chapbook *Dauerwunder: a brief record of facts* (2023). Her work has been supported by the Stadler Center for Poetry at Bucknell

University, Bread Loaf, CantoMundo, a National Endowment for the Arts fellowship, as well as a residency fellowship from the Lannan Foundation. A longtime editor, she helps edit poetry at *The Rumpus*, as well as the online zine *Visible Binary*. From 2023-2025 she is the Bonderman Assistant Professor of poetry at Brown University.

Christine Shan Shan Hou is a poet and collage artist of Hakka Chinese dissent. Recent publications include the chapbook, *Evolution of the Bullet* (2023), co-written with Vi Khi Nao, *Playdate* (2022), and *The Joy and Terror are Both in the Swallowing* (2021). Their artwork has been exhibited at White Columns and Deli Gallery in New York City.

Cindy Juyoung Ok is the author of *Ward Toward* (2024). She teaches creative writing at Kenyon College.

Daisuke Shen is the author of the forthcoming short story collection *Vague Predictions & Prophecies* (2024), and the novella *Funeral* (with Vi Khi Nao, 2023). They live in New York City.

A poet and multimedia artist, Diana Khoi Nguyen is the author of *Ghost Of* (2018), which was a finalist for the National Book Award, and *Root Fractures* (2024). Her video work has recently been exhibited at the Miller Institute for Contemporary Art. Diana is a Kundiman fellow and member of the Vietnamese artist collective She Who Has No Master(s). A recipient of a fellowship from the National Endowment for the Arts, and winner of the 92Y Discovery Poetry Contest and 2019 Kate Tufts Discovery Award, she currently teaches in the Randolph College Low-Residency MFA and is an Assistant Professor at the University of Pittsburgh.

desveladas is Sheila Maldonado, Macarena Hernández, and Nelly Rosario. Sheila Maldonado is a poet, author of *one-bedroom solo* (2011) and *that's what you get* (2021). She teaches English for the City University of New York and is working on *bloodletters*, a book about a lifelong obsession with the ancient Maya. Macarena Hernández is a multimedia journalist, formerly an editorial columnist at *The Dallas Morning News*; the Rio Grande Valley Bureau Chief for *The San Antonio Express-News*; and the Fred Hartman Distinguished Professor of Journalism at Baylor University. Currently, she is an educational consultant and is working on a play about the media's obsession with the U.S.-Mexico border. Nelly Rosario is a fiction and prose writer, author of *Song of the Water Saints: A Novel* (2002). She currently serves as Assistant Director of Writing for the MIT Black History Project and as Associate Professor in the Latina/o Studies Program at Williams College. desveladas is the recipient of a 2016 Creative Capital Award in Literature.

Divya Victor is the author of *Curb* (2021), winner of the 2022 PEN America Open Book Award and the 2022 Kingsley Tufts Poetry Award. She is also the author of *Kith* (2017), *Scheingleichheit: Drei Essays* (trans. Lena Schmidt, 2020), *Natural Subjects* (2014), *Unsub* (2014), and *Things To Do With Your Mouth* (2014). Her work has been collected in numerous venues, including *BOMB, The Best American Experimental Writing, Poetry* magazine, and more. A 2023 PEN Affiliated Fellow at Civitella Ranieri and collaborator on an Andrew Mellon Just Futures grant, as well as recipient of other awards, her work has been performed or installed at the Museum of Contemporary Art (MoCA) Los Angeles, The National Gallery of Singapore, the Museum of Modern Art (MoMA), and other places. She teaches at Michigan State University, where she is the Director of the Creative Writing Program.

Gabrielle Civil is a black feminist performance artist, poet, and writer, originally from Detroit, MI. She has premiered over fifty performance artworks worldwide including *Black Weirdo School* (Pop Up Critique) (2023), *the déjà vu—live* (2022) and *Jupiter* (2021). Her performance memoirs include *Swallow the Fish* (2017), *Experiments in Joy* (2019), *(ghost gestures)* (2021), *the déjà vu* (2022) and *In & Out of Place* (2024). Her writing has also appeared in *New Daughters of Africa, Kitchen Table Translation, Migrating Pedagogies, DanceNotes*, and *Experiments in Joy: a Workbook*. A 2023 Franconia Performance Fellow, she earned her Ph.D. in Comparative Literature from New York University and teaches at the California Institute of the Arts. The aim of her work is to open up space.

IMANI ELIZABETH JACKSON is a poet and artist from Chicago. She is the author of two chapbooks, *saltsitting* (2020) and *Context for arboreal exchanges* (2023), and her first book, *Flag*, is forthcoming from Futurepoem, for which she received the press's 2020 Other Futures Award.

JENNE HSIEN PATRICK is a writer and artist based in Seattle, WA. She writes poetry, comics, and hybrid text/image works often incorporating textiles and papercutting. Jenne is a Hugo House Fellow, a Tin House Workshop alum, and their work has appeared in publications such as *Hayden's Ferry Review, wildness/Platypus Press*, and *Honey Literary*, among others.

JENNIFER PERRINE is the author of four books of poetry: *Again* (2020), *The Body Is No Machine* (2007), *In the Human Zoo* (2011), and *No Confession, No Mass* (2015). Their latest poems and essays appear in *Cincinnati Review, Pleiades, Nimrod, New Letters, Poetry Northwest, Orion Magazine, Harpur Palate, Oregon Humanities*, and *Cascadia Field Guide: Art, Ecology, and Poetry*. Jennifer lives in Portland, Oregon, where they cohost the Incite: Queer Writers Read series, teach writing, and guide nature-based mindfulness experiences.

JENNIFER S. CHENG's work includes poetry, lyric essay, and image-text forms, exploring immigrant home-building, shadow poetics, and the interior wilderness. Her hybrid book *Moon: Letters, Maps, Poems* (2018) was selected by Bhanu Kapil for the Tarpaulin Sky Award and named a *Publishers Weekly* "Best Book of 2018." She is also the author of *House A* (2016), selected by Claudia Rankine for the Omnidawn Poetry Prize, and *Invocation: An Essay* (2010), an image-text chapbook published by New Michigan Press. A National Endowment for the Arts Literature Fellow, she has received awards and fellowships from Brown University, the University of Iowa, San Francisco State University, the U.S. Fulbright program, Kundiman, Bread Loaf, MacDowell, and the Academy of American Poets. Having grown up in Texas and Hong Kong, she lives in San Francisco.

JHANI RANDHAWA is a nonbinary Kenyan-Punjabi/Anglo-American counterdisciplinary maker and collaborator based between the U.S. and the U.K.. Author of *Time Regime* (2022), winner of the 2023 California Book Award for Poetry, Jhani's work is interested in fugue states, ecological grief-tending, and formations of friendship across species and consciousness. They are the co-founding editor of *rivulet*, an experimental journal dedicated to investigations of the interstitial.

KATHY WU (she/they) is a cross-disciplinary artist, writer, and educator based in Providence, RI (Narragansett land). She moves between and across textiles, code, book arts, and language. Her work is interested in scientific epistemology, nomenclatures, fossils, and land markers. She is currently a Literary Arts MFA candidate at Brown University.

KELLY PUIG is a Cuban-American writer and interdisciplinary artist. She holds an MFA in Fiction from Brown University where she was the recipient of the Weston Prize for best graduate work in addition to the Frances Mason Harris Prize for best manuscript of poetry or prose fiction written by a woman. Her forthcoming cross-genre debut, *The Book of Embers*, was selected by Amaranth Borsuk for the 2022 Essay Press Book Prize and will be published as a traditional book object in 2025. Her poetry and fiction have appeared in *Denver Quarterly, Witness, Wag's Revue, The Columbia Review*, and *Möbius Strip*. She lives in Boulder, Colorado.

KIMBERLY ALIDIO (she/they) is the author of *Teeter* (2023), *why letter ellipses* (2020), *: once teeth bones coral :* (2020), and *after projects the resound* (2016). In addition to her full-length poetry collections, she has published four chapbooks: *ROOM TONE* (2023), *a cell of falls* (2019), *shaping and edging* (2015), and *solitude being alien* (2013). Her most recent poetic-critical essays are published on The Poetry Foundation and the anthology, *Filipino Studies*. She recently published visual-concrete poems in *Juf* magazine and in Hauser & Wirth's *Ursula* magazine. A video-poem is nominated for Best-of-the-Net by *The Denver Quarterly*. Her writing has been nominated for the United States Artists Fellowship and awarded the Nightboat Poetry Prize. She writes and lives on Munsee-Mohican lands along the Mahicannituck River, otherwise known as New York's Upper Hudson Valley.

MONICA ONG is the author of *Silent Anatomies* (2015), winner of the Kore Press First Book Award. A Kundiman poetry fellow, Ong's visual poetry is exhibited widely at special collections and galleries including the Center for Book Arts (NYC), The Institute Library (New Haven), and the Poetry Foundation (Chicago). *Planetaria*, her recent exhibition of visual poetry, has been exhibited at the Poetry Foundation and Hunterdon Art Museum. You can find her work in *Poetry* magazine, *Scientific American*, *Tab Journal*, and *ctrl+v*. In 2021, Monica founded Proxima Vera, a micropress specializing in literary art & objects, which are now part of many distinguished institutional collections worldwide.

NADIA HAJI OMAR was born in Melbourne, Australia in 1985 and lives and works in Warren, Rhode Island. She received a Bachelor of Arts from Bard College in 2007 and a MFA from the School of Visual Arts in 2014. Nadia has had solo exhibitions at Providence College Galleries, the Visual Arts Center of New Jersey, Kristen Lorello, and Bard College, among other venues, and has been included in group exhibitions at The Center for Contemporary Art, Bedminster, NJ, the Katonah Museum of Art, Katonah, NY, Bronx Art Space, and Deli Gallery, among other venues. Her works are included in the collections of the RISD Museum, Providence, RI, Hallmark Art Collection, Kansas City, MO, Providence College Galleries and Collections, Providence, RI, Capital Group, Los Angeles, CA, and Art in Embassies, U.S. Department of State, Permanent Collection, U.S. Embassy, Colombo, Sri Lanka, among others. Her exhibitions have been reviewed in *Hyperallergic* and *New York Magazine*, among other publications.

PAISLEY REKDAL is the author of four books of nonfiction and seven books of poetry, including *Nightingale* (2019), *Appropriate: A Provocation* (2021), and, most recently, *West: A Translation* (2023). She is the editor and creator of the digital archive projects *West*, *Mapping Literary Utah*, and *Mapping Salt Lake City*. Her work has received the Amy Lowell Poetry Traveling Fellowship, a Guggenheim Fellowship, an NEA Fellowship, Pushcart Prizes, the Academy of American Poets Laureate Fellowship, a Fulbright Fellowship, and various state arts council awards. The former Utah poet laureate, she teaches at the University of Utah where she directs the American West Center.

QUYÊN NGUYỄN-HOÀNG is a writer and translator born in Việt Nam. Her most recent publication is *Chronicles of a Village* (2022), a translation of a novel by Nguyễn Thanh Hiện. Her work has appeared in *Poetry* magazine, *Jacket2*, *Modern Poetry in Translation*, and other venues. She is a Stanford University graduate and has received support from the PEN/Heim Fund and the Institute for Comparative Modernities, among other honors.

SAMIYA BASHIR, called a "dynamic, shape-shifting machine of perpetual motion" by Diego Báez, writing for *Booklist*, is a poet, writer, librettist, performer, and multimedia poetry maker whose work, both solo and collaborative, has been widely published, performed, installed, printed, screened, experienced, and Oxford comma'd from Berlin to Düsseldorf, Amsterdam to Accra, Florence to Rome, and across the United States. Sometimes she makes poems of dirt. Sometimes zeros and ones. Sometimes variously rendered text. Sometimes light. Samiya is the author of three poetry collections, most recently *Field Theories* (2017), winner of the 2018 Oregon Book Award's Stafford/Hall Award for Poetry.

SANDY TANAKA is a writer, artist, and designer. She has been working in the comics industry for ten years. Before that, she was an art director, music supervisor, and band manager in Los Angeles. She has a B.A. in film from the University of California, Santa Barbara, and an MFA in creative writing from Warren Wilson College. She was a nominee for the Pushcart Prize. In 2021, she received the Oregon Literary Career Fellowship. She lives in Portland, Oregon with her family.

SASHA STILES is a Kalmyk-American poet, language artist, and AI researcher widely recognized as a pioneer of algorithmic authorship and blockchain poetics. Author of the "instant techno-classic" *Technelegy* (2022), her work has been published and exhibited around the world, featured by institutions from MoMA to Christie's, and referenced in publications including *Artforum, Lit Hub* and the *Washington Post*. Sasha is also co-founder of acclaimed literary gallery theVERSEverse and has been named one of the "Top Artists Shaping the Digital Art Scene." Other honors include a Future Art Award, the Lumen Prize shortlist, the IoDF 100 Innovators List, and nominations for the Forward Prize, Pushcart Prize, and Best of the Net. Sasha has served as Poetry Mentor to the AI humanoid BINA48 since 2018, and lives near New York City with her husband and creative partner, Kris Bones.

SHIN YU PAI is the author of twelve books of poetry, including most recently *No Neutral* (2023) and *Less Desolate* (2023), a collection of haiku comics. In 2020, Entre Rios Books published *Ensō*, a 20-year survey of her work across poetry, photography, performance, installation, and public art. Her poetry films have screened at Zebra Poetry Film Festival, The Cadence Video Poetry Festival, Madrid International Short Film Festival, Tokyo International Short Film Festival, and other outlets. Shin Yu is host and creator of *Ten Thousand Things*, an award-winning, chart-topping podcast on Asian American stories, produced in collaboration with KUOW, Seattle's NPR affiliate station. For her work in podcasting and public radio, she has received recognition from the Signal Awards and the Asian American Podcasters Association. Shin Yu is currently Civic Poet for the City of Seattle.

The work of STEPHANIE ADAMS-SANTOS spans poetry, prose, and screenwriting. Often grappling with themes of strangeness and belonging, their work reflects a fascination with the weird, numinous, and primal forces that shape inner life. They are the author of several full length poetry collections and chapbooks, including *Dream of Xibalba* (2023), selected by Jericho Brown as winner of the 2021 Orison Poetry Prize, and *Swarm Queen's Crown* (2016), finalist for a Lambda Literary Award. Stephanie served as Staff Writer and Story Editor on the television anthology horror series *Two Sentence Horror Stories* (Netflix), and was winner of a 2022 Gold Telly Award in TV Writing. They have received grants and fellowships from Sundance, Film Independent, Vermont Studio Center, Regional Arts and Culture Council, and Oregon Arts Commission. In addition to their literary work, Stephanie is illustrating an original Major Arcana tarot deck called *Tarot de La Selva*.

VAUHINI VARA is the author of *This is Salvaged* (2023), named one of the most anticipated books of 2023 by *Lithub*, *Electric Literature*, and *The Millions*, and *The Immortal King Rao* (2022), which was a finalist for the Pulitzer Prize and was shortlisted for the National Book Critics Circle's John Leonard Prize and the Dayton Literary Peace Prize. She is also a journalist, writing for *Wired*, *The New York Times Magazine*, and others. She teaches at Colorado State University as a 2023-24 Visiting Assistant Professor of Creative Writing and at the Lighthouse Writers Workshop's Book Project. She is also the secretary of Periplus, a mentorship collective serving writers of color.

VI KHI NAO is the author of many books and is known for her work spanning poetry, fiction, play, film, and interdisciplinary collaborations. Her forthcoming novel, *The Italian Letters*, is scheduled for publication by Melville House in 2024. In the same year, she will release a co-authored manuscript titled, *The Six Tones of Water*, with Sun Yung Shin, through Ricochet. Recognized as a former Black Mountain Institute fellow, Vi received the Jim Duggins, PhD Outstanding Mid-Career Novelist Prize in 2022.

VICTORIA CHANG's forthcoming book of poems, *With My Back to the World*, will be published in 2024 by Farrar, Straus & Giroux. Her latest book of poetry is *The Trees Witness Everything* (2022). Her nonfiction book, *Dear Memory*, was published in 2021. *OBIT* (2020), her prior book of poems, received the Los Angeles Times Book Prize, the Anisfield-Wolf Book Award in Poetry, and the PEN/Voelcker Award. She has received a Guggenheim Fellowship and the Chowdhury International Prize in Literature. She is the Bourne Chair in Poetry at Georgia Tech and Director of Poetry@Tech.

EDITOR BIOS

DAO STROM is a poet, musician, writer, and multimedia artist who works with three "voices"—written, sung, visual—to explore hybridity and the intersection of personal and collective histories. The author of several hybrid works, including the poetry-art collection *Instrument* (2020), which won the 2022 Stafford/Hall Oregon Book Award for Poetry, and its musical companion, *Traveler's Ode*, her work has received support from the Creative Capital Foundation, NEA, and others; she is also the author of two books of fiction. In 2017 Dao co-founded De-Canon as a literary art and social engagement "pop-up library" project to center works by writers of color. She is a founding member of the Vietnamese women and nonbinary artist collective, She Who Has No Master(s). Born in Vietnam, she grew up in the Sierra Nevada foothills of northern California and now lives in Portland, Oregon.

JYOTHI NATARAJAN is an editor, writer, and cultural worker and has collaborated with Dao Strom as part of De-Canon since 2021. She spent nearly a decade working at the Asian American Writers' Workshop, where she edited the digital literary magazine *The Margins* and helped to establish The Margins Fellowship for emerging writers. Jyothi now works as Program Manager at Haymarket Books, where they administer a fellowship program for writers impacted by carceral systems. They are the recipient of the 2017 Wai Look Award for Outstanding Service to the Arts and, with Dao, are part of the 2023-24 IPRC re/source residency. Having grown up in Southern Virginia, Jyothi is now based out of Portland, Oregon.

FONO GRAF

Other Fonograf Ed. titles

1. **Eileen Myles**—*Aloha/irish trees* (LP)
2. **Rae Armantrout**—*Conflation* (LP)
3. **Alice Notley**—*Live in Seattle* (LP)
4. **Harmony Holiday**—*The Black Saint and the Sinnerman* (LP)
5. **Susan Howe & Nathaniel Mackey**—*STRAY: A Graphic Tone* (LP)
6. **Annelyse Gelman & Jason Grier**—*About Repulsion* (EP)
7. **Joshua Beckman**—*Some Mechanical Poems To Be Read Aloud* (print)
8. **Dao Strom**—*Instrument/ Traveler's Ode* (print; cassette tape)
9. **Douglas Kearney & Val Jeanty**—*Fodder* (LP)
10. **Mark Leidner**—*Returning the Sword to the Stone* (print)
11. **Charles Valle**—*Proof of Stake: An Elegy* (print)
12. **Emily Kendal Frey**—*LOVABILITY* (print)
13. **Brian Laidlaw and the Family Trade**—*THIS ASTER: adaptations of Emile Nelligan* (LP)
14. **Nathaniel Mackey and The Creaking Breeze Ensemble**—*Fugitive Equation* (compact disc)
15. **FE Magazine** (print)
16. **Brandi Katherine Herrera**—*MOTHER IS A BODY* (print)
17. **Jan Verberkmoes**—*Firewatch* (print)
18. **Krystal Languell**—*Systems Thinking with Flowers* (print)
19. **Matvei Yankelevich**—*Dead Winter* (print)
20. **Cody-Rose Clevidence**—*Dearth & God's Green Mirth* (print)
21. **Hilary Plum**—*Hole Studies* (print)
22. **John Ashbery**—*Live at Sanders Theatre, 1976* (LP)
23. **Alice Notley**—*The Speak Angel Series* (print)
24. **Alice Notley**—*Early Works* (print)
25. **Joshua Marie Wilkinson**–*Trouble Finds You* (print)
26. **Timmy Straw**–*The Thomas Salto* (print)
27. **Audre Lorde**–*At Fassett Studio, 1970* (LP)
28. **Gabriel Palacios**–*A Ten Peso Burial For Which Truth I Sign* (print)
29. **Isabel Zapata, trans. Robin Myers**–*A Whale Is a Country* (print)
30. **Callum Angus**–*Cataract* (print)

Fonograf Editions is a registered 501(c)(3) nonprofit organization. Find more information about the press at: fonografeditions.com. Find more information about De-Canon at de-canon.com